FILM CRITICISM:

An Index to Critics' Anthologies

by

RICHARD HEINZKILL

The Scarecrow Press, Inc.
Metuchen, N.J.   1975

Library of Congress Cataloging in Publication Data

Heinzkill, Richard, 1933-
    Film criticism.

    1. Moving-pictures--Reviews--Indexes.   I.   Title.
PN1995.H4   016.79143'7   75-20159
ISBN 0-8108-0840-4

PREFACE

I owe a debt of acknowledgment and gratitude to the Oregon State System of Higher Education and specifically to the University of Oregon for making research leave possible. My thanks are due to Dr. Carl W. Hintz, University Librarian Emeritus, and Dr. H. William Axford, University Librarian, for allowing released time from my position within the library. Recognition must be paid my departmental colleagues, Robert McCollough, Edmund Soule and Nina Casto, who in my absence split my duties among them. Additional appreciation is due Robert McCollough without whose interest in films and books this index could never have become a reality. I especially want to thank Linda Batty who was kind enough to share her indexing experience with me, as well as the following for various degrees of assistance: Karen Jones, The Danish Film Museum, Copenhagen; Michelle Snapes, The National Film Archive, London; Herman Weinberg, New York City; Graham Petrie, McMaster University, Hamilton, Ontario; Bernard Karpel, Museum of Modern Art Library, New York City; David R. Smith, Walt Disney Archives, Burbank; Zagreb Film, Zagreb; Rodolf J. Broullon, Tricontinental Film Center, New York City; Leonard Maltin, Teaneck; and Oliva Lujbomir, Ceskoslovensky Filmexport, Prague.

This volume is dedicated to Mary H. Cajina, Carl and Tecla Hassmann and Barbara H. Sabo, who were there when I needed them a long time ago.

INTRODUCTION

Why this particular book? Essays and reviews buried in anthologies have always been a problem to locate. Through this Index, film criticism in these places will be more accessible. The anthologies chosen for analysis are only those that contain the work of a single critic.

To the casual browser this Index may appear to be nothing more than a scissors and paste job, that the indexes already in the anthologies were simply interfiled into one alphabet. Such is not the case. First of all, many of the anthologies do not have an index. Secondly, in order to have entries uniform existing indexes were not used. Each work was freshly indexed so that the present work would reflect a consistent viewpoint of what was to be included and what was to be excluded. (See "Guidelines for Use," following.) And lastly, this Index uses a special set of subject words that are specifically intended to index film criticism most effectively.

This work is intended to serve several kinds of readers. First, it will benefit the person in Middletown, U.S.A., who will discover that his public library can probably afford the anthologies indexed here, but cannot afford the long runs of film journals and metropolitan newspapers in which many of these reviews first appeared. Next for the beginning student of the film, anxious to learn more about a particular film, this Index is just one of several reference works that can direct him to sources for further study. For the more serious student who is interested in reading something besides another review, this volume should prove a useful research tool. And for anyone, this cumulative Index should save nervous leafing through many individual volumes in search of pertinent commentary.

GUIDELINES FOR USE

<u>actors and actresses</u> Items listed under a person's name re-
fer to discussions of that person's career or life. For material on specific performances, see title of the film.

<u>alphabetization</u> Diacritical marks (in particular the umlauts
of Germanic languages) are disregarded in alphabetizing
the entries.

<u>book reviews</u> Listed by author (in a separate entry from
the person as subject) with underlined title immediately
following name entry.

<u>directors</u> Items listed under a person's name refer to dis-
cussion of that person's career or life. For material on
specific productions, see title of the film.

<u>form of entry</u> Film title entries are underlined; subjects
are CAPITALIZED; persons, objects, societies, and non-
film titles are in normal print. A book title following a
name entry is underlined (see "book reviews," above).

<u>page numbers</u> Numbers cited in parentheses following a
critic's name refer to pages on which only a brief mention
of the subject appears.

<u>quotations</u> References to passages in which a person is di-
rectly quoted appear in separate name entries that are fol-
lowed by "(quoted)".

<u>titles</u> Not every film title that is mentioned in the texts has
been indexed; for instance, very often in the course of a
review, previous films by the same director, or starring
the same actor, may be mentioned. These occurrences
are not indexed.

In discussion of a national cinema--e.g., AMERI-
CAN FILMS or FRENCH FILMS--I have tended not to in-

dex all the titles that are mentioned. The same can be
said for title coverage in the discussion of genres--e.g.,
WESTERNS or HORROR FILMS.

Lists are indexed under BEST FILMS. Film titles
appearing on these lists are not usually indexed separately.

Translations of foreign titles, alternative titles,
etc. are not treated consistently. Usually the title best
known to American audiences is used, with cross references from variants.

Films are listed without identification. Feature
films, documentaries, animated films, etc. are not labeled
as such. The director's name may follow some titles in
order to avoid confusion with a film having a similar title.

Note that in alphabetizing, the first article is ig-
nored, e.g. The Birds as Birds, The; La Dolce Vita as
Dolce Vita, La; L'Avventura as Avventura, L'.

use   The form of a title used as an entry in this Index may
not appear on the page of the book to which the user has
been directed by the citation. This is because for the
overall purposes of this Index one form had to be selected
of a film title that has several variants. If there is any
doubt as to which film on a given page an Index entry re-
fers to, the user can look up all titles on that page in this
Index and will find that one of them is cross-referenced to
the entry with which the user began the search. (Cross
references are used to direct the user from variants of
the titles to the title used in this Index; alternative--or
original--titles do not appear with the main title entry.)

ANTHOLOGIES INDEXED
AND THEIR ABBREVIATIONS

Adler   Adler, Renata. Year in the Dark. New York: Random House, 1969. (Reviews from her stint on the staff of the New York Times, 1968-69.)

Agate (a)   Agate, James Evershed. Around Cinemas. London: Home and Van Thal, 1946. (Except for seven articles, this anthology is a selection of his reviews and musings as they appeared in the Tatler between 1929 and 1945.)

Agate (b)   _____. Around Cinemas, 2d ser. London: Home and Van Thal, 1948. (A second collection of Agate's reviews from the Tatler.)

Agee   Agee, James. Agee on Film, vol. 1. New York: McDowell, Obolensky, 1958. (A selection of his reviews from Nation, December 1942 through September 1948, where the review of Monsieur Verdoux and his appreciation of D. W. Griffith first appeared. Also included are his reviews from Time, November 1941 through February 1948, plus three other magazine articles: a review of Sunset Boulevard and Life articles on silent comedy and John Huston. His essay on Negro and American folk music is not indexed.)

Alpert   Alpert, Hollis. The Dreams and Dreamers. New York: Macmillan, 1962. (Reprints and revisions of articles from Saturday Review, Woman's Day, Theatre Arts, Gentlemen's Quarterly, and Cosmopolitan.)

Brown (a)   Brown, John Mason. Seeing More Things. New York: McGraw-Hill, 1948. (Brown's

ix

column, "Seeing Things, " in the Saturday Review of Literature was his vehicle for recording his thoughts on a variety of things; only his views on movies have been indexed.)

Brown (b)   . Seeing Things. New York: McGraw-Hill, 1946. (The first anthology of his column, "Seeing Things. ")

Brown (c)   . Still Seeing Things. New York: McGraw-Hill, 1950. (Another collection of his contributions to the Saturday Review of Literature.)

Crist   Crist, Judith. The Private Eye, the Cowboy and the Very Naked Girl. Chicago: Holt, Rinehart and Winston, 1968. (For the most part these reviews are from the New York Herald Tribune and the World Journal Tribune between 1963 and 1967.)

Durgnat   Durgnat, Raymond. Films and Feelings. Cambridge, Mass.: M. I. T. Press, 1967. (Although Durgnat's main concerns are problems of film aesthetics and criticism, these essays from British journals reflect a wide range of interests--e. g., the portrayal of women in film, science fiction films and films on art.)

Farber   Farber, Manny. Negative Space. New York: Praeger, 1971. (Manny Farber has been a columnist in the New Republic, Cavalier, and New Leader, in addition to contributing to several other magazines. About half of the material for this anthology is from Nation, Artforum, and Commentary.)

Ferguson   Ferguson, Otis. The Film Criticism of Otis Ferguson. Philadelphia: Temple University Press, 1971. (The Preface states that 80 percent of his film writing for the New Republic, 1934-42, is gathered here, including observations on his trip to Hollywood in 1941.)

Gilliatt   Gilliatt, Penelope. Unholy Fools: Wits, Comics, Disturbers of the Peace: Film &

Theater. New York: Viking, 1973. (Gilliatt
writes film and theater criticism and miscel-
laneous essays for various publications on
both sides of the Atlantic. Only her comments
on the cinema, which comprise over two-
thirds of this anthology, have been indexed.)

Greene   Greene, Graham. Graham Greene on Film.
New York: Simon and Schuster, 1972.
(Greene was film critic for the Spectator,
1935-40. The latter half of 1937 he reviewed
for Night and Day.)

Kael (a)   Kael, Pauline. Deeper into Movies. Boston:
Little, Brown, 1973. (Reviews from the New
Yorker between September 1969 and March
1972.)

Kael (b)   _____. Going Steady. Boston: Little,
Brown, 1970. (Pauline Kael became a regu-
lar columnist for the New Yorker in January 1968. With the exception of an article
for Harper's, "Trash, Art and the Movies,"
all of the reviews appeared in the New Yorker, 1968-69.)

Kael (c)   _____. I Lost It at the Movies. Boston:
Little, Brown, 1965. (The first half dates
mostly from the 1950's; the second half cov-
ers 1961-63 and includes her critique of
Kracauer's Theory of Film and the frequently
cited analysis of the auteur school, "Circles
and Squares. ")

Kael (d)   _____. Kiss Kiss Bang Bang. Boston:
Little, Brown, 1968. (Kael gathered reviews
she did 1965-67 for the first two-thirds of
this anthology. The last third consists of
program notes on 280 movies.)

Kauffmann (a) Kauffmann, Stanley. Figures of Light. New
York: Harper & Row, 1971. (In December
1967 Kauffmann returned to the New Republic
as film critic. The majority of these pieces
appeared there between that time and June
1970.)

Kauffmann (b)   . A World on Film. New York:
Harper & Row, 1966. (Almost all of these
reviews are from the New Republic between
1958 and 1965.)

Lejeune   Lejeune, Caroline Alice. Chestnuts in Her
Lap, 1936-46. London: Phoenix House, 1947.
(A selection of her reviews and articles as
they were printed in Observer (London). A
short note appended to some updates her ini-
tial reactions.)

Macdonald   Macdonald, Dwight. Dwight Macdonald on
Movies. Englewood Cliffs, N.J.: Prentice-
Hall, 1969. (The greater part of this book is
made up of the reviews he did for Esquire,
1960-69. A few of the articles appeared else-
where and earlier. Although Macdonald says
he did not rewrite, he did edit and annotate
several of the selections.)

Pechter   Pechter, William. S. Twenty-four Times a
Second. New York: Harper & Row, 1971.
(Film criticism written between 1960 and 1971
for several publications.)

Reed (a)   Reed, Rex. Big Screen, Little Screen. New
York: Macmillan, 1971. (Movie reviews
from 1969 and 1970 that appeared in Women's
Wear Daily, Holiday, and several other uni-
dentified sources. The first third is taken up
by television reviews and is not indexed.)

Reed (b)   Conversations in the Raw. New
York: World, 1969. (A collection of interviews and impressions of visits to events and
places between 1966 and 1969. Some of the
interviews are from the New York Times.
Sketches not directly connected with the world
of movie making are not indexed.)

Reed (c)   Do You Sleep in the Nude? New
York: New American Library, 1968. (Another series of interviews, again mostly from
the New York Times, dated 1966-67. These
interviews manage to incorporate more de-
tails of the subject's life and career than those

in the other volumes he did. Interviews with
stage personalities are not indexed.)

Sarris (a)   Sarris, Andrew. Confessions of a Cultist.
New York: Simon and Schuster, 1970. (Ex-
cept for 14 pieces, the reviews are from The
Village Voice, 1955-69.)

Sarris (b)   _____ The Primal Screen. New York:
Simon and Schuster, 1973. (Articles, reviews
and essays that he wrote since 1960 gathered
here from various publications. The last 34
pages on literary personages are not indexed.)

Schickel   Schickel, Richard. Second Sight; Notes on
Some Movies, 1965-70. New York: Simon
and Schuster, 1972. (The Preface claims
this anthology represents a little less than
half of his reviews from Life. Following
many of them are postscripts of Schickel's
further thoughts on what he originally wrote.
A lengthy introductory essay discusses the
role of the film critic.)

Sheed   Sheed, Wilfrid. Morning After. New York:
Farrar, Straus & Giroux, 1971. (Essays and
reviews on writers, writing, theater and
films. Only the film reviews, all from Esquire, are indexed.)

Simon (a)   Simon, John Ivan. Acid Test. New York:
Stein and Day, 1963. (An anthology divided
into sections on film, books, theater, fine
arts, poetry and critics. Those chapters per-
taining to the film world are indexed.)

Simon (b)   _____ . Movies into Film. New York:
Dial Press, 1971. (Reviews from the New
Leader, 1967-70.)

Simon (c)   _____ . Private Screenings. New York:
Macmillan, 1967. (Mostly reviews as they
appeared in the New Leader, 1963-66, along
with four other pieces.)

Sontag (a)   Sontag, Susan. Against Interpretation and
Other Essays. New York: Farrar, Straus &

Giroux, 1966. (Only six essays from this
collection are indexed, on: Bresson (1964),
Godard (1964), sci-fi films (1965), Jack
Smith (1964), Resnais (1963), and novels and
films (1961).)

Sontag (b)   Styles of Radical Will. New York:
Farrar, Straus & Giroux, 1969. (Three es-
says are indexed: Theater and film (1966),
Bergman's Persona (1967) and Godard (1968).)

Van Doren   Van Doren, Mark. The Private Reader. New
York: Holt, 1942. (An anthology which includes Van Doren's chronicle of films for Nation, 1935-38. Other pieces are not indexed.)

Warshow   Warshow, Robert. The Immediate Experience.
Garden City, N.Y.: Doubleday, 1962. (War-
show wrote for Commentary and Partisan Review. Those portions of this anthology per-
taining to films are indexed.)

Weinberg   Weinberg, Herman. Saint Cinema; Selected
Writing, 1929-70. New York: Drama Books
Specialists, 1970. (Weinberg has written for
a broad spectrum of film journals. This collection draws from these and includes selections from his volumn for the anniversary
issues of Variety during the 1960's.)

Winnington   Winnington, Richard. Drawn and Quartered.
London: Saturn Press, 1948. (Reviews and
drawings which appeared mainly in the News
Chronicle (London), 1943-48.)

Young   Young, Vernon. On Film. Chicago: Quad-
rangle Books, 1972. (Principally, articles
from the Hudson Review during the middle
1950's through 1969. Vernon Young is a student of European films, especially those from
Sweden.)

FILM CRITICISM INDEX*

A bout de soufflé see Breath-
less
A nous la liberté
  Kael (d) 320
A tout prendre see Take It
  All
Abbott and Costello (comedy
  team)
  Agee (18)
Abdul the Damned
  Agate (a) 132-33
Abe Lincoln in Illinois
  Ferguson 288-89
About a Person Whom Some
  Call St. Lazarus and Some
  St. Babalou
  Adler 354
Abraham Lincoln (D. W. Grif-
  fith)
  Agate (a) 88-90
Abschied von Gestern see
  Yesterday Girl
Abysses, Les
  Kauffmann (b) 263-66
Abyssinia
  Graham 6
Accattone!
  Adler 107-08
  Kauffmann (a) 58-61
  Young (235)
Accent on Youth
  Graham (37)
Accident
  Crist 239-40
  Farber 188
  Kael (d) 105-09
  Reed (b) 142-44
  Simon (b) 337-42
  Young 312-13

Accused (Thornton Freeland)
  Lejeune 17
Ace in the Hole
  Simon (a) 27-28
Acerea de una persona que unos
  llaman San Lazaro y otros
  Babalou see About a Per-
  son Whom Some Call St.
  Lazarus...
Across the Pacific (John Huston)
  Agate (b) 214
Act of the Heart, The
  Kael (a) 205-06
  Reed (a) 308
Act One
  Simon (c) 102-03
ACTING
  Agate (a) 154-57
  Agate (b) 196
  Agee 31
  Alpert 45, 56-58, 249-50
  Durgnat 45-49
  Farber 3-4, 118-19, 145-54,
    181, 186-87, 190
  Ferguson (70)
  Kael (a) 11-12, 352-53
  Kael (b) 21-22
  Kael (d) 90-91
  Kauffmann (b) 59-60
  Weinberg 37-38, 204
  Young 57
ACTION FILMS (see also AD-
  VENTURE FILMS; GANGSTER
  FILMS)
  Farber 12-24
Action for Slander
  Graham 167
Activist, The
  Simon (b) 90-93

---

*Page numbers in parentheses refer to brief mention only of subject.

ACTORS AND ACTRESSES (see
   also VAMPS; STARS)
   Agate (a) 54-56
   Agate (b) 52-53, 188
   Agee 223, 239-40
   Alpert 245, 249-50
   Crist 209
   Durgnat 46
   Farber 19, 118-19, 145-54,
      180-83, 186-87
   Ferguson 455-56
   Kael (a) 350, 352-53
   Kael (c) 285
   Macdonald 189
   Pechter 263
   Sarris (a) 340
   Sarris (b) 32, 34
   Simon (c) 297-303
   Sontag (a) 184-85
Actors' Studio (New York)
   Alpert 45
Actress, The (Sidney Franklin)
   Agate (b) (15)
ACTRESSES see ACTORS
   AND ACTRESSES
Acts of the Apostles, The
   Adler 221-24
Ådalen '31
   Farber (245)
   Kael (a) 41-42
   Kauffmann (a) 207-08
   Reed (a) (255)
   Schickel 274-76
   Simon (b) 395-97
   Young 351-52
Adam at 6 A. M.
   Reed (a) 307
Adam's Rib
   Kael (d) 228
ADAPTATIONS (see also THEA-
   TRE AND THE CINEMA)
   Crist 228-31
   Durgnat 194
   Ferguson 46, 192-93, 223-24
   Kael (a) 216, 236-37
   Kael (b) 20-21, 29-30, 230
   Kael (d) 68-70
   Kauffmann (a) (1), 142, 220-
      21
   Kauffmann (b) 70, 93, 97-98
   Lejeune 111-13
   Sarris (a) 433
   Sarris (b) 57

Schickel 166-67
Simon (b) 25-26
Simon (c) 92-93, 213-14
Sontag (a) 242-45
Sontag (b) 100-01, 105
Van Doren 292-97
Weinberg 179
ADAPTATIONS--BEST FILMS
   Simon (c) 93
Adding Machine, The
   Reed (a) 253
Address Unknown
   Agee (92)
Adler, Renata
   Adler xiii-xxv
Admirable Crichton, The (Lewis
   Gilbert) see Paradise La-
   goon
ADOLESCENTS see YOUNG
   PEOPLE
Adventure (Michelangelo Antoni-
   oni) see Avventura, L'
Adventure (Victor Fleming)
   Lejeune 174-75
   Winnington 48-49
ADVENTURE FILMS (see also
   ACTION FILMS)
   Simon (c) 124
Adventure for Two
   Winnington 13-14
Adventure in Blackmail
   Lejeune 73-74
Adventurer, The (Charlie Chap-
   lin)
   Weinberg (347)
Adventurers, The (Lewis Gilbert)
   Kael (a) 132-36
   Reed (a) (281)
Adventures in Bokhara
   Weinberg 27
Adventures of a Young Man
   Kael (c) 222-25
Adventures of Chico, The
   Van Doren 393-95
Adventures of Huckleberry Finn,
   The (Richard Thorpe)
   Ferguson 252
Adventures of Marco Polo (Arch-
   ie Mayo)
   Ferguson (216)
Adventures of Mark Twain, The
   Agee (92)
Adventures of Michael Strogoff

see Soldier and the Lady, The
Adventures of Robin Hood, The
  Lejeune 41-42
  Van Doren 406-08
Adventures of Robinson Crusoe,
The
  Kael (d) 228-29
Adventures of Sherlock Holmes,
The
  Ferguson 271
  Graham 273-74
Adventures of Tartu, The
  Agee 53
Adventures of Tom Sawyer, The
  (Potter and Taurog)
  Ferguson 213-14
Adventuress, The
  Agee 244
ADVERTISING FILMS
  Adler 149-50
ADVERTISING FOR FILMS
  Alpert 16, 24
  Crist 131-33
  Ferguson 281
  Kael (a) 151, 232, 234, 236
  Kael (c) 322-23, 329
  Kael (d) 27
  Reed (a) 387-88
Aerograd see Frontier
AESTHETICS (see also "AUTEUR"
  THEORY; CRITICISM; PLOTS,
  DISCUSSION OF; SUBJECTS OF
  FILMS)
  Adler 12-14, 144, 167, 200-
  02, 317-18
  Agate (a) 17, 23-24, 28
  Agate (b) 62-63, 73, 193-94,
  197, 215-16, 267
  Agee ii, 111-13, 136-39, 415
  Alpert 220-21, 236, 247, 251
  Crist 23-25, 271
  Durgnat 13-16, 19-30, 32-34,
  39-42, 117, 135, 138, 152-
  58, 173-77, 186, 198-201,
  268
  Farber 3-11, 14-15, 71-72,
  81-83, 135-36, 143-44, 184,
  190-91, 194, 197, 203, 215,
  247
  Ferguson 3, 5, 56-58, 69-
  70, 227, 231
  Graham 94
  Kael (a) 5, 66, 117, 236-37,

274
  Kael (b) 3-4, 59-63, 87-88,
  92, 94-99, 101-09, 112-
  17, 127-29, 253
  Kael (c) 11-27, 269-92
  Kael (d) 24-25, 172, 218-27
  Kauffmann (a) (38), 163-64,
  (248-49), 281-83
  Kauffmann (b) 249, 414-18
  Macdonald ix-xiii, xix, 64-
  68, 155-57, 366, 456-58
  Pechter 13, 39, 121, 201-02,
  262, 277, 280-83, 285,
  301, 310, 313-16
  Sarris (a) 174-75, 227
  Sarris (b) 12-18, 65, 70,
  73-74, 78, 84, 89-90, 99-
  105, 139
  Schickel 25, 31-32, 302
  Simon (b) 1-4, 18-20, 23,
  181, 336
  Simon (c) 96-97, 123-24,
  134, 196, 210, 272
  Sontag (a) 177, 179-85, 198
  Sontag (b) 99, 103, 110,
  119-22, 139, 179-80
  Van Doren 287-90, 297-98
  Warshow 19
  Weinberg 15-17, 38, 186,
  191, 194, 201
  Winnington 123, 125-26
  Young ix-xi, xvii, 20, 45,
  49, 78, 185-87, 242, 305-
  06, 328
Affair of the Heart, An
  Crist 248-49, (269)
  Kauffmann (a) 52-55
  Sarris (a) 316
  Simon (b) 375
Affair of the Skin, An
  Crist (35)
  Simon (c) 100
Affairs of Cellini, The
  Ferguson 42
Affairs of Susan, The
  Agee 153-54
African Holiday
  Ferguson 185
African Queen, The
  Farber (77)
  Kael (d) 229
African Report
  Agee (42)

Africa's Skyways
    Graham   269
Agate, James
    Agate (a)   7-8
    Agate (b)   30-32, 35-38
Agate, James (quoted)
    Alpert   244
Age d'Or, L'
    Sontag (b)   (121), (158)
    Weinberg   178, (192)
Agee, James
    Agee   i-ii
    Farber   84-88, (176)
    Ferguson   x-xii
    Kael (b)   49-50
    Macdonald   4-14, 123-24
    Pechter   261-75, 276, 279
    Sarris (a)   144
    Sarris (b)   (13), 64, (69), 74,
        76-77
    Schickel   23-24
    Simon (a)   287
    Simon (b)   (5), 406
Agee, James (quoted)
    Macdonald   4-5
    Pechter   262-69
    Simon (a)   268
Agee, James. Agee on Film
    Farber   86-88
    Pechter   261-75
    Simon (a)   269-71
Aghnihat elmoutakasra   see
    Broken Wings
Ah, Wilderness!
    Ferguson   (7), 107-09
Air Force
    Agee   28-29
Airport
    Kael (a)   136-37
    Reed (a)   (281)
    Schickel   (22-23)
Aka hige   see   Red Beard
Albuquerque
    Agee   294
Aldrich, Robert
    Farber   23
    Macdonald   55
Alerte en Méditerranée, La   see
    S.O.S. Mediterranean
Alex in Wonderland
    Kael (a)   224-27
Alexander   see   Very Happy Al-
    exander

Alexander Nevsky
    Agee   247-48, (341)
    Durgnat   51-52
    Farber   (9)
    Ferguson   250
    Young   (86), 153
Alexander's Ragtime Band
    Ferguson   231
Alexandre le bienheureux   see
    Very Happy Alexander
Alfie
    Crist   182
    Schickel   81-83
    Simon (b)   372
    Simon (c)   244-48
Alfred the Great
    Kael (a)   67-68
Algiers
    Ferguson   225-27, (342)
Alibi, L' (Pierre Chenal)
    Graham   192
Alice Adams (George Stevens)
    Ferguson   89-91
    Kael (d)   229-30
Alice's Restaurant
    Gilliatt   199-201
    Kael (a)   5-6
    Kauffmann (a)   198-200, (202)
    Pechter   103-05
    Reed (a)   183
    Sarris (a)   457-59
    Simon (b)   118-19
All About Eve
    Alpert   151-52
    Farber   61
    Kael (d)   230
All Fall Down
    Kael (c)   137-38
    Kauffmann (b)   108-11
    Macdonald   142-44
All I Desire
    Alpert   89
All My Sons
    Agee   300
All Quiet on the Western Front
    Agate (a)   68-71
    Ferguson   (9), 184, (236)
    Kael (d)   230-31
    Macdonald   (76), 101-02
    Weinberg   (179)
All That Money Can Buy
    Agate (b)   199-200
All the Loving Couples

Kael (a) 57-58
All the Way Home
  Simon (c) 93-94
All These Women
  Kauffmann (b) 289-90
Alloway, Lawrence
  Sarris (b) 66-80
Alloway, Lawrence (quoted)
  Sarris (b) 66-67, 75-76
Almost a Man
  Simon (c) 252-53
Aloma of the South Seas (Alfred
  Santell)
  Lejeune 80-81
Alpert, Hollis
  Alpert 1-5
  Sarris (b) 123
Alphaville
  Simon (b) (167)
  Simon (c) 183
  Young (282), 324-26
Älskande par see Loving
  Couples
Älskarinnan
  Young 198-99
Alvarez, Alfred (quoted)
  Young 381
Alvarez, Santiago
  Adler 352
Alvarez Kelly
  Crist 201-02
Always in My Heart
  Agate (b) 218-19
Amant de cinq jours see Five
  Day Lover
Amanti (Vittorio de Sica) see
  Place for Lovers
Amants, Les see Lovers, The
  (Louis Malle)
Amazing Dr. Clitterhouse, The
  Ferguson 228-29
America America
  Crist (39)
  Kauffmann (b) 155-56
  Macdonald 144-45, (152)
  Sarris (a) 115-16
  Simon (c) 103-04
American Dream, An
  Crist 181-82, 211
  Kael (d) (131), (134)
American Film Insti-
  tute
  Adler (275), 337-38

Sarris (b) 95-98
AMERICAN FILMS (see also
  HOLLYWOOD)
  Durgnat 79, 186, 268
  Ferguson 4-12
  Macdonald 38-39, 76-77,
    134-35
  Reed (a) 227-28
  Sarris (a) 168-69
  Sarris (b) 48, (50)
  Schickel 338
  Young 13, 17, 78, 387-88,
    399
AMERICAN FILMS (1930's)
  Ferguson 23, 42
  Macdonald xix
AMERICAN FILMS (1940's)
  Agee 238
  Kauffmann (a) 201
  Sarris (b) 74
AMERICAN FILMS (mid-1950's)
  Durgnat 63-64
  Farber 113-24
AMERICAN FILMS (1960's)
  Kael (a) 238, 280
  Kael (b) 179-81
  Macdonald 174-78
AMERICAN FILMS (mid-1960's)
  Farber 160, 166
  Pechter 97
  Simon (c) 119-20
AMERICAN FILMS (late 1960's)
  Kael (a) 145-53, 315
  Kauffmann (a) 21-24, 201-04,
    277-79
  Schickel 338
AMERICAN FILMS (early 70's)
  Kael (a) 426
American Romance, An
  Agate (b) 253-54
  Lejeune 128-29
  Winnington 24
American Tragedy, An (Sergei
  Einsenstein)
  Weinberg 277
American War, The
  Adler 349-51
Americanization of Emily, The
  Sarris (a) 362
Amiche, Le
  Kauffmann (b) 313
Amici per la pelle see Woman
  in the Painting

Among People see Maxim
  Gorky Trilogy
Amore, L' see Ways of Love
Amour à travers les âges see
  Anticipation
Amour à vingt ans see Love at
  Twenty
Amour avec des "si"...
  Young 258-59
Amourist, The see Pornogra-
  pher, The
Amphitryon (Reinhold Schuenzel)
  Weinberg 47, (259), (283),
  (344)
Anatahan
  Weinberg 112-15, 159, 350
Anatolian Smile see America
America
Anchors Aweigh
  Agee 168
And God Created Woman
  Alpert 198
  Durgnat (231)
And Now for Something Com-
  pletely Different
  Gilliatt 272-75
And Now Tomorrow (Irving Pi-
  chel)
  Agee 130
  Winnington 34
And Quiet Flows the Don
  Macdonald (460)
And the Angels Sing
  Agee 94
  Lejeune 107-08
And Then There Were None
  Agee (178)
Andalusian Dog see Chien An-
  dalou
Anderson, Lindsay
  Durgnat (72)
Anderson, Robert
  Reed (c) 107-13
Anderson Platoon, The
  Kauffmann (a) (57)
Anderson Tapes, The
  Kael (a) 285
Andrews, Harry
  Crist 147
Andromeda Strain, The
  Kael (a) 275-76
Andy Hardy (series)
  Pechter 7

Andy Hardy's Blonde Trouble
  Winnington 21
Andy Hardy's Double Life
  Lejeune 87
Angel
  Lejeune 18-20
Angel and the Bad Man, The
  Agee (244)
Angel exterminador, El see
  Exterminating Angel
Angels over Broadway
  Ferguson 321-22
Anger, Kenneth. Hollywood Baby-
  lon.
  Kael (c) 35-36
Angry Silence, The
  Kauffmann (b) 192-94
Animal Farm
  Weinberg 124-27
ANIMAL FILMS
  Kael (d) 181-83
ANIMATED FILMS
  Adler 18-19, 295
  Kael (b) 189, 191-92
  Lejeune 36
ANIMATED FILMS, HISTORY OF
  Sarris (b) 194-99
Anna and the King of Siam (John
  Cromwell)
  Agee 206
  Winnington 64
Anna Karenina (Clarence Brown)
  Graham 25-26
Anna Karenina (Julien Duvivier)
  Agee 386
  Winnington 98-99
Anne of Green Gables (George
  Nicholls, Jr.)
  Ferguson (66)
Anne of the Thousand Days
  Kael (a) 95-97
  Reed (a) 269
  Simon (b) 401
Année dernière à Marienbad
  see Last Year at Marienbad
Anne-Marie
  Graham 73
Annenkovscina see Enemies of
  Progress
Anniversary, The
  Adler 89-90
Another Park of the Forest
  Agee 305

Ansiktet see Magician
Anthony Adverse
    Agee (142)
    Ferguson 143-45
    Graham 103-04
Anticipation
    Sontag (b) 145
Antonioni, Michelangelo
    Farber 142-43, 197
    Kael (c) (23-24), (296)
    Kauffmann (a) 238-45
    Macdonald (475-76)
    Pechter 246, 311
    Reed (c) 1-6
    Sarris (a) 29-33, 70-73
    Sontag (a) (245)
    Young 187-89, 278-79, 288
Antonioni, Michelangelo (quoted)
    Kauffmann (b) 315
Anxious Years see Dark Jour-
    ney
Any Wednesday
    Reed (a) 335
Anything Goes (Lewis Milestone)
    Graham 53
Apa see Father
Aparajito
    Kael (c) (290)
    Kauffmann (b) 367-69
Apartment, The
    Crist (96)
    Kael (c) 41
    Kauffmann (b) 149
    Macdonald (187), 280-83
    Simon (a) 26
Appaloosa, The
    Crist 211
Appointment with Danger (Lewis
    Allen)
    Farber 60
APPRECIATION see AESTHET-
    ICS; CRITICISM; STUDY
    AND TEACHING OF FILMS
April Fools, The
    Reed (a) 235-36
Apur sansar see World of Apu,
    The
Arch of Triumph, The
    Agee (305)
ARCHITECTURE AND THE CINE-
    MA
    Durgnat 99-104
ARCHIVES, FILM (see also LI-

BRARIES, FILM; PRESERVA-
    TION OF FILMS)
    Sarris (b) 91-94, 97
    Young xi
Are We All Murderers? see
    We Are All Assassins
'Arf a Mo' Hitler
    Graham 248
Ariane
    Ferguson 33
Arise My Love
    Ferguson 316
Arizona (Wesley Ruggles)
    Ferguson 319-20
Arms and the Girl (Sidney Lan-
    field)
    Ferguson 96-97
    Graham 36-37
Arnheim, Rudolf. Film as Art.
    Macdonald xix
Aroma-Rama
    Alpert 178-80
Around the World under the Sea
    Kael (d) 183
Arrangement, The
    Kael (a) 48-53
    Simon (b) 324-26
Arrast, Harry d'Abbadie d'
    Macdonald 85-86
    Weinberg 306-22
Arrowsmith
    Agate (b) 63-65
Arsenal Stadium Mystery, The
    Graham 266-68
Arsenic and Old Lace
    Kael (d) 231-32
ART, FILMS ON (see also
    PAINTING AND THE CINEMA)
    Durgnat 118-32
    Young 68-76
ART AND THE CINEMA [includes
    not only fine arts but material
    on all the arts and cinema]
    Durgnat 19-21, 99
    Kael (a) 236, 238
    Kauffmann (a) 38
    Pechter 113
    Sarris (b) 56-57
    Sontag (a) 245
    Sontag (b) 116, 119-20
    Weinberg 195
ART CINEMAS
    Agee (150)

Alpert 16
Farber 205, 246
Kael (b) 215
ART DIRECTION
Ferguson 445
Artamonov Affair see Arta-
    monov and Sons
Artamonov and Sons
    Winnington 54
Artaud, Antonin
    Sontag (b) 121-22
Artaud, Antonin (quoted)
    Sontag (b) 114-15
Artist, The
    Weinberg (292)
Artisten in der Zirkuskuppel see
    Artists under the Big Top
Artists at the Top of the Big Top
    see Artists under the Big
    Top
Artists under the Big Top
    Adler 237
As You Like It (Paul Czinner)
    Agate (a) 173-77
    Agate (b) 124-26
    Graham 98, 100
Ascenseur à l'échafaud, L'
    Durgnat 108
Ashes and Diamonds
    Gilliatt 96-98
    Kauffmann (b) 355-56
Asphalt Jungle
    Farber 34-36, (62)
Assassins et voleurs see Lov-
    ers and Thieves
Assignment in Brittany
    Agate (a) 241-42
Astaire, Fred
    Durgnat (44)
    Sarris (b) 175-76
Astruc, Alexandre (quoted)
    Sarris (b) 85
    Sontag (a) 181
At Dawn We Die see Tomor-
    row We Live (George King)
At Land
    Agee 191
Atalante, L'
    Agee 265-66
    Weinberg (258)
Atlantis
    Young 21
Attack!--The Invasion of New

Britain
    Agee 97, 99-100
ATTENDANCE see AUDI-
    ENCES
Atti degli apostoli see Acts of
    the Apostles
Au Hasard Balthazar
    Sarris (b) 157-60
Auden, W. H. (quoted)
    Agee i
AUDIENCES
    Adler 84, 207, 273
    Agate (b) 73-74, 197, 227-
    28
    Agee 34-35, 66, 86, (150)
    Alpert 6, 231, 236-38
    Crist xi-xii, 265
    Durgnat 22, 30, 135, 152-56
    Farber 23-24, 54-57
    Ferguson 227, 229-31, 332,
    352-53, 441-42
    Kael (a) 3-5, 7-8, 13-14,
    117, 145-53, 274
    Kael (b) 28, 60-62, 87-89,
    91-92, 104, 215
    Kael (c) 8-15, 31, 324
    Kael (d) 172
    Kauffmann (a) 279
    Kauffmann (b) 340, 397, 415-
    28
    Lejeune 152-53
    Macdonald 36, 42, (65), 175
    Schickel 28-29, 312, 337-38
    Simon (c) 121-22, 134, 177-
    78
    Sontag (b) 107, 121
    Winnington 126
    Young xiv, (57)
Audran, Stéphane
    Farber 4
"AUTEUR" THEORY [also see
    names of exponents, e. g.
    André Bazin, Andrew Sarris]
    Durgnat 61-86
    Kael (a) 78-79
    Kael (c) 292-319
    Kauffmann (a) 96-99, 256
    Macdonald 135, (453)
    Sarris (a) 360-65
    Sarris (b) 38-61, 68
    Schickel 32-33, 36
    Simon (b) 6-13, 21
    Sontag (b) 112

Auto-Destructive Art
  Durgnat 127
Autumn Fire
  Weinberg (292)
AVANT-GARDE FILMS (see also
  EXPERIMENTAL FILMS)
  Sontag (a) 227, 244
Avec des si... see Amour avec
  des "si"...
Aventures du Roi Pausole see
  Roi Pausole
Aveu see Confession (Costi
  Costa-Gavras)
Avventura, L'
  Alpert 188-90
  Durgnat (70-71), 109-10,
    (232), (234)
  Kael (c) 148-49
  Kauffmann (b) 299-302
  Macdonald 34-36, 332-33
  Pechter 43-50
  Sarris (a) 34-35
  Simon (a) 17-21
  Simon (c) 29-31
  Sontag (b) (133-34), (147)
  Weinberg 238
  Young (189), 193-94, (328)
AWARDS (see also FESTIVALS;
  OSCARS)
  Schickel 216
Awful Truth, The (Leo McCarey)
  Ferguson 205-06

-B-

B-MOVIES
  Farber 55-57
Babes in Arms
  Agate (b) 171-73
Babes on Broadway
  Agate (a) 236-38
Baby Doll
  Alpert 225-26
  Kael (d) 232
Baby Love
  Reed (a) 161-62
Baby Maker, The
  Kael (a) 157-58
Bacall, Lauren
  Agee 355
  Durgnat 142
Bacharach, Burt

Reed (b) 189-97
Bachelor Girl Apartment see
  Any Wednesday
Bachelor Mother (Garson Kanin)
  Ferguson 261-62
Bachelor Party, The
  Farber 121-22
Back to the Wall
  Kauffmann (b) 221-22
Background to Danger (Lewis Al-
  len) see Appointment with
  Danger
Background to Danger (Raoul
  (Walsh)
  Agee 45
Bad and the Beautiful, The
  Kael (d) 232-33
Bad Day at Black Rock
  Kael (d) 233
Bad Sister (Bernard Knowles)
  Winnington 83-84
Bad Sleep Well, The
  Kauffmann (b) 382-83
Bahama Passage
  Lejeune 71-72
Baie des anges see Bay of the
  Angels
Baisers volés, Les see Stolen
  Kisses
Baker's Wife, The
  Agate (b) 166-68
  Ferguson 293-94
  Graham 227
  Kael (d) 233
  Weinberg 91-92
Bal du Comte d'Orgel see Ball
  of Count D'Orgel
Balázs, Béla
  Sontag (b) 120
Ball, Lucille
  Reed (c) 55-60
Ball of Count D'Orgel, The
  Reed (a) 396
Ballad of a Soldier
  Kael (c) 42, (196)
  Kauffmann (b) 362-63
  Macdonald 269-70
Ballad of Cable Hogue, The
  Kauffmann (a) 266-67
  Reed (a) 279-80
  Schickel 294-96
Ballada o soldate see Ballad
  of a Soldier

Ballerina (Jean Benoît-Lévy)
  see Mort du Cygne, La
Balthazer see Au Hasard Bal-
  thazar
Baltic Deputy
  Ferguson 196-97
Bambi
  Agate (b) 206-08
  Lejeune 77
Bambini ci guardano, I see
  Children Are Watching Us,
  The
Bananas
  Gilliatt 36-39
  Kael (a) 369-70
Band Concert, The
  Agate (b) 116
  Ferguson 85-86
  Weinberg 329
Band Wagon, The
  Kael (d) 234
Banda Casaroli, La
  Young 234
Bande à part see Outsiders
  (Jean-Luc Godard)
Bandéra, La
  Graham 38-39
Bandit, The (Lima Barreto)
  Young 83-85
Banditi a Milano see Violent
  Four
Bandits of Orgosolo, The
  Kauffmann (b) 342-43
  Macdonald 359-60
  Young 209-10
Bank Dick, The
  Ferguson 326-27
Barbarella
  Adler 267-70
  Kael (b) 171-73
  Reed (a) 201
  Simon (b) 142-43
Barbarian and the Geisha,
  The
  Kauffmann (b) 146
Barbary Coast
  Graham 32
Barber of Seville, The (Mario
  Costa)
  Agee 251
Barcarole
  Graham 8-9
Bardot, Brigitte

Alpert 198-99
Durgnat 143-44, 150, 159
Barefoot Contessa, The
  Alpert 154-55
  Kael (d) 234-35
Bariera see Barrier (Jerzy
  Skolimowski)
Baron Münchhausen
  Weinberg (190)
Barrage contre le Pacifique, Le
  see Sea Wall, The
Barren Lives see Vidas Secas
Barretts of Wimpole Street, The
  (Sidney Franklin)
  Ferguson 46-47
Barrier (Jerzy Skolimowski)
  Farber 225-26
  Sarris (a) 314-15
  Simon (b) (378)
Bartleby
  Kael (a) 417-18
Bas-Fonds, Les see Lower
  Depths, The (Jean Renoir)
Basilischi see Lizards
Bataan
  Agee 44-45
Bataille, La see Thunder in
  the East
Bataille du Rail, La see Bat-
  tle of the Rails, The
Bathing Beauty
  Agee 101, 349
Battaglia di Algeri, La see
  Battle of Algiers, The
Battaglia di Napoli, La see
  Four Days in Naples
Battcock, Gregory. The New
  American Cinema.
  Young 322-27
Battle for Beauty
  Winnington 42
Battle for the Marianas, The
  Agee 118
Battle of Algiers, The
  Adler (106), (217)
  Crist 259-60
  Farber 228
  Simon (b) 373-74
Battle of Britain, The (Frank
  Capra)
  Agee 56
Battle of Britain, The (Guy Ham-
  ilton)

Reed (a) 253-54
Battle of Russia, The
  Agee 56-57, (66)
Battle of San Pietro see San
  Pietro
Battle of the Rails, The
  Winnington 83
Battle of the River Plate, The
  see Pursuit of the Graf Spee,
  The
Battle on the Neretva, The
  Simon (b) 400
Battle Stripe see Men, The
  (Fred Zinnemann)
Battleship Potemkin see Po-
  temkin
Battling Bellhop see Kid Gala-
  had (Michael Curtiz)
Bay of the Angels
  Kael (d) 235
  Sarris (a) 171-72
  Simon (c) 139
Bazin, André
  Durgnat 29, (41), 67-69
  Pechter (13)
  Sarris (b) 39-46, 84, 139
  Simon (b) (6)
Bazin, André (quoted)
  Sarris (b) 88-89
Bazin, André. What Is Cinema?
  v. 1
  Sarris (b) 87-90
Be Like a Rose see Kimiko
Beachcomber, The (Erich Pom-
  mer)
  Ferguson 244-45
Beast with Five Fingers, The
  Kael (c) (6)
Beat the Devil
  Crist (72-73)
  Kael (d) 235-36
Beatty, Warren
  Reed (c) 13-37
Beau Geste (William A. Wellman)
  Ferguson 263-64
  Graham 237-38
Beau Serge, Le
  Alpert 200-01
Beautiful Cheat see What a
  Woman!
Beauty and the Beast
  Agee (289)
  Durgnat (53)

Kael (d) 236
  Weinberg (202)
Beaver Dam
  Weinberg 218
Becker, Jacques
  Sontag (a) (183)
Becket
  Crist 52-54
  Kauffmann (b) 63-64
Becky Sharp
  Ferguson 80-81
  Graham 8
Bed and Board
  Kael (a) 243-45
Bed Sitting Room, The
  Kael (a) 16-17
  Kauffmann (a) 204-06
Bedelia
  Agate (b) 269-70
Bedknobs and Broomsticks
  Kael (a) 359-60
Bedlam
  Agee 192
Bedtime Story
  Macdonald 163-66
Beethoven see Life and Loves
  of Beethoven, The
Beethoven's Great Love see
  Life and Loves of Beethoven,
  The
Before Him All Rome Trembled
  Agee 244
Before the Revolution
  Kael (d) 124-25
  Sarris (a) 201-02
  Sontag (b) (140)
Beggar's Opera, The
  Kael (c) 116-19
Beginners see First Time
Beginning see Début
Beginning or the End, The
  Agee 242-43
Begone Dull Care
  Durgnat (20)
Behind the Great Wall
  Alpert 179
Behind the Iron Curtain see
  Iron Curtain
Behind the Rising Sun
  Agate (b) 239-41
Bell'Antonio, Il
  Kael (d) 236-37
  Young 131-33, (173), (232)

Belle de Jour
  Adler 117-19, 326
  Farber 272-74
  Kauffmann (a) 77-79
  Sarris (a) 353-59
  Simon (b) 139-41
  Sontag (b) (129)
  Young 310-11
Belle et la bête, La see
  Beauty and the Beast
Belle of the Nineties
  Ferguson 52-53
Bellocchio, Marco
  Kael (b) 7-8
Bells of St. Marys, The
  Agee 184-85
Belmondo, Jean Paul
  Reed (c) 176-80
  Sarris (a) 262-68
Ben Hur (Fred Niblo)
  Weinberg 176
Ben Hur (William Wyler)
  Kauffmann (b) 22-23
  Macdonald 424-27
  Weinberg (160-61), (163)
Benayoun, Robert (quoted)
  Simon (b) 7-8
Benefit of the Doubt, The
  Simon (b) 380
Benjamin
  Adler 94-95
  Kael (b) 72-73
  Sarris (a) 344-46
  Simon (b) 260-61
  Young 335-36
Benjamin, Richard
  Kael (a) 347-48
Bentley, Nicolas (quoted)
  Winnington 9-10
Bergman, Ingmar
  Alpert 62-77
  Durgnat 64
  Kael (c) 245-46, 303-04
  Pechter 133-46, 311
  Simon (a) 30-34
  Simon (b) 224-26
  Weinberg 158, 245
  Young 203-04, 276-77, 287-92
Bergman, Ingmar (quoted)
  Macdonald 416
Bergman, Ingmar. Four screen-
  plays.
  Simon (a) 33

Bergman, Ingrid
  Reed (b) 38-44
Bergner, Elizabeth
  Agate (b) 188
Berkeley, Busby
  Kael (a) (382-83)
  Sontag (b) (110), (112)
Bern, Paul
  Weinberg 218, 248
Beroringen see Touch
Bertolucci, Bernardo
  Kael (b) 7
BEST FILMS [also entered here
  are lists of films that may
  not be "best" but examples of
  a particular type]
  Adler 83
  Agate (a) 217-19
  Agee 228
  Ferguson 120, 169-70, 206
  Graham 94
  Kael (a) 152
  Kael (c) 24-25, 81
  Kael (d) 180, 184-85
  Kauffmann (a) 202
  Lejeune 16-61
  Macdonald ix-x, xix-xx, 64,
    66-67, 135, 174
  Pechter 308, 311
  Reed (a) 385
  Sarris (b) 116, 231
  Schickel 308
  Simon (b) 363
  Simon (c) 15, 86
  Weinberg 60-61, 143, 184,
    246, 294
  Young 274, 318
BEST FILMS, 1940's
  Sarris (b) 23-24, 27-29
BEST FILMS, 1940
  Ferguson 327-28
BEST FILMS, 1942
  Agee 23-24
BEST FILMS, 1943
  Agee 65-67
BEST FILMS, 1944
  Agee 136-39
BEST FILMS, 1945
  Agee 186-89
BEST FILMS, 1946
  Agee 236-39
BEST FILMS, 1947
  Agee 287-90

Winnington 94
BEST FILMS, 1951
  Farber 58-60
BEST FILMS, 1963
  Crist 39-40
BEST FILMS, 1964
  Crist 87-91
BEST FILMS, 1965
  Crist 148-52
BEST FILMS, 1966
  Crist 208-18
BEST FILMS, 1967
  Crist 257-71
BEST FILMS, 1968
  Adler 206, 324-29
  Farber 232
BEST FILMS, 1969
  Reed (a) 255
BEST FILMS, 1970
  Reed (a) 302-03
Best Foot Forward
  Lejeune 106
Best Man, The (Franklin Schaff-
ner)
  Crist 68-69
  Kauffmann (b) (400)
  Sarris (a) 156-60
Best of Everything
  Weinberg (244-45)
Best Years of Our Lives, The
  Agee 229-33, (235)
  Durgnat (29-30)
  Warshow 155-61
Bête humaine, La see Human
Beast, The
Betragen bis zum Jungsten Tag
see Duped Till Domesday
Betrayal from the East
  Agee 146
Between Two Worlds (Marco Bel-
locchio) see Fist in His
Pocket
Between Two Worlds (Edward
Blatt)
  Agee 91-92
Beware of Pity (Maurice Elvey)
  Agate (b) 272-73
Bewitched
  Agee 171
Beyond the Law (Norman Mailer)
  Farber 231
  Kauffmann (a) 115-17
  Sarris (a) 396-400

Beyond the Valley of the Dolls
  Simon (b) 154-60
Bezhin Meadow
  Kauffmann (a) 142-43
  Young (152)
Bible, The (John Huston)
  Crist 184-87
  Reed (a) 367-70
BIBLICAL FILMS
  Macdonald 430-31
Biches, Les
  Adler 250-51
  Farber 233, 239-40
  Kael (b) 148
  Reed (a) 202
  Simon (b) 10-12, 261-64
Bicycle Thief, The
  Brown (c) 282-87
  Durgnat 106-07
  Sarris (a) 30
Bidone, Il see Swindlers, The
Big Bounce, The
  Reed (a) 153-54
Big Broadcast of 1937
  Ferguson 159
Big Brown Eyes
  Graham (82)
Big Carnival see Ace in the
Hole
Big City (Frank Borzage)
  Graham 173
Big City (Satyajit Ray)
  Schickel 126-28
Big Clock, The (John Farrow)
  Agee 306
Big Day, The
  Kael (d) 290
Big Deal at Dodge City see
  Big Hand for the Little Lady,
A
Big Deal on Madonna Street
  Kael (d) 238
  Macdonald (361-62)
Big Gamble, The (Richard
Fleischer)
  Durgnat 37
Big Hand for the Little Lady, A
  Reed (a) 331
Big Heart see Miracle on 34th
Street
Big Job, The see Stöten
Big Knife, The
  Kael (d) 238

Big Mouth, The
  Sarris (a) 302
Big Parade, The
  Durgnat (57-59)
  Weinberg (179), (291)
Big Shot, The (Lewis Seiler)
  Agate (b) 212
Big Sleep, The
  Agee 215
  Durgnat (224
  Farber 6, (145)
  Kael (d) 6-7, 238-39
  Sontag (b) (161), (184)
  Winnington 69
Big Street, The
  Agee 338-39
Biggest Bundle of Them All, The
  Adler 16-17
Bill and Coo
  Agee (300)
Bill of Divorcement, A (John
  Farrow)
  Lejeune 54
Billy Budd
  Kael (c) 234-39
  Kauffmann (b) 116-17
Billy Jack
  Kael (a) 341-47
Billy Liar
  Kauffmann (b) 203-05
  Sarris (a) 111-12
  Young (225)
Billy the Kid (King Vidor)
  Agate (b) 41-43
Birds, The
  Kauffmann (b) 156-58
  Macdonald 302-07
  Pechter 183-91
  Sarris (a) 84-86
Birth of a Nation, The
  Agee (26), (151), (164), 313-
    14
  Ferguson 304-05
  Graham 74
  Macdonald (xiv), (268), (460)
  Sarris (b) (139-40), 217-22
  Weinberg (196), 248-49, (258),
    (292)
Birth of the Blues, The
  Ferguson 387-88
Birthday Party, The
  Adler (318)
  Kael (b) 211-13

Kauffman (a) 128-29
Reed (a) (212-13)
Sarris (a) 409-14
Sheed 227-29
Biruma no tategoto see Bur-
  mese Harp
Biscuit Eater, The
  Ferguson 297
Bitter Sweet (W. S. van Dyke)
  Lejeune 58-59
Bitter Tea of General Yen, The
  Agate (a) 115-16
  Ferguson 152
BLACK AND WHITE FILMS (see
  also COLOR FILMS)
  Agee 26
  Kael (a) 372
  Macdonald 460
Black Angel
  Agee 217
Black Eyes (Victor Tourjansky)
  see Dark Eyes
Black Flower for the Bride see
  Something for Everyone
Black Fox
  Simon (c) 68-69
Black Fury
  Ferguson 8, 73-74, (135)
Black Girl
  Farber 10
Black God, White Devil
  Young (12)
Black Legion
  Ferguson 165-67
  Graham 151, 164
Black Like Me
  Crist (99)
Black Narcissus
  Agee 272-73
Black Orpheus
  Durgnat (235)
Black Peter
  Simon (c) 186
Black Room, The
  Graham 22-23
Black Sabbath see Black Sunday
  (Mario Bava)
Black Sunday (Mario Bava)
  Durgnat (147-48)
Black Waters
  Agate (a) 47
Blackboard Jungle
  Kael (c) 58-60

BLACKLISTING see "HOLLY-
  WOOD TEN"
Blackmail (Alfred Hitchcock)
  Durgnat (150), (233)
BLACKS IN FILMS
  Adler 63-66
  Agee 80
  Crist 98-99
  Kauffmann (b) 87
  Sarris (a) 236-37, 307-09
Blackwaters see Black Waters
Blanche Fury
  Winnington 101
Blaue Engel, Der see Blue
  Angel, The (Josef von Stern-
  berg)
Blaze of Noon
  Agee (244)
Blesh, Rudi. Keaton
  Farber 175-76
Blind Alley
  Graham 239
Bliss of Mrs. Blossom, The
  Sarris (a) 415-16
Blithe Spirit
  Agee 178
  Lejeune 145-47
Blockade (William Dieterle)
  Ferguson 222-23
Blonde in Love see Loves of a
  Blonde
Blonde Venus, The
  Agate (a) 112-13
  Macdonald 96-97
Blood Feast see Fin de Fiesta
Blood Money see Requiem for
  a Heavyweight
Blood of a Poet, The
  Durgnat 53-54, 101
  Kael (d) 239
  Macdonald xvi, (371)
Blood on the Sun
  Lejeune 153-54
Bloody Mama
  Reed (a) 285
Blow Job
  Reed (a) 193-94
Blow-Up
  Crist 206-08, 217, (251),
    267-68
  Kael (d) 31-37
  Kauffmann (a) 5-13
  Reed (a) 378-79

Sarris (a) 280-84
Schickel 91-94
Sheed 185-88
Simon (c) 264-71
Blue
  Reed (a) 344-46
Blue, Monte
  Weinberg 215
Blue Angel, The (Josef von Stern-
  berg)
  Agate (a) 75-76, 218-19
  Durgnat (32), (47)
  Kael (d) 239-40
  Young 177-80
Blue Angel (Edward Dmytryk)
  Weinberg 162
Blue Dahlia, The
  Agee 202-03
Blue Movie
  Reed (a) 194-95
  Sarris (b) 106-07
Bluebeard (Claude Chabrol) see
  Landru
Bluebeard's Eighth Wife (Ernst
  Lubitsch)
  Ferguson 218
Bob & Carol & Ted & Alice
  Farber 220-21
  Kael (a) 8-13
  Reed (a) 244-45
  Schickel 259-62
  Simon (b) 382-85
Boccaccio 70
  Sarris (b) 52-53
Body and Soul (Robert Rossen)
  Agee 281
  Kauffmann (a) 210, 214-15
  Pechter 148-49
Bodyguard see Yojimbo
Bofors Gun, The
  Kael (a) 89-90
  Reed (a) 389-90
Bogart, Humphrey
  Sarris (a) 262-63
Bogata nieviesta see Rich
  Bride, The
Bohème, La (Franco Zeffirelli)
  Simon (c) 192-93
Bombay Talkie
  Kael (a) 195-96
Bondu Saved from Drowning
  Kael (d) 140-42
  Pechter 203-08

Sarris (a)   287-89
Bonheur, Le
Simon (c)   228-32
Bonjour Tristesse
Alpert   114-17
Bonne Chance
Graham   55-56
Bonnes Femmes, Les
Sarris (a)   243-45
Bonnie and Clyde
Crist   243-44, (253), 257-58,
267-68
Farber   155-56
Kael (d)   47-63
Kauffmann (a)   18-24
Pechter   86-90
Sarris (a)   (353)
Schickel   140-44
Sheed   196-97
Simon (b)   168-71, 401
Young   391-92
Booloo
Graham   200-01
Boom!
Simon (b)   313-14
Boomerang! (Elia Kazan)
Agee   243-45
Winnington   78
Borinage
Van Doren   (335)
Born Free
Kael (d)   180-81
Reed (a)   348
Born to Win
Kael (a)   351-52
Born Yesterday
Gilliatt   74-77
Kael (d)   240
Borsalino
Reed (a)   296, 323-24
Bossak, Jerzy
Kauffmann (b)   404-05
Boston Strangler, The
Adler   271-72
Kael (b)   166-67
Reed (a)   203-04
Boucher, Le
Kael (a)   403-05
Box, The
Adler   128
Box of Pandora, The   see
Pandora's Box
BOX OFFICE   see   EXHIBITION

BOXING IN FILMS   see   FIGHT
FILMS
Boy (Nagisa Oshima)
Simon (b)   389
Boy Friend, The
Kael (a)   379-83
Boy in the Tree, The
Young   252
Boy Named Charlie Brown, A
Kael (a)   91-92
Boy Slaves
Ferguson   248-49
Boy Ten Feet Tall, A
Crist   117
Boys in the Band, The
Kael (a)   137-38
Reed (a)   283
Boys' School
Graham   239-40
Boys' Town
Ferguson   235
Boys Will Be Boys (William
Beaudine)
Graham   16
Brains Trust
Lejeune   98-99
Brakhage, Stan
Kael (c)   (318)
Sarris (a)   (290-91)
Brando, Marlon
Adler   (211)
Alpert   40-61
Crist   145-46
Durgnat   141
Kael (c)   45-46
Kael (d)   189-95
Kauffmann (b)   32-34
Brauner, Arthur
Weinberg   254
Breach of Promise   see   Adven-
ture in Blackmail
Break of Hearts
Graham   20-21
Break the News
Agee   150
Breakfast at Tiffany's
Gilliatt   218-19
Breaking Point (Michael Curtiz)
Farber   (61)
Breaking the Sound Barrier
Kael (d)   240-41
Breakup
Young   246

Breathless
  Alpert   119-20, 206-08
  Durgnat   (45), (232)
  Farber   (148-49)
  Kael (c)   127-32, (211-12),
    (215)
  Kauffmann (b)   238-41
  Macdonald (xiv), (175), 372-
    75
  Pechter   17-36, 312
  Sarris (a)   (262), (265)
  Sarris (b)   (62)
  Sontag (a)   (235)
  Weinberg   (176)
  Young   280
Brecht, Bertold
  Sarris (a)   (378)
  Sontag (a)   178, 180-81, 183
Breer, Robert
  Sontag (b)   (103)
Bresson, Robert
  Sarris (b)   (48)
  Sontag (a)   177-95, (245)
  Sontag (b)   (104), (112), (149-
    50), 175-77, 182-83, (185)
Brewster McCloud
  Kael (a)   227-28
Bride by Mistake
  Agee   (122)
Bride Comes Home, The
  Graham   45-46
Bride of Frankenstein, The
  Durgnat   106
  Ferguson   79, (174)
  Graham   5-6
  Sarris (b)   (59)
Bride of the Lake, The
  Ferguson   50
Bride Wore Black, The
  Adler   183-85, 195, 327
  Kael (b)   (108)
  Sarris (a)   380-82
  Simon (b)   182-84
  Young   337-38
Bride Wore Red, The
  Lejeune   25-28
Brides of Dracula
  Durgnat   38
Bridge, The (Bernhard Wicki)
  Kauffmann (b)   349-50
Bridge on the River Kwai, The
  Alpert   (21)
  Durgnat   (182)

Kael (c)   (8)
Sarris (a)   226-27
Weinberg   (258)
Brief Ecstasy
  Graham   167
Brief Encounter
  Agate (b)   261-62
  Agee   214-15, 235
  Lejeune   161-63
  Winnington   42-43
Brig, The
  Simon (c)   204
  Weinberg   (272)
Brighton Rock
  Winnington   98
Bring on the Girls
  Agee   146
Bringing Up Baby (Howard Hawks)
  Ferguson   215-16
  Kael (a)   (431)
  Kael (d)   241
British Agent
  Ferguson   47-48
British Film Institute
  Kauffmann (b)   402
BRITISH FILMS
  Alpert   22
BRITISH FILMS (1930's)
  Agate (b)   170
  Ferguson   50, 232
  Graham   29-40, 78-80, 243
BRITISH FILMS (1940's)
  Agate (b)   267, 269
  Winnington   82, 126
BRITISH FILMS (1950's)
  Kael (c)   62-64, 75-78
  Young   8-10, 138-40
BRITISH FILMS (1960's)
  Kael (b)   180-81
  Macdonald   395, 411
  Young   8-10, (300)
Broadway Bill (Frank Capra)
  Ferguson   58-59
Broadway by Light
  Durgnat   131-32
Broadway Melody of 1936
  Ferguson   94-96
Broadway Rhythm
  Agee   (93)
Broca, Philippe de
  Alpert   209-11
  Kauffmann (b)   407-08
Broken Arrow

Kael (d) 241-42
Broken Blossoms (D. W. Griffith)
  Agate (a) 22, 218
Broken Wings, The
  Adler 81-82
Bronenosets Potyomkin see Potemkin
Brother Sun and Sister Moon
  Kael (a) (182-83)
Brotherhood, The
  Kael (b) 243-47
Brotherly Love
  Kauffmann (a) 256-58
Brothers, The (Davie Macdonald)
  Agee (306
Brown, Ivor
  Agate (a) 38-39
Brücke see Bridge (Wicki)
Brute Force
  Agee 276
Buchman, Sidney
  Kael (d) 68, 78-81, 95
Büchse der Pandora, Die see
  Pandora's Box
Buck Benny Rides Again
  Ferguson (303)
BUDGETING see FINANCING;
  LOW BUDGET FILMS
Buffalo Bill
  Agee 93
BUFFS see FANS
Build My Gallows High see Out
  of the Past (Jacques Touineur)
Bullets or Ballots
  Graham 121
  Weinberg (55)
Bullfight
  Young 77-80
Bullfighter and the Lady, The
  Kael (d) 242
Bullitt
  Adler 270-71
  Kael (b) 165-66
  Kauffmann (a) 118-20
  Schickel 209-11
  Simon (b) 294-95
  Young 392-93
Bunny Lake Is Missing
  Sarris (a) 212-14
Buñuel, Luis
  Durgnat 64
  Farber 275-81
  Kael (b) 254-62

Kael (c) (340)
  Pechter 215-25
  Sarris (b) (51), 86
  Weinberg 252-53
  Young 288-89, 377-86
Buona Sera, Mrs. Campbell
  Reed (a) 143-45
Burgomaster of Stilemonde, The
  Agate (a) 34-37
Burmese Harp, The
  Simon (c) 249-50
  Young 103
Burn!
  Kael (a) 175-80
Bush Christmas
  Agee (294)
Busman's Honeymoon see
  Haunted Honeymoon
Butch Cassidy and the Sundance
  Kid
  Kael (a) 5-6
  Schickel 253-55
  Simon (b) 177-78, (401)
  Young 394-95
Butterfield 8
  Simon (a) (17), (21)
By Love Possessed
  Durgnat (224-25)
Bye Bye Braverman
  Adler 53-54
  Kael (b) 51-53
  Simon (b) 311

-C-

C. C. and Company
  Kael (a) 173-74
Cabaret
  Kael (a) 409-13
Cabinet of Dr. Caligari, The
  Durgnat 34, 103
  Ferguson (79)
  Kael (d) 242-43
  Macdonald xvi-xvii, (170)
  Pechter (304)
  Sontag (b) (102-03), (117)
Cabiria see Nights of Cabiria
Cactus Flower
  Reed (a) 249-50
Caesar and Cleopatra
  Agate (b) 262-64)
  Agee 212-13, 216

Lejeune 166-68
Café Metropole
  Graham 172
Cafe of Seven Sinners see Sev-
  en Sinners (Gay Garnett)
Cage aux Rossignols see Cage
  of Nightingales, A
Cage of Nightingales, A
  Agee 245
Cagney, James
  Agate (b) (178)
  Ferguson (6), 198-99
Cahiers du Cinéma (magazine)
  Alpert 200
  Durgnat 65-67, 146
  Macdonald (372)
  Simon (b) 6-10
Caldwell, Zoe
  Reed (b) 86-92
Call It a Day
  Graham 156
Call Me Genius
  Gilliatt 11-12
Call Northside 777
  Agee (300)
Camelot
  Simon (b) 328-29
Camera (Poland) see Kamera
  Unit
CAMERA WORK see CINEMA-
  TOGRAPHY
CAMERAMEN see CINEMA-
  TOGRAPHY
Cameron, Ian
  Sarris (b) 49
Camille (George Cukor)
  Agate (b) 143-44
  Durgnat 37-38
  Ferguson 170-71
  Kael (d) 243
Camille (Fred Niblo)
  Agate (a) 49-51
Camille without Camellias
  Simon (c) 184
CAMP see AESTHETICS
Can Hieronymus Merkin Ever...
  Reed (a) 158-60
Candlelight in Algeria
  Agee 106
Candy
  Adler 320-21
  Kael (b) 223-25
  Kauffmann (a) (134)

Reed (a) (214)
  Simon (b) (352)
Cangaceiro see Bandit (Lima
  Barreto)
Cannes Film Festival see In-
  ternational Film Festival,
  Cannes
Can't Help Singing
  Agee (135)
Canterbury Tale, A
  Lejeune 121
  Winnington 22
Canterville Ghost, The
  Agee 105-06
Cape Fear
  Macdonald 57-59
Caporal épinglé, Le see Elu-
  sive Corporal, The
Capra, Frank
  Farber 105-07
  Kael (a) (5)
  Pechter (54), (57), 123-62,
    (308)
  Sarris (b) (103)
Caprice
  Sarris (a) (298)
Capricious Summer
  Farber 232-33
Captain Blood (Michael Curtiz)
  Graham 54
Captain Eddie
  Agee 168
Captain from Castille
  Agee (294)
Captain Hates the Sea, The
  Ferguson 9, 112-16
Captain January (David Butler)
  Graham 92
Captain Kidd
  Agate (b) 260-61
Captains Courageous
  Ferguson 182-83
  Sarris (b) (16)
  Van Doren 365-67
Captain's Paradise, The
  Kael (d) 243
Captivation
  Agate (b) 47-48
Captive Heart, The
  Agee 251-52
  Lejeune 178-79
Carabiniers, Les
  Adler 126-27, 137-39, 326-27

Farber 270-71, 273-74
Gilliatt 91-95
Kael (b) (106)
Kauffmann (a) 81-83
Sheed 202-04
Simon (b) (380)
Caravan (Arthur Crabtree)
Lejeune 183
Card, The see Promoter, The
Card, James G.
Adler 335-38
Young 20-21
Cardinal, The
Kael (c) (9)
Macdonald 152-57
Sarris (a) 109-111
Simon (c) 97-98
Caressed
Simon (c) 186
Caretaker (Clive Donner) see
Guest
Carnal Knowledge
Kael (a) 282-85
Carné, Marcel
Farber 165
Sontag (a) (245)
Carnegie Hall
Agee 251
Carnet de Bal, Un
Graham 184
Kael (d) 243-44
Van Doren 396-98
Carnival in Costa Rica
Agee 252
Carnival in Flanders see Ker-
messe Héroïque, La
Carola
Kael (c) (300)
Caron, Leslie
Reed (b) 183-88
Carrington, V. C. see Court-
Martial (Anthony Asquith)
Carroll, Sydney (quoted)
Agate (b) 37, 64, 147
Carrosse d'or, Le see Golden
Coach, The
Carry On... (series)
Gilliatt 283-87
CARTOONS see ANIMATED
FILMS
Casablanca
Agee 29, (66)
Farber (180)

Kael (d) 245
Sarris (b) (31), 59
Casanova Brown
Agee 113-14
Casbah
Agee (306)
Case of Jealousy, A see Pizza
Triangle, The
Case of Lena Smith, The
Macdonald (xv)
Case of Sergeant Grischa, The
see Sergeant Grischa
Case of the Lucky Legs, The
Graham 49
Case of the Missing Switchboard
Operator see Affair of the
Heart, An
Cash see For Love or Money
(Zoltan Korda)
Casino Royale
Gilliatt 248-49
Casque d'Or
Kael (d) 245-46
Young 145-46
Cassavetes, John
Kael (b) 195-99
Young (145)
Castellari, Enzo G.
Adler 240
CASTING
Kael (d) 72-74, 90
Castle in Flanders, A
Graham 165
Cat and Mouse (H. Pohland)
Reed (a) 268
Cat and Two Women, A
Kael (d) 246
Cat Ballou
Crist (124-26), (149)
Kael (d) 29
Simon (c) 170
Cat Food
Farber 253
Cat on a Hot Tin Roof
Kauffmann (b) 79-81
Cat People, The
Kael (d) 246-57
Catch-22
Kauffmann (a) 271-76
Sarris (b) 230-36
Schickel 309-12
Simon (b) 326-27
Catch Us If You Can see

Having a Wild Weekend
Catherine the Great
    Ferguson 30-32
Caught (Max Ophuls)
    Kael (d) (296)
    Young 26-27
Cavalcade
    Agate (b) 78-80
    Kael (a) (16)
Caza, La see Hunt, The
Ceiling Zero
    Ferguson 11
Censored
    Adler 91-92
CENSORSHIP (see also Legion of
    Decency; PRODUCTION CODE;
    TRIALS, CENSORSHIP)
    Adler 341
    Agee 200, 238, 245
    Alpert 8-9, 134, 217-32, 246
    Ferguson (109), 214-15, 234,
        267, 399, 402-04
    Gilliatt 106
    Graham 11, 35, (69), 229,
        262, 269
    Kael (a) 377
    Kael (c) 43-44
    Kauffmann (a) 105, 147-48
    Lejeune 101-02
    Macdonald 55-57, 288-89,
        (327)
    Sarris (b) 106-10, 129, 256-
        58
    Schickel 158-59
    Simon (a) (34)
    Simon (c) (64), (15), (154)
    Van Doren 378-79, 408-11
Censorship in Denmark
    Simon (b) 153-54
Centre National du Cinéma
    (France)
    Adler 156-58
C'era una volta il West see
    Once in the Glorious West
Cerny Petr see Black Peter
Cerro Pelado
    Adler 353
Chabrol, Claude
    Simon (c) (127-28)
Chain, The
    Kauffmann (b) (399)
    Kauffmann (b) 397-98
Chairman, The

Reed (a) 240
Challenge, The (Milton Rosmer)
    Agate (b) 154-57
Chamade, La
    Reed (a) 183
    Simon (b) 264-66
Champion
    Farber 65-66
Champion, Gower
    Reed (c) 61-65
Champs-Elysées
    Graham 259
Chance see Chans
Changes
    Simon (b) 111-12
Chans
    Young 199-201
Chant du Styrène, Le
    Sarris (a) 103
Chapeau de Paille d'Italie, Le
    see Italian Straw Hat, The
Chaplin, Charles
    Agate (a) (7), 13-16, 168
    Agee 8-10, 17
    Ferguson 118-19
    Gilliatt 143-51, 156-57
    Macdonald (xi)
    Pechter (308)
    Sarris (b) 35-36
    Simon (a) 287
Chaplin, Charles, Jr. My Father,
    Charlie Chaplin
    Gilliatt 156-57
Chaplin, Geraldine
    Reed (c) 199-204
Chapman Report, The
    Kauffmann (b) (60)
Chappaqua
    Reed (a) 337-39
CHARACTER ACTORS
    Ferguson 6
CHARACTERIZATION
    Durgnat 178-81, 186, 194-96,
        208
    Farber 117-18
Charade
    Kael (c) (26)
    Sarris (a) 113-14
Charge of the Light Brigade, The
    (Michael Curtiz)
    Agate (b) 140-41
    Lejeune 22
Charge of the Light Brigade, T'

(Tony Richardson)
Kael (b) 145-48
Kauffmann (a) 106-09
Reed (a) 202-03
Sheed 232
Simon (b) 315-16
Charley's Aunt (Archie Mayo)
Lejeune (76)
Charlie Bubbles
Adler 44-46, 58-59, 325
Farber 189, 211-13
Kael (b) 47-48
Sarris (a) 339-42
Schickel 168-70
Simon (b) 309-10
Charlie Chan at the Circus
Graham 89
Charlie Chan in Shanghai
Graham 50
Charly
Kael (b) 150-52
Young 348-49
Charmes de l'existence, Les
Durgnat 124-25, 131
Charulata
Young (11)
Chase, The (Arthur Penn)
Farber 163-64
Kael (d) 151-53
Reed (a) 355-58
Chasse à l'Homme, La see
Male Hunt, The
Che!
Reed (a) 234-35
Cheat, The see Tricheurs, Les
Cheaters, The see Tricheurs,
Les
Cheers for Miss Bishop
Ferguson 348-49
Chelovek No. 217 see Girl
Number 217
Chelsea Girls, The
Crist (269)
Reed (a) 193
Sarris (a) 274-76
Simon (c) 261-62
Cheyenne Autumn
Kauffmann (b) 169-70
Cheyenne Social Club, The
Reed (a) 295
Chicago, Chicago see Gaily,
Gaily
Chien Andalou, Un

Kael (c) (286), (290)
Sontag (b) (121), (158)
Child Is Waiting, A
Simon (c) 55-56
Childhood of Maxim, The see
Maxim Gorky Trilogy
CHILDREN, EFFECTS OF FILM
ON
Agate (a) 84
Alpert 225-26
Macdonald 449-50
CHILDREN AND THE CINEMA
Crist 111-14
Kael (b) 99-100
Kael (d) 179-80, 184-85
Macdonald (59)
Reed (a) 223
Sarris (b) 12-13
Children Are Watching Us, The
Kael (d) 247
Children at School
Ferguson (207)
Graham 174
CHILDREN IN FILMS
Ferguson 155, 214-15
Schickel 84
Children of Paradise, The
Agee 246-47
Durgnat (77)
Kael (b) 115
Kael (d) 247
Macdonald (371), 456-58
Sarris (a) (227)
Simon (c) 19-20, 119-20
Young 22-23
Children on Trial
Winnington 67-68
CHILDREN'S FILMS see CHIL-
DREN AND THE CINEMA
Children's Hour, The
Kael (c) 175-76
Sarris (b) (62)
Chimes at Midnight see Fal-
staff (Orson Wells)
China (John Farrow)
Agate (b) 227
China Is Near
Adler 8-9
Farber 205-06
Kael (b) 4-6
Kauffmann (a) 50-52
Sarris (a) 336-39
Simon (b) 286-90

Chinese Girl, The   see   Chinoise,
  La
Chinoise, La
  Adler 105-06, 122-23, 149
  Farber (8), 269-72
  Kael (b) 76-84
  Kauffmann (a) 66-70
  Sarris (a) 349-52
  Sarris (b) 99
  Schickel 171-73
  Simon (b) 249-60
Chitty Chitty Bang Bang
  Adler 321-23
  Kael (b) 225-27
Chocolate Soldier, The
  Lejeune 70-71
Choses de la Vie, Les
  Reed (a) 407
Christine see Carnet de Bal
Christmas Holiday
  Agee (102)
  Lejeune 127-28
Christmas in July
  Ferguson 335
Christmas Morn
  Young 248-49
Christopher Strong
  Kael (a) 341, 346
Chronicle of a Summer
  Kauffmann (b) 266-67
Chu Chin Chow (Walter Forde)
  Ferguson 50-51
Chump at Oxford, A
  Graham 273
Chushingura (Hiroshi Inagaki)
  Crist 189-90
Chute de la Maison Usher, La
  Durgnat 94
Ciascuno il suo see We Still
  Kill the Old Way
Ciel et la boue, Le see Sky
  Above, the Mud Below, The
Cimarron (Wesley Ruggles)
  Agate (a) 91-94
  Agate (b) 50
Cina è vicina see China Is Near
Cincinnati Kid, The
  Crist 138-39, 165-66
CINEMA DIRECT see CINEMA
  VERITE
Cinema 16 (society, New York)
  Agee 307-09
  Macdonald 312-16

CINEMA VERITE
  Kael (b) 12-16
  Kauffmann (a) 151, 155
  Sarris (b) 104
  Young 221-22, (343)
Cinemascope
  Alpert 19
Cinémathèque (Paris)
  Adler 254-58
CINEMATIC see AESTHETICS;
  CINEMATOGRAPHY; EDITING
CINEMATOGRAPHY (see also
  AESTHETICS, EDITING)
  Agate (a) 192
  Agee (79)
  Alpert 251
  Durgnat 27, 29-30, 34-35,
    40, 49-59, 79, 93-94, 96-
    98, 100-05
  Farber 3-11, 62, 75-77, 192,
    197
  Ferguson 194, 447-50, 457
  Kael (d) 13-14, 93-94
  Kauffmann (a) 163
  Kauffmann (b) 419
  Macdonald 5, 44
  Pechter 152, 154, 264
  Sarris (b) 36, 218
  Sontag (a) 228-29
  Sontag (b) 106, 108-10
  Young 18-19
Cinerama
  Alpert 19
Ciociaria, La see Two Women
Circle, The see Vicious Circle
Circus (Charles Chaplin)
  Kauffmann (a) 223-26
Circus Clown, The
  Ferguson (42)
Citizen Kane
  Agate (a) 227-31
  Farber 78-81, 144
  Ferguson 359, 363-65, 368-
    71
  Kael (d) 247-48
  Lejeune 62-63
  Macdonald xiv, (484)
  Pechter 167-69, 310-11
  Sarris (b) 44-45, (61), 111-
    36
  Simon (b) (66)
  Simon (c) 33-35
  Young 408-09

City Lights
    Agate (b)   51
    Agee   10
    Pechter   (303)
City of Gold
    Kael (d)   248
City That Stopped Hitler--Heroic
    Stalingrad, The
    Agee   51-52
Clair, René
    Agate (b)   (203)
    Agee   75-76
    Ferguson   21
    Pechter   306-07
Claire's Knee
    Kael (a)   264-67
Clarens, Carols. An Illustrated
    History of the Horror Film
    Simon (b)   403-06
CLASSIFICATION OF FILMS   see
    RATINGS FOR FILMS
Claudia
    Agee   50-51
Clear Skies
    Crist   (35)
Cleo from 5 to 7
    Kauffmann (b)   252-54
    Young   (260)
Cleopatra (Joseph Mankiewicz)
    Crist   (xvii-xviii), 9-13
    Macdonald   301-34
    Simon (c)   78-81
Climax, The (George Waggner)
    Agate (b)   256-57
Clock, The (Vincente Minelli)
    Agee   164-66, 357-58
Clockwork Orange, A
    Kael (a)   373-77
Closely Watched Trains
    Adler   (347)
    Gilliatt   129
    Kauffmann (a)   29-30
    Schickel   152-54
    Simon (b)   279
Close-Up (magazine, 1927-31)
    Durgnat   (43)
Clouds over Europe
    Ferguson   260
Clowns, The
    Gilliatt   15-20
Club des Femmes, Le
    Van Doren   378
CLUBS, FILM   see   SOCIETIES,

FILM
Cluny Brown
    Agee   203
    Kael (d)   248-49
Coastal Command
    Lejeune   83-84
Cobra (Mario Sequi)
    Adler   97
Cobra Woman
    Lejeune   132
Cobweb, The
    Kael (c)   (58)
    Kael (d)   249
Cobweb Castle, The   see
    Throne of Blood
Cocteau, Jean
    Kael (c)   (296)
    Pechter   280
    Sontag (a)   191, 193-95, 199-
    200
Cocteau, Jean (quoted)
    Sontag (a)   197
    Sontag (b)   109
Cold Wind in August, A
    Kael (d)   249-50
COLLECTIONS OF FILMS   see
    PRIVATE COLLECTIONS OF
    FILMS
Collector, The
    Crist   121-23
    Kauffmann (b)   132-34
    Sarris (a)   195-99
    Sarris (b)   62
    Simon (c)   162-66
College   see   Hohe Schule
Colonel Blimp
    Agee   152-53
COLOR FILMS (see also
    BLACK AND WHITE FILMS)
    Adler   273, 300-01
    Agee   224
    Durgnat   53, 55, 97-98, 115-
    116
    Graham   (1), 8
    Kael (a)   371-73
    Macdonald   459-60
    Sarris (a)   154-55, (196),
    (323)
    Sarris (b)   62-63
COLOR IN FILMS   see   COLOR
    FILMS
COLOR SYSTEMS
    Durgnat   116

Colossus see Forbin Project,
  The
Colt 45
  Sarris (b) 71-72
Columbia Revolt
  Adler 287-88
Come and Get It (Hawks and Wy-
  ler)
  Ferguson (7), (371)
Come Dance with Me
  Macdonald 443
Come out of the Pantry
  Graham 39
Comedians, The
  Simon (b) 308-09
COMEDIANS
  Ferguson 322-23
  Lejeune 90-91, 166
  Pechter 305
  Sarris (b) 13
COMEDIES
  Agate 170
  Agee 2-3, 17-18, 202
  Ferguson xi, 18-24, 113
  Gilliatt 168
  Kael (a) 10-11, 372-73
  Kael (d) 6
  Macdonald 160-66, 405
COMEDIES--BEST FILMS
  Ferguson 19, 24, 161
  Kael (a) 10
  Kael (c) 148
  Macdonald 160, 406-07
COMEDIES, SILENT
  Agee 2-19
  Farber 93-94
  Ferguson 20
COMEDIES, SOUND
  Ferguson 22
COMEDY
  Ferguson 405
  Gilliatt 194-95
Comic, The
  Kael (a) 60-62
Coming Apart
  Kael (a) 36
  Reed (a) (255)
  Schickel 266-69
  Simon (b) 151
Commandos Strike at Dawn, The
  Agee 26-27
COMMERCIALS see ADVER-
  TISING FILMS

Communicants see Winter Light
COMMUNISM AND THE CINEMA
  Kael (c) 43-44, 326-46
Compagni, I see Organizer,
  The
COMPOSERS see MUSIC, FILM
Compulsion
  Kael (d) 250
Comrade X
  Ferguson 333
Concerto see I've Always Loved
  You
Concerto for Sub-Machine Gun
  Adler 19
Conclusion see Two Daughters
Condamné à mort s'est eschappé,
  Un see Man Escaped, A
Condemned of Altona, The
  Kauffmann (b) 123-24
Confession, The (Costi Costa-
  Gavras)
  Kael (a) 200-05
Confession of Felix Krull, The
  Kael (d) 251
Confessions of a Nazi Spy
  Ferguson 253
  Graham 229
Confidential Agent
  Agee 178-79
  Kael (d) 251
Confidential Report see Mr.
  Arkadin
Conflict (Curt Bernhardt)
  Agee 169
Conformist, The
  Kael (a) 270-75
Congress Dances
  Agate (b) 57-60
Conklin, Chester
  Agee (5)
Connection, The
  Kauffmann (b) 113-16
  Macdonald (56-57)
Conquer by the Clock
  Agee 27
Conqueror Worm, The
  Adler 209
Conquest (Clarence Brown)
  Graham 187, 190
CONSERVATION OF FILMS see
  PRESERVATION OF FILMS
Constant Nymph, The (Edmund
  Goulding)

Lejeune 140-41
Contempt
  Crist 86
  Kauffmann (b) 243-44
  Sarris (a) 184-89
  Simon (c) 145
CONTINUITY (see also EDITING)
  Farber 191
Cool Hand Luke
  Kauffmann (a) 28
  Schickel 149-51
  Simon (b) 72-73
Cool World, The
  Crist 71-72
  Kauffmann (b) 164-66
  Macdonald 323-27, (344)
  Sarris (a) 135-36
Cooper, Gary
  Durgnat 139-40
Copacabana
  Agee (273)
Coppola, Francis Ford
  Pechter (156)
  Reed (b) 260-65
Corn Is Green, The
  Agee 157
Corner in Wheat, A
  Adler 80
Cornered (Edward Dmytryk)
  Agee 189-90
Corruzione, La
  Young 232-33
Corsican Brothers, The (George
    Ratoff)
  Lejeune 72-73
Corvette K-225
  Agate (b) 244
  Agee 54
Costello, Lou see Abbott and
    Costello
COSTUMES
  Durgnat 37-38
Counsellor-at-law
  Kael (d) 251-52
Count of Monte Cristo, The (Row-
    land V. Lee)
  Ferguson 53-54
Counter-Attack
  Agee 160-61
Countess from Hong Kong, A
  Crist 237-38
  Gilliatt 143-54
  Sarris (a) 292-96

County Doctor, The (Henry King)
  Graham 80-81
Courage of Lassie
  Winnington 60
Court-Martial (Anthony Asquith)
  Sarris (a) 20-21
Cousins, The
  Alpert 204-05
  Durgnat 201-08
  Kael (c) 132-36
Cover Girl
  Agee 86-88, (93)
Cover to Cover
  Graham 100
Covered Wagon, The
  Agee (228)
Coward, Noel
  Lejeune 162-63
Cowboy and the Lady, The (H. C.
    Potter)
  Ferguson 241
Cowboys, The (Mark Rydell)
  Kael (a) 390-93
Crack in the World
  Crist 116-17
Cracksman, The
  Gilliatt 158-63
Cranes Are Flying, The
  Kael (c) 42
  Kauffmann (b) (362)
  Macdonald 268-70
Crash Dive (Archie Mayo)
  Agate (b) 229
Crawford, Joan
  Agate (b) (188)
  Farber 150-51
Crawford, Michael
  Reed (c) 152-57
Crazy Quilt
  Crist 216
Crazy Ray, The
  Agee (151)
CREDIT TITLES (see also
    TITLING)
  Kael (c) 39-40
  Macdonald 458-59
Crime and Punishment (Marcel
    Aymé)
  Kael (d) 252
Crime and Punishment (Josef von
    Sternberg)
  Graham 61-62
  Van Doren 308

Crime et Châtiment (Pierre Che-
    nal)
    Graham   57-58
    Van Doren   308
Crime de Monsieur Lange, Le
    Durgnat   (77)
    Sarris (a)   131-33
    Simon (c)   118
CRIME FILMS (see also DE-
    TECTIVE FILMS; GANGSTER
    FILMS; VIOLENCE IN FILMS)
    Crist   75, 251-53
    Kael (b)   182
Crime School
    Ferguson   220-21
Crime without Passion
    Ferguson   48-49
Crimes of Dr. Mabuse, The   see
    Last Will of Dr. Mabuse, The
Criminal Life of Archibaldo de la
    Cruz, The
    Kauffmann (b)   352
Crimson Pirate, The
    Alpert   32
    Kael (d)   252
Crisis (Drew and Leacock)
    Kauffmann (b)   397
Crist, Judith
    Crist   xi-xix
Cristo Proibito, Il
    Kael (d)   252-53
CRITICISM (see also AESTHET-
    ICS; "AUTEUR" THEORY)
    Adler   xv-xxv, 82-85, 201,
        262, 304-08
    Agate (a)   7, 23-24, 98, 249
    Agate (b)   37, 189-90, 213-14
    Agee   i, 22-23
    Alpert   5-10
    Crist   xiv-xix
    Durgnat   13-16, 19-21, 41, 43,
        66, 71-75, 164, 268-69
    Farber   12, 14, 24, 176, 184
    Ferguson   44, 56, 58, 187,
        272, 411-13
    Graham   243
    Kael (a)   230-34
    Kael (b)   vii-viii, 97, 108-09,
        127
    Kael (c)   23-27
    Kael (d)   21
    Lejeune   148
    Macdonald   175-76, 462-63, 471

Reed (a)   387
Pechter   39, 98, 266-69, 282-
    83, 285, 312-13, 315
Sarris (a)   14-15, 361-62
Sarris (b)   16-18, (26-27), 41,
    47-48, 63, 66-80, 83-84
Schickel   19, 24, 27, 34, 36-
    37, 200-01
Simon (b)   (1), (22-24), 403
Simon (c)   1-16
Warshow   19
Winnington   94
Young   ix-xi, xiii-xv, 44, 329,
    394
CRITICS
    Agate (a)   7-8
    Agate (b)   31-32, 93, 206, 218
    Agee (188)
    Alpert   6-9
    Durgnat   13-14, 74, 152-53
    Farber   57, 71-72
    Ferguson   x, xiii, 67-68, 412,
        434
    Kael (c)   228-34
    Macdonald   xi-xii, 29
    Sarris (a)   114
    Sarris (b)   11, 22, 30
    Schickel   13-14, 18, 24-28,
        35-37, 69-70
    Simon (a)   267
    Simon (b)   2-6, (136), 336-37
    Simon (c)   13-15
    Winnington   123
    Young   xiv, 289, 306, 381
Cromwell
    Kael (a)   181
Cronaca familiare, La   see   Fam-
    ily Diary, The
Cross of Lorraine, The
    Agee   62
Crossfire (Edward Dmytryk)
    Agee   269-70
    Brown (a)   50-53
    Kael (d)   253
    Winnington   96-97
Crowley, Mart
    Reed (b)   174-82
Crowther, Bosley
    Adler   (xiv), (xviii)
    Sarris (a)   292-93
Crowther, Bosley (quoted)
    Kael (d)   207
Crusades, The

Graham 16-18
Cry, The see Grido, Il
Cry Havoc
Agate (b) 244-45
Agee 62
Csillagosok, Katonák see Red
and the White, The
CUBAN FILMS (early 1960's)
Young 268-69
CUBAN FILMS (late 1960's)
Adler 339-54
Cukor, George
Kael (c) 303-05
Cul-de-Sac
Crist 195-96, 210-11
Simon (c) 257-58
Curée see Game Is Over
Current
Kauffmann (b) (399)
Curse of the Cat People, The
Agee 85-86, (137)
Farber 48-49
Custer of the West
Adler 192
CUTS IN FILMS see VERSIONS,
ABBREVIATED
CUTTING see EDITING
Cynara
Agate (b) 83-85
Cyrano de Bergerac (Alexander
Korda)
Agate (a) 188
Czar to Lenin
Van Doren 359-60
Warshow 273-80
CZECH FILMS (mid-1960's)
Gilliatt 127-29
Simon (b) 277-78, 283
CZECH FILMS (late 1960's)
Adler 225-28
Kael (b) 98

-D-

Daisies, The
Gilliatt 130-31
Simon (b) (278), 282
Dama s sobatchkoi see Lady
with a Dog
Dame aux Camélias, La (Abel
Gance)
Agate (b) 121

Dame aux Camélias, La (Fred
Niblo) see Camille
Dames du Bois de Boulogne, Les
Sarris (a) 133-35
Simon (c) 117-18
Sontag (a) (241)
Damned, The (Joseph Losey)
see These Are the Damned
Damned, The (Luchino Visconti)
Kael (a) 86-88
Kauffmann (a) (245)
Schickel 291-92
Simon (b) 190-96
Weinberg 337-38
DANCE AND THE CINEMA
Kael (b) 70-71
Kael (c) 279-80
DANCE FILMS
Simon (c) 176-77
Dance Programme see Carnet
de Bal
Dancing Mothers
Kael (d) 253
Dandy in Aspic, A
Adler 101-02
Dangerous
Graham 81-82
Dangerous Journey
Agee 123
Danish Parish Churches (Carl
Dreyer)
Durgnat 118
Dark Angel, The (Sidney Frank-
lin)
Graham 25
Dark at the Top of the Stairs,
The
Macdonald (459)
Dark Corner
Agee 217-18
Dark Eyes
Graham 211
Dark Journey
Graham 141
Dark Mirror, The (Robert Siod-
mak)
Agee 226-27
Dark of the Sun
Adler 191-92
Dark Rapture
Ferguson 240
Graham 270
Dark Victory

Ferguson 259-60
Dark Waters
  Agee 130
Darling
  Crist 148
  Sarris (a) (206)
  Schickel 39-42
  Kael (d) 158-59
  Kauffmann (b) 206-09
Darling Lili
  Reed (a) 281
Darrach, Brad
  Macdonald 463-64
D'Arrast, Harry see Arrast,
  Harry d'Abbadie d'
Date with a Lonely Girl, A see
  T. R. Baskin
Daughters Courageous
  Graham 250-52
David and Lisa
  Crist 17-18
  Farber 147
  Kael (c) (246)
  Simon (c) 50-51
David Copperfield (George Cukor)
  Agate (a) 134-37
  Agate (b) 112-14
  Ferguson 67
Davis, Bette
  Agate (b) 196
  Reed (b) 11-21
Dawn Patrol, The (Edmund Gould-
  ing)
  Graham 207, 210
Day at the Races, A
  Ferguson 183-84
  Graham 160-61
  Van Doren 367-69
Day in the Country, A
  Kael (d) 254
  Winnington 82-83
Day of the Great Adventure, The
  Graham 62, 64
Day of Wrath
  Agee 303-05
  Durgnat 105-06
  Kael (d) 254
  Warshow 261-67
  Winnington 72-73
Day the Earth Caught Fire, The
  Kael (c) 176-79
Day the Earth Stood Still, The
  Farber 59-60

Day with Timmy Page, A
  Adler 130-31
Daybreak (Michael Carné)
  Agee 273
  Durgnat 226
  Ferguson 216
  Graham 193
  Kael (c) (298)
  Winnington 53
Daydreams (Ivor Montagu)
  Kael (d) 253-54
Days and Nights
  Agee 200
Days of Glory
  Agee 102
Days of Wine and Roses
  Farber (154)
de Broca, Philippe see Broca,
  Philippe de
de Haviland, Olivia see Havi-
  land, Olivia de
Dead End
  Agate (b) 147-49
  Ferguson 192
  Graham 180-81
Dead Heat on a Merry-Go-Round
  Sarris (b) 188-90
Dead Man see Death
Dead of Night
  Agee 213
  Kael (d) 254-55
Deadline at Dawn
  Agee 197
Deadly Invention, The
  Kael (b) 192
  Kael (d) 255-56
Deadly Is the Female see Gun
  Crazy
Dealers in Death
  Ferguson 60-62
Dean, James
  Alpert 44
Dear John
  Crist 215
  Reed (a) 327-28
  Schickel 62-64
  Simon (c) 214-18
Death
  Weinberg (178)
Death of a Gunfighter
  Reed (a) 177-79
Death of a Salesman
  Pechter 279-80

Warshow 173-88
Debut, The
   Kael (a) 311
Dee, Sandra
   Alpert 93-94
Déep End
   Gilliatt 101-03
Deep Waters (Henry King)
   Agee (309)
Deerslayer (Lew Landers)
   Agee 61
Defector, The
   Crist 202-03
Defiant Ones, The
   Kael (d) 205-06
Dehn, Paul (quoted)
   Agate (b) 144
Déjeuner sur l'herbe, Le
   Durgnat (78)
   Weinberg 202
Delfini see Dolphins
Delo Artamonovich see Arta-
   monov and Sons
Demanty noci see Diamonds of
   the Night
DeMille, Cecil B.
   Agee 379-80
   Weinberg 218
Demi-Paradise see Adventure
   for Two
Demoiselles de Rochefort see
   Young Girls of Rochefort
Demon (Kaneto Shindo) see
   Onibaba
Demonio, Il
   Young 225
Dennis, Sandy
   Reed (c) 76-81
Départ, Le
   Crist (269)
   Farber 228
   Gilliatt 99-100
   Sarris (a) 314-15
   Simon (b) 378
   Sontag (b) (140)
Deputat Baltiki see Baltic
   Deputy, The
Derrière la façade see 33
   [trente-trois] rue de Mont-
   martre
DeSade
   Kael (a) 18-19
Descendant of Genghis Khan see

Storm over Asia
Deschner, Donald. The Films of
   Spencer Tracy
   Sarris (a) 434-35
Desert Victory
   Agee 33-35, (65)
Deserter, The (Vsevolod Pudov-
   kin)
   Graham 132-33
Deserter and the Nomads, The
   Simon (b) 390
Deserto rosso, Il see Red Des-
   ert, The
DeSica, Vittorio
   Kael (a) 360-66
   Kael (c) (247-48), (341)
   Kauffmann (b) 406
Desire (Frank Borzage)
   Graham 64
Desire Under the Elms
   Kauffmann (b) 70-73
Desnois, Edmundo
   Adler 343
Desperadoes (Charles Vidor)
   Agate (a) 424-43
Desperate Characters
   Gilliatt 81-86
Destination Tokyo
   Agee 68
Destiny of a Man see Fate of
   a Man
Destroy, She Said
   Simon (b) 386-87
Destry Rides Again (George Mar-
   shall)
   Graham 270-71
   Kael (d) 256
Detective, The
   Kael (d) 256
DETECTIVE FILMS (see also
   CRIME FILMS; GANGSTER
   FILMS; THRILLERS)
   Crist 177-79
   Graham 48
Detective Story
   Farber 42-44, 73-74
Detstvo Ivana see My Name Is
   Ivan
Deus eo diabo na terra do sol
   see Black God, White Devil
Deutschland, Erwache see Ger-
   many Awake!
Deux ou trois choses que je sais

d'elle see Two or Three
  Things I Know About Her
Deuxième bureau see Second
  Bureau
Deveti krug see Ninth Circle
Devi
  Kael (c) 245-55
Devil and Daniel Webster, The
  see All That Money Can Buy
Devil and Miss Jones, The
  Agate (a) (224)
  Ferguson 357-59
Devil and the Nun, The see
  Mother Joan of the Angels
Devil and the Ten Commandments,
  The
  Kauffmann (b) 262-63
Devil by the Tail, The
  Gilliatt 222-23
Devil Dogs of the Air
  Ferguson 68
Devil in the Flesh, The
  Durgnat 55
  Kael (d) 257
Devil Is a Sissy, The
  Ferguson 6-7, 156-57
Devil Is a Woman, The
  Durgnat 95
  Weinberg (178)
Devil Strikes at Night, The
  Kael (d) 257-58
Devil Takes the Count, The see
  Devil Is a Sissy, The
Devils, The
  Kael (a) (315)
Devil's Disciple, The
  Alpert 31-32
Devil's Envoys, The
  Agee 275-76
Devil's Eye, The
  Gilliatt 244-45
  Kauffmann (b) 281-82
Devil's General, The
  Kael (d) 258
  Young 81
Devil's Passkey, The
  Weinberg 213
Devotion (Curtis Bernhardt)
  Agee 198
  Winnington 63
Dewhurst, Colleen
  Reed (b) 116-24
Dezertir see Deserter (Vsevo-

lod Pudovkin)
Diable au corps, Le see Devil
  in the Flesh, The
Diable et les dix commandements,
  Le see Devil and the Ten
  Commandments, The
Diable par la queue Le see
  Devil by the Tail, The
Diabolique
  Kael (d) 258-59
Diaboliques, Les see Diabol-
  ique
Dial M for Murder
  Kael (d) 259
DIALOG
  Agate (a) 29-30
  Agate (b) 44, 197
  Alpert 244-45
  Brown (c) 253
  Farber 61, 116
  Ferguson 431-32
  Lejeune 112-13
  Macdonald (388)
  Pechter 306, 308, 310-11
  Sontag (a) 182, 200-02
Diamond Earrings see Earrings
  of Madame de..., The
Diamonds and Crime see Hi
  Diddle Diddle
Diamonds Are Forever
  Kael (a) 388-89
Diamonds of the Night
  Adler 79-80
  Simon (b) 285-86
  Young 279
Diary of a Chambermaid (Luis
  Buñuel)
  Kauffmann (b) 352
  Weinberg (220)
  Young (256)
Diary of a Country Priest
  Kael (d) 259
  Sontag (a) (201)
Diary of a Mad Housewife
  Reed (a) 293-94
Diary of Anne Frank, The
  Alpert 145-47
  Pechter (8)
Diary of David Holzman, The
  Adler 275
Dietrich, Marlene
  Reed (c) 238-45
Dietstvo Gorkovo see Maxim

Gorky Trilogy
Dieu créa la femme, Et see
    And God Created Woman
Dieux s'amusent see Amphitry-
    on (Reinhold Schuenzel)
Diga sul Pacifico, La see Sea
    Wall, The
Dimanches de Ville-d'Avray,
    Les see Sundays and Cybèle
Dinner at Eight
    Agate (b) 90-92
    Farber (145)
Diogenes Perhaps
    Adler 19
DIRECT CINEMA see CINEMA
    VERITE
DIRECTING
    Durgnat 34-36, 40-42
    Ferguson 13, 16-17, 23,
        (70), 335
    Kael (b) 94-97, 205
    Pechter 156-57
    Sarris (b) 81-86
    Weinberg (153)
DIRECTORS
    Agate (a) 8, 213
    Agate (b) 203
    Agee 190, 330
    Alpert 130-33, 162
    Crist 183-84
    Durgnat 23, 30, 61, 63, 76,
        80-81, 117-18, (135)
    Farber 9, 11-18, 203
    Ferguson 9-10, 362
    Kael (d) 14, 16, 59
    Kauffmann (a) 22-23, (165)
    Kauffmann (b) 406
    Lejeune 169
    Macdonald xi-xiii, 25, 64-67,
        76-77, 103, 185-86, 306,
        (350), 446, 453
    Pechter 67
    Sarris (a) (45), (251), (282),
        340
    Sarris (b) 23, 26-37, 46-47,
        75, 81-82, 130, 142
    Simon (b) 12, 180-81, 275-
        77
    Sontag (a) 245
    Sontag (b) 112, 170-71
    Weinberg 143
    Winnington 125-26
    Young 347

Dirty Dozen, The
    Adler (3), (5), 64
    Crist (253)
    Kael (a) (315)
    Sarris (a) 296-98
    Sheed 198-99
Dirty Harry
    Kael (a) 385-88
Dishonored (Josef von Sternberg)
    Weinberg 219, 263
Disney, Walt
    Agee (18)
    Brown (b) 91-98
    Crist (112-14)
    Ferguson 373
    Kael (b) 191
    Lejeune 36-37
    Pechter 6
    Weinberg 329-32 [NB: Disney
        Studios not familiar with
        cartoon referred to here;
        correct title unable to be
        identified]
Disorder
    Simon (c) 123
Disparus de St. Agil, Les see
    Boys' School
Disputed Passage
    Graham 257
DISTRIBUTION (see also EX-
    HIBITION)
    Alpert 13, 15-17
    Crist 115
    Ferguson 298-300
    Sarris (b) 96
    Schickel 21-22, 79-80, 207-
        08
Dive Bomber
    Ferguson 386-87
Divided World, A
    Young 240-41, 244, 248-49
Divine Lady, The
    Agate (b) 18-20
Divorce American Style
    Kael (b) (21-22)
    Sarris (a) 306
    Schickel 119-22
Divorce--Italian Style
    Farber 152
    Young 172-74
Djävulens öga see Devil's Eye
Djungelsaga see Flute and the
    Arrow

Dni i nochi   see   Days and Nights
Do You Love Me?
    Agate (b)   275-77
Doc
    Kael (a)   349
Dr. Caligari   see   Cabinet of
    Dr. Caligari, The
Dr. Ehrlich's Magic Bullet
    Ferguson   292
Doctor Faustus   (Burton and Cog-
    hill)
    Adler   34-35
    Kael (b)   40-41
    Young   317-18
Dr. Kildare's Wedding Day
    Ferguson   389
Dr. Monica
    Ferguson   40
Dr. Socrates
    Graham   50-51
Dr. Strangelove
    Crist   43-46, (67), 88
    Gilliatt   119-22
    Kael (d)   62-63
    Kauffmann (b)   14-19
    Macdonald   289-93
    Sarris (a)   119-22
    Simon (c)   105-07
    Weinberg   240
Dr. Zhivago
    Crist   155-58
    Kael (d)   136-37
    Sarris (a)   225-29
    Schickel   46-49
    Simon (c)   204-08
Doctor's Dilemma, The
    Kauffmann (b)   90-93
Doctors' Wives
    Kael (a)   250-60
DOCUMENTARY FILMS   (see al-
    so CINEMA VERITE)
    Durgnat   (61)
    Graham   223
    Kauffmann (a)   79-80
    Sarris (a)   313-14
    Sarris (b)   101-03
    Schickel   186
    Sontag (b)   101, (113), 116
    Van Doren   334-36, 403-05
    Young   242
Dodsworth
    Graham   113
Does, The   see   Biches, Les

Doesburg, Theo Van   see   Van
    Doesburg, Theo
Doknotcheno pismo   see   Letter
    That Was Not Sent
Dolce Vita, La
    Alpert   191-95
    Durgnat   (233-34)
    Kael (c)   (44), (149), (182-84),
        192-94
    Kauffmann (b)   (67-68), (207-
        08), 320-22
    Pechter   37-43
    Macdonald   348-49
    Sarris (a)   33
    Simon (a)   17-21
    Weinberg   177-78
Doll, The (A. Mattssonn)   see
    Wax Doll, The
Dollar Between the Teeth, A
    see   Stranger in Town, A
Dollaro tra i denti, Un   see
    Stranger in Town, A
Dolphins, The
    Young   135-36
Domicile conjugal   see   Bed and
    Board
Don Quixote (Grigori Kozinstev)
    Weinberg   (176)
Don Quixote (Georg Pabst)
    Ferguson   64-65
    Kael (d)   259-60
Donat, Robert
    Agate (a)   165-66
Don't Look Back
    Kael (b)   14-15
    Sarris (a)   309-14
    Sheed   206-07
Don't Lose Your Head
    Gilliatt   287-88
Don't Make Waves
    Sarris (a)   297-98
Don't Raise the Bridge, Lower the
    River
    Gilliatt   169-71
Donzoko   see   Lower Depths
    (Akira Kurosawa)
Dood Wasser
    Graham   18-19
Doors of the Night   see   Gates
    of the Night
Dorado, El (Howard Hawks)
    Kael (d)   45
    Sarris (a)   299-302

Dos au mur   see   Back to the
   Wall
Double Indemnity
   Agee   119-20, (138)
   Simon (a)   (27-28)
   Winnington   24-25
Double Life, A (George Cukor)
   Winnington   114
Double Man, The
   Adler   134
Double Tour, A   see   Leda
Doubting Thomas
   Ferguson   91
Dovzhenko, Alexander
   Pechter   302-03
   Sarris (b)   141
Down Argentine Way
   Agate (b)   181-82
Down to Earth (Alexander Hall)
   Agee   272, 375
Downhill Racer, The
   Kael (a)   45-47
   Reed (a)   (260)
   Schickel   270-73
   Simon (b)   301-03
Dragon Seed
   Agee   109-10
   Lejeune   129
   Winnington   80
Dramatic School
   Lejeune   45-46
Drame de Shanghai
   Graham   235-36
Dramma della gelosia   see   Piz-
   za Triangle, The
Drawing of Leonardo da Vinci,
   The
   Durgnat   119
Dreaded Mafia   see   Salvatore
   Giuliano
Dream of Kings, A
   Reed (a)   252-53
Dream of Olwen   see   While I
   Live
Dreamer, The (Dan Wolman)
   Reed (a)   (403)
   Simon (b)   305-06
Dreaming Lips, The (Paul Czin-
   ner)
   Agate (b)   85-87
   Graham   133
   Kael (d)   260
Dreams That Money Can Buy

Agee   309-10
Dreigroschenoper, Die   see
   Threepenny Opera, The
   (Georg Pabst)
Dreyer, Carl
   Durgnat   27, 38-49
   Kauffmann (b)   404
   Pechter   280-81
   Sarris (a)   346-48
   Weinberg   273
Dreyfus Case (Kraemer and Ros-
   mer)
   Agate (a)   96
DRIVE-INS
   Adler   108-10
   Alpert   15, 223
Drums
   Ferguson   240
Drums Along the Mohawk (John
   Ford)
   Ferguson   277
Dry Martini
   Weinberg   315-17
Du Barry Was a Lady
   Agate (b)   227-29
Du Rififi chez les hommes   see
   Rififi
Du sollst nicht ehebrechen   see
   Thérèse Raquin (Jacques Fey-
   der)
DUBBING
   Adler   136-37, 145
   Alpert   187
   Kauffmann (b)   64-69, 332
   Sarris (a)   (116)
Duca, Lo. L'Erotisme au Cinéma
   Durgnat   157-58
   Kael (c)   35
Duck Soup
   Sarris (b)   131
   Weinberg   (164)
Duel in the Sun
   Durgnat   (78), (230), (265)
Duet for Cannibals
   Farber   244-45
   Kael (a)   35-36
   Kauffmann (a)   208-09
   Simon (b)   389-90
Duffy
   Kael (b)   149-50
Duffy's Tavern
   Agee   178
Duke, Patty

Reed (b) 287-95
Dumbo
   Ferguson 392-93
Duped Til Domesday
   Young 107-10
Duras, Marguerite
   Pechter (67-71)
Dutchman, The
   Crist 230
   Reed (a) 365-66
   Simon (b) 70-71
Dylan Thomas
   Simon (c) 69
Dzien wielkiej przygody see
   Day of the Great Adven-
   ture, The

                  -E-

Each Dawn I Die
   Farber 22
   Ferguson 264-65
Eady Plan
   Alpert 22
Earl of Chicago, The
   Ferguson 303-04
Earrings of Madame de..., The
   Durgnat (51)
   Kael (c) 97-101, (298)
Earth
   Agate (a) 100-02
   Kael (d) 260
   Pechter (303)
   Warshow 280-82
Earth Trembles, The see
   Terra Trema, La
East Meets West (Herbert Ma-
   son)
   Graham (101)
East of Eden
   Kael (c) 55-57
Easter Parade
   Agee (310)
Eastern Valley
   Graham 186-87
Eastman House see George
   Eastman House
Easy Life, The
   Crist (40)
   Young 228-29
Easy Rider
   Farber 218-19

Kael (a) 3-4
   Kauffmann (a) 185-88
   Pechter 100-102
   Reed (a) 232-34
   Sarris (a) 445-47
   Schickel 240-43
   Simon (b) 115-17
   Young 353-54
Easy Street
   Ferguson 185
Eau à la Bouche see Game of
   Love (Jacques Doniol-Valcroze)
Eclipse, The
   Farber (148-50), (154)
   Kauffmann (b) 307-13
   Macdonald 337-39, (478)
   Sarris (b) 61
   Simon (c) 47-50
   Young 194-95, 210-11
Ecran Français, L' (magazine)
   Durgnat 66
Ecstasy
   Kael (d) 260-61
   Weinberg 52, (237), (283)
Edge, The
   Sarris (a) 350-51
Edge of the City
   Kael (d) 261
Edge of the World, The (Michael
   Powell)
   Ferguson 233-34
Edison, The Man
   Ferguson 303
EDITING
   Agate (a) (29)
   Durgnat 31-32, 35, 50, 57-
   60
   Farber 188, 191-92
   Ferguson 16-17, 55-57, 450
   Kael (d) 99
   Kauffmann (a) 248-49
   Pechter 117, 121-22, 153,
   155-56, 160, 301
   Sarris (b) 62-63, 88, 141,
   239
   Sontag (b) 109
   Simon (c) 161
   Young 18, 20-21, 45
   Weinberg 258, 291-92
EDUCATION, USE OF FILMS IN
   (see also STUDENTS AND THE
   CINEMA)
   Adler 20-21

Eeny Meeny Miney Mo see Old
  Dole Doff
Egg and I, The
  Agee 252
8-1/2 [eight and a half]
  Crist 14-16, (39)
  Durgnat 148-49
  Farber 168-69
  Gilliatt 344-46
  Kael (c) 261-66
  Kauffmann (b) 322-27
  Macdonald (xiii), 16-31, 350-
    51, 473
  Pechter 77-84
  Simon (c) 74-75
1812 [Eighteen twelve] (Vladimir
  Petrov)
  Agee (122)
Eighth Day of the Week
  Young (171-72)
Eisenstein, Sergei
  Agee (238), 299
  Kael (c) (341)
  Macdonald 67, (70-73), 250-
    65
  Pechter 111-22, (293-94),
    301-03
  Sarris (a) (323)
  Sarris (b) 44, 88, 141
  Weinberg 68, (194), 241, 265
  Young 149-55
Eisenstein, Sergei (quoted)
  Agate (b) 236
  Pechter 113-15, 117, 119
Eisenstein, Sergei. The Film
  Sense
  Agate (b) 235-36
  Macdonald 250-55
  Sarris (b) 83
El see This Strange Passion
Eleanor Roosevelt Story, The
  Crist 141-43, 150
  Sarris (a) 219-21
Electra (Michael Cacoyannis)
  Simon (c) 51
  Young 205-08
Elektra (Nicholas and Zarpas)
  see Elektra at Epidaurus
Elektra at Epidaurus
  Simon (c) 84
  Weinberg 193
Elephant Boy, The
  Ferguson 172-74

Graham 143-44
Elephant Never Forgets, An
  Graham 224
Elter, Anielka (quoted)
  Weinberg 207-08
Elusive Corporal, The
  Gilliatt 325-26
  Kauffmann (b) 5-7
  Macdonald 464-65
  Pechter 208-13
  Sarris (a) 73-74
Elvira Madigan
  Kauffmann (a) 34-36
  Sarris (a) 317
  Simon (b) 377
  Young 308-09
Emil and the Detectives
  Agate (b) 81-82
Emperor Jones, The
  Kael (d) 262
Emperor Waltz, The
  Agee 310
Emperor's Candlesticks, The
  Graham (78)
Empty Canvas, The
  Young 232
Enamorada, La
  Weinberg 254
Enchanted Cottage, The (John
  Cromwell)
  Agee 156-57
End As a Man see Strange
  One, The
End of St. Petersburg, The see
  Petersburg Nights
End of the Road, The
  Kael (a) 110-12
  Simon (b) 52-55
Enemies of Progress
  Ferguson 29
Enemies of the People see
  Enemies of Progress
Enemy Below, The
  Kauffmann (b) 7-8
Enfance nue, L' see Naked
  Childhood
Enfant sauvage, L' see Wild
  Child, The
Enfants du Paradis, Les see
  Children of Paradise
Enfants terribles, Les see
  Strange Ones, The (Jean-Pi-
  erre Melville)

Enfer de Rodin, L'
Durgnat 123-24
Engagement, The see Fiancés, The
ENGLISH FILMS see BRITISH FILMS
Englishman's Home, An (Albert de Courville)
Graham 244-45
Ensayo de un crimen, El see Criminal Life of Archibaldo de la Cruz, The
Enter Laughing
Gilliatt 77-79
Entertainer, The
Farber (3), 182
Kael (c) 70-72
Kauffmann (b) 183-85
Entertaining Mr. Sloane
Gilliatt 239-42
Entr'acte
Durgnat 58
Pechter (305)
EPIC FILMS
Young 18-19
Epic That Never Was, The see I, Claudius
Episode
Graham 32-33
Weinberg 75-76
EPISODE FILMS
Weinberg 201
Ercole alla conquista di Atlantide see Hercules Conquers Atlantis
Eroica
Gilliatt 57-58
Kael (c) (153-54)
EROTICISM IN FILMS
Adler 92-94
Alpert 126-29, 198, 217-18, 221-23, 227-29
Crist 171, 262-63, 267-71
Durgnat 160-63
Kael (a) 18-19
Kael (b) 207
Kael (c) 43-44
Kauffmann (a) 148-50
Kauffmann (b) 86-87, 419-20
Macdonald 288-89, 327, 398, 443-44
Reed (b) 175
Sarris (a) 266, 403, 416, 432-

33
Sarris (b) 106-09
Schickel 31, 64-65
Simon (b) 131-32, 159
Weinberg 20, 49-55, 58-60, 342-43, 349
Young (330), 348
Erste liebe, Die see First Love (Maximilian Schell)
Escapade (John Harvel) see Captivation
Escape (Mervyn LeRoy)
Ferguson 318-19
Escape (Joseph Mankiewicz)
Agee 310
Escape from Yesterday (Julien Duvivier) see Bandéra
Escape Me Never (Paul Czinner)
Agate (a) 140-42
Agate (b) 115-16
Escape to Happiness see Intermezzo (Gregory Ratoff)
Espoir see Man's Hope
Estate Violenta, La
Young (134)
ESTHETICS see AESTHETICS
Et Dieu créa la femme see And God Created Woman
Eternal Husband, The
Kael (d) 262
Eternal Return, The
Winnington 45-46
Eternel Retour, L' see Eternal Return, The
Etrange aventure de Lemmy Caution, Une see Alphaville
Eugene Atget
Durgnat 124
Europa 51 see Greatest Love, The
Eva
Crist 118-20
Evans, Edith
Reed (c) 134-39
Eve of St. Mark, The
Agate (a) 264-65
Agee 95
Evening with the Royal Ballet, An
Simon (c) 176
Events While Guarding the Bofors Gun see Bofors Gun, The
Everson, William
Sarris (b) (97)

Every Night at Eight
  Kael (c) 292-93
  Sarris (b) 53
Everybody Go Home!
  Kauffmann (b) 235-36
Everything Is Thunder
  Graham 94-95
Everything You Always Wanted
  to Know About Sex But Were
  Afraid to Ask
  Gilliatt 39-44
Evil Eden see Mort en Ce
  Jardin, La
Evil Street see Germany, Year
  Zero
Exclusive
  Graham 176
Executioner, The see Not on
  Your Life!
EXHIBITION (see also DISTRI-
  BUTION)
  Crist 115
  Ferguson 225, 298-300
  Simon (c) 122
Exile, The (Max Ophuls)
  Agee 383-84
Exiles, The (Kent Mackenzie)
  Kael (d) 263
Experiment in Terror
  Macdonald 57-59
EXPERIMENTAL FILMS (see
  also UNDERGROUND FILMS)
  Agee (42)
  Farber 253
  Kael (d) 12-13, 18-19
  Macdonald 313-14
  Pechter (279)
  Simon (c) 260-61
  Weinberg 292-93
Expo '67 (Montreal)
  Crist 264-66
EXPRESSIONISM
  Durgnat 87-98, 103-106
Expresso Bongo
  Kael (c) 65
  Kael (d) 263
  Kauffmann (b) 189-92
Extase see Ecstasy
Exterminating Angel, The
  Gilliatt 9-11
  Schickel 136-39
  Simon (c) (83)
  Weinberg 226-27, (253),

(269-70)
EXTRAS
  Ferguson 452-53
Eye for an Eye, An
  Kael (d) 264
  Young 112-14
Eyes without a Face see Hor-
  ror Chamber of Dr. Faustus,
  The

-F-

Fabulous Dorseys, The
  Agee (247)
Fabulous World of Jules Verne,
  The see Deadly Invention,
  The
Face see Magician
Face at the Window, The
  (George King)
  Graham 245
Face in the Crowd, A
  Farber (115-17), (120)
  Sarris (a) 21-23
Face of Fu Manchu, The
  Durgnat (75)
Face of War, A
  Kauffmann (a) 79-81
  Schickel 183-85
Faces
  Adler 235-36, 303-04, 326
  Farber 231, 233-34
  Kael (b) 197-99
  Kauffmann (a) 120-21
  Sarris (a) 406-09
  Schickel 217-19
  Simon (b) 296-97
Fahrenheit 451
  Crist 196-97, 210
  Kael (d) 146-50
  Reed (a) 358-59
  Simon (c) 258-60
  Young 293-95
Faim see Hunger
Fairbanks, Douglas, Sr.
  Lejeune 50-51
Fairies, The see Queens, The
Falcons, The
  Reed (a) 402
Fall of the Roman Empire, The
  Crist 62-65
  Simon (c) 114

Fallen Sparrow, The
  Agee 50
Falstaff
  Crist 260
  Kael (d) 200-02
  Kauffmann (a) 4-5
  Sarris (a) (279-80), 292-94
  Simon (b) 30-31
Fame Is the Spur
  Winnington 83
Family Diary, The
  Sarris (a) 202-05
  Simon (c) 175-76
FAMILY IN FILMS
  Durgnat 269-70
Family Way, The
  Sarris (a) 304-06
  Schickel 105-07
Fanfan the Tulip
  Kael (d) 264
Fanny (Marc Allégret)
  Agee (300)
Fanny by Gaslight see Man of
  Evil
FANS
  Adler 304-05
  Agate (a) 54-56
  Agate (b) 92-93
  Simon (b) 4-5
Fantasia
  Agate (a) 222-24
  Durgnat 237
  Ferguson 317-18
  Kael (b) (192)
Fantastic Voyage, The
  Kael (d) 156-57
Fantomas (series)
  Weinberg 268
Far from the Madding Crowd
  Crist 255-57
  Simon (b) 33-34
  Young 318-20
Far from Vietnam
  Adler 164-65
  Farber 229
  Kauffmann (a) (57)
  Sarris (a) 317
  Simon (b) (381-82)
Farber, Manny
  Macdonald 134-35
  Sarris (b) 64, (69), 77
Farceur, Le see Joker, The
Farewell, My Lovely see

Murder, My Sweet
Farewell to Arms (Frank Borz-
  age)
  Agate (a) 192-94
Farewell to Arms, A (Charles
  Vidor)
  Kauffmann (b) (73)
Farmer's Daughter, The (H. C.
  Potter)
  Agee 247
Farrébique
  Agee 296-99
  Winnington 105
  Young 264
Farrow, John
  Farber 13
Fascist, The
  Sarris (a) 199-200
  Simon (c) 167-69
Fastest Guitar Alive, The
  Adler 46
Fate, Le see Queens
Fate of a Man
  Kauffmann (b) 364
Father (István Szabó)
  Crist 249-50, 260
  Simon (b) 379
Father Brown see Detective,
  The
Fatuous Fire, The see Fire
  Within, The
Faulkner, William
  Kael (a) (237)
Faust (A. E. C. Hopkins)
  Graham 53
Faust (Friedrich Murnau)
  Weinberg 118-24
Federale, Il see Fascist, The
Feldman, Charles K.
  Kael (d) 67-69
Fellini, Federico
  Durgnat 111-12
  Kauffmann (b) 406-07
  Sarris (a) 29-33
  Sontag (a) (245)
  Young 276-77, 286-92
Fellini, Federico (quoted)
  Macdonald 352-53
Fellini Satyricon
  Kael (a) 127-32
  Kauffmann (a) 250-54
  Reed (a) 265-66
  Schickel 289-91

Simon (b) 211-19
Weinberg 338-44, 346
Femme Disparait, La see Por-
  trait of a Woman
Femme Douce, Une
  Farber 242-43
  Simon (b) 388-89
Femme du boulanger, La see
  Baker's Wife, The
Femme est une femme, Une see
  Woman Is a Woman, A
Femme Infidèle, La
  Farber (4-5), 10-11
  Kael (a) 53-54
  Simon (b) 266-70
Femme mariée, La see Mar-
  ried Woman
Fenin, George N. and William K.
  Everson. The Western
  Sarris (b) 208-11
Ferdinand the Bull
  Ferguson 241
Ferguson, Otis
  Farber 24
  Ferguson ix-xiii, xv, 187
  Sarris (b) 64
Fernandez, Emilio
  Weinberg 261
Fest der Schönheit see Olympia,
  Festival of the Nations
Fest der Völker see Olympia,
  Festival of the Nations
Festival of Beauty see Olym-
  pia, Festival of the Nations
Festival of New Czechoslovak
  Cinema, 1967
  Simon (b) 278
Festival of the Nations see
  Olympia, Festival of the Na-
  tions
FESTIVALS
  Simon (b) 368-69
Feu Follet, Le see Fire With-
  in, The
Feuillade, Louis
  Sontag (b) 160-63
Feverish Years, The
  Sarris (a) 315
  Simon (b) 374-75
Feydeau, Georges
  Weinberg 323-24
Fiancés, The
  Kauffmann (b) 337-40

Macdonald 356-59
Simon (c) 108-09
FICTION see ADAPTATIONS;
  LITERATURE AND THE
  CINEMA
Fidanzati, I see Fiancés, The
Fiddler on the Roof
  Kael (a) 327-33
Fields, W. C.
  Agee 17-18
  Crist 225-28
  Ferguson 87-89
  Gilliatt 257-63
Fiends see Diabolique
Fifth Avenue Girl
  Ferguson 268
Fifth Chair see It's in the Bag
Fifth Horseman Is Fear, The
  Simon (b) 280, (283)
  Adler 139-41, 327
FIGHT FILMS
  Farber 64-65
Fight for Life, The
  Ferguson 292-93
Fight for Peace, The
  Van Doren 405
Fighting Father Dunne
  Agee (310)
Fighting Lady, The (U.S. Navy)
  Brown (b) 271-76
  Winnington 105-06
Fighting Seabees, The
  Agee 80-81
Fighting Seventh, The see Lit-
  tle Big Horn
Fighting Sullivans, The see
  Sullivans, The
Fille du puisatier, La see
  Well-Digger's Daughter, The
Filly see Roots
FILM... [for combinations in
  which film is first word look
  under second word; e.g., film
  societies are listed as SOCIE-
  TIES, FILM]
Film (Alan Schneider)
  Kauffmann (b) 409
  Sarris (b) 168-69
  Simon (c) 187
FILM COURSES see STUDY
  AND TEACHING OF FILMS
Film Culture (magazine)
  Sarris (a) 11-13

FILM MAKING (see also STU-
    DENT FILMS)
  Kael (d) 67-100
  Pechter 114
  Reed (b) 93-101, 206-09,
    235-40, 251-54
  Reed (c) 146-51
  Schickel 28
Film Polaski see Kamera
  Unit
Film without a Name
  Kael (d) 264
Fin de Fiesta
  Young 369-71
Final Test, The
  Kael (d) 265
FINANCING
  Agee 196, 237
  Alpert 35-36, 197-98
  Kael (b) 92-93
  Kauffmann (a) 203
  Ferguson 442-43
  Pechter 5
  Reed (a) 263
  Sarris (b) 135
  Schickel 212
  Young (86)
Finian's Rainbow
  Adler 266
  Kael (b) (96), 159
Finnegans Wake see
  Passages from
  James Joyce's
  Finnegans Wake
Finney, Albert
  Reed (b) 159-65
Fire over England
  Graham 135-36
Fire Raisers, The
  Agate (b) 93-95
Fire Within, The
  Crist 89
  Kael (a) 308
  Sarris (a) 122-24
  Simon (c) 112-14
  Young 222-23
Firemen's Ball, The
  Adler 258-60
Fires on the Plain
  Kael (c) 225-28
First Comes Courage
  Lejeune 101
  Winnington 13

First Cry, The
  Simon (b) 283-85
First Love (Henry Koster)
  Graham 258
First Love (Maximilian Schell)
  Kael (a) 162-63
  Reed (a) 308
First Mrs. Fraser, The
  Agate (b) 65-67
First Spaceship on Venus
  Durgnat 254-55, 267
First Time, The
  Reed (a) 222
First World War, The
  Ferguson (60)
Fist Fight
  Simon (c) (188)
Fist in His Pocket
  Adler 159-60
  Kael (b) 6-7
  Kauffmann (a) 86-87
  Reed (a) 389
  Simon (c) 187
Fistful of Dollars, A
  Adler (239)
  Crist 251-52
  Sarris (a) 388
Fitzgerald, Barry
  Agee 348-49
Five-Card Stud
  Sarris (a) 390
Five-Day Lover, The
  Gilliatt 220-21
  Kael (d) 265
  Kauffmann (b) 235-36
  Pechter 51-58
Five Easy Pieces
  Kael (a) 251-52
  Reed (a) 303-05
  Schickel 320-23
Five Faces of Malaya
  Graham 201
Five Graves to Cairo
  Weinberg 160-61
Five Star Final
  Agate (b) 61-62
  Weinberg 54-55
Fixed Bayonets
  Farber 58
Fixer, The
  Adler 313-14
  Kael (b) 208-10
  Reed (a) 201-02

Sheed 230-32
Simon (b) 321
Flaherty, Robert
  Kael (c) 248
  Pechter 304
  Sarris (b) 101-02
  Weinberg 109-12, 243
  Young 243
Flame of New Orleans, The
  Agate (a) 224
Flaming Creatures
  Kael (c) (19)
  Kauffmann (b) (424)
  Macdonald (327)
  Sontag (a) 226-31
  Weinberg 244-45
FLASHBACKS
  Simon (c) 161
Fleet That Came to Say, The
  Agee (168)
Flesh
  Reed (a) 195
Flight
  Agate (a) 58-59
Flight Command
  Ferguson 344
Flight of the Phoenix, The
  Crist 166-68
  Farber 185-86
Flower Thief, The
  Weinberg 193
Flowers and Trees
  Lejeune (36)
Flute and the Arrow, The
  Young 252
Follies of 1929, The
  Agate (a) 47-48
Follow Me, Boys
  Crist 210
Follow the Boys
  Agate (b) 249-50
  Agee (93), 345-46
Follow the Fleet
  Graham 67, 69
Folly to Be Wise
  Kael (d) 265-66
Fonda, Henry
  Farber 176-78
Fonda, Jane
  Farber 3-4
  Kauffmann (b) 60-61
Fonda, Peter
  Reed (c) 219-37

Fool Killer, The
  Gilliatt (258)
Foolish Wives
  Agate (a) 21-22
  Agee (228)
  Macdonald (106)
  Weinberg 70-71, (185), (200),
    (353)
Fools for Scandal
  Graham 200
För att inte tala om dessa kvin-
  nor see All These Women
For Ever and a Day see For-
  ever and a Day
For Love of Ivy
  Kauffmann (a) 93-95
For Love or Money (Zoltan Korda)
  Ferguson 44
For Me and My Gal
  Agate (b) 233-34
For the First Time
  Adler 354
For the Love of Ivy
  Adler 212-13
For Valour (Tom Walls)
  Graham 140
For Whom the Bell Tolls
  Agee 46-49
  Lejeune 103-04
For You Alone/ see When You're
  in Love
Forbidden Games
  Kael (c) 111-13
  Simon (c) 19-20
  Young 30-31
Forbidden Paradise (Ernst Lub-
  itsch) see Trouble in Para-
  dise
Forbidden Planet
  Durgnat 256
  Kael (d) 266
Forbin Project, The
  Sarris (b) 200-02
  Schickel 300-02
Force of Evil
  Kauffmann (a) 209-10, 214-15
  Pechter 148-51
Ford, John
  Durgnat 78
  Ferguson 8-9
  Pechter 234-41
  Sarris (b) (36), 38-39, 132
  Young 88-94

Foreign Affair, A
  Agee   310-11
  Simon (a) 24
  Weinberg (215)
Foreign Correspondent, The
  Ferguson 308-09
Foreman, Carl
  Alpert 21
Forest Rangers, The
  Agate (b) 214
Forever Amber
  Agee 380-81
Forever and a Day
  Agate (b) 226-27
Forever in Love see Pride of
  the Marines, The
Forgotten Men
  Agate (b) 107-09
Forgotten Village, The
  Agate (b) 274
  Ferguson 399-400
  Winnington 21-22
Forman, Milos
  Adler (153), (156)
Fort Apache
  Agee 311
Fortune Cookie, The
  Crist (189)
  Schickel 87-89
Forty Days of Musa Dagh, The
  Weinberg 257
48 [forty-eight] Hours
  Agee 104
Forty-First, The (Grigori Chukh-
  rai)
  Kael (d) 266
Forty Guns
  Sarris (b) 61
49th [forty-ninth] Parallel see
  Invaders (Michael Powell)
Forty-Seven Ronin see Chushin-
  gura (Hiroshi Inagaki)
Forty Thousand Horsemen
  Agate (b) 190-91
Fountain
  Ferguson 46
Four Bags Full
  Kael (d) 267
Four Days of Naples, The
  Macdonald (463)
  Sarris (a) 82-84
  Young 237
Four Feathers (Zoltan Korda)

  Ferguson 264
  Graham 218
Four Horsemen of the Apoca-
  lypse, The (Rex Ingram)
  Agate (a) 17-19, 218
400 [four hundred] Blows,
  The
  Durgnat (97)
  Kauffmann (b) 223-24
  Macdonald 375-76, (390)
  Sarris (b) (63)
  Simon (b) (185)
  Weinberg (257)
  Young 180-82, (328)
Four Jills in a Jeep
  Lejeune 115-16
  Winnington 21
Four Men and a Prayer
  Ferguson 226-27
491 [four ninety-one]
  Sheed 213-14
Four Stars
  Farber 247-48
Four Steps in the Clouds
  Winnington 116-17
Fourteenth of July, The
  Durgnat 56
Fox, The (Mark Rydell)
  Adler 57-58
  Farber 206-08
  Kael (b) 30-35
  Simon (b) 137-39
Fox Fire see Fire Within,
  The
Fox Hunt, The
  Graham 115
Française et l'amour, La see
  Love and the Frenchwoman
Freaks
  Kael (d) 39
Fredlös
  Graham 115
FREE CINEMA see BRITISH
  FILMS
Freedom to Love
  Simon (b) 153
French Can-Can
  Durgnat (35), 52
  Sarris (a) 41-42
French Connection, The
  Kael (a) 315-19
FRENCH FILMS
  Ferguson 21

Graham (205)
FRENCH FILMS (pre-1914)
  Pechter 295
FRENCH FILMS (1920's)
  Durgnat 93-94
FRENCH FILMS (mid-1930's)
  Graham 39
FRENCH FILMS (pre-1940)
  Pechter 304-05
  Sarris (b) 104
FRENCH FILMS (1950's)
  Young 10-11
FRENCH FILMS (1960's)
  Adler 155-58
  Macdonald 372
  Young 10-11, 144-46, 253-62
FRENCH FILMS (1970's)
  Simon (b) 247-48
French without Tears
  Graham 248
Frenchman's Creek
  Agee 120-21
Frenchwoman and Love, The
  see Love and the French-
  woman
Frenzy (Alf Sjöberg)
  Agate (b) 274-75
  Winnington 56-57
Freshmen, The
  Agee 12
Freud
  Durgnat 150
  Farber (150), (153-54)
  Simon (c) 45-46
  Weinberg 212-13
Freudlose Gasse see Streets of
  Sorrow (Georg Pabst)
Freund, Karl (quoted)
  Weinberg 207, 281
Fric-Frac
  Agee (306)
Frieda
  Agee 273
Friend Will Come Tonight, A
  Agee 311-12
Friends for Life see Woman in
  the Painting
Friends of Mr. Sweeney
  Ferguson 43
'Frisco Kid
  Graham (57)
Frog, The
  Graham 150

Fröken Julie see Miss Julie
From Here to Eternity
  Alpert 228-29
  Kael (c) (49)
  Schickel (150)
From Russia with Love
  Kauffmann (b) 128
  Simon (c) 115-16
From the Earth to the Moon
  Durgnat 264
From the Manger to the Cross
  Graham 194
From This Day Forward
  Agee 196-97
  Winnington 54, 56
Front Page, The
  Sarris (b) 59
  Weinberg 54
Frontier
  Agee (164)
  Van Doren 320-21
Frou-Frou see Toy Wife
Frozen Limits, The
  Graham 252-54
Fu Mattia Pascal see Late
  Mathias Pascal (Pierre Che-
  nal)
Fugitive, The (John Ford)
  Agee 288-89
  Winnington 108-09
  Young 92
Fugitive Kind, The
  Kauffmann (b) 83-85
  Macdonald 146-48
Full Confession
  Ferguson 269-70
Fuller, Samuel
  Farber 56, 129-33
  Simon (b) (8), (12)
  Sontag (b) (173)
Funeral in Berlin
  Kael (d) 10
Funny Girl
  Adler xx, (161), 243-44
  Kael (b) 133-37
  Kauffmann (a) 114-15
  Reed (a) 352-55
  Sarris (a) 392-95
Funny Thing Happened on the
  Way to the Forum, A
  Crist (189)
  Kael (d) 138-39
  Reed (a) 334

Funnyman
    Sarris (a)   315
    Simon (b)   380-81
Furia
    Agee   294
Furthman, Jules
    Kael (d)   59
Fury (Fritz Lang)
    Ferguson   8, 136-37, (187)
    Graham   84-85, (96-97), (145)
Futz
    Kael (a)   54-57
    Simon (b)   361-63

-G-

G.I. Joe   see   Story of G.I. Joe,
    The
G-Men
    Ferguson   76-77
Gai Savoir, Le
    Farber   244
    Simon (b)   387
Gaily, Gaily
    Kael (a)   73-74
    Reed (a)   251-52
Game Is Over, The
    Reed (a)   359-61
Game of Life, The
    Agate (a)   20
Game of Love (Jacques Doniol-
    Valcroze)
    Durgnat   113
Games
    Crist   246-47, (266)
    Sarris (a)   321
    Sheed   (200-01)
Gance, Abel
    Sarris (a)   (318)
Gang War (Carol Reed)   see   Odd
    Man Out
Gang's All Here, The (Busby
    Berkeley)
    Agate (b)   246-48
    Agee   64
GANGSTER FILMS (see also
    CRIME FILMS; DETECTIVE
    FILMS)
    Agate (b)   211-12
    Ferguson   81-83
    Kael (b)   244-45
    Kael (c)   (46)

Kal (d)   48-49, 54
    Warshow   129-33, 135-37,
        139-40
    Weinberg   201
Gangster's Boy
    Lejeune   45
Gangway
    Graham   173
Ganze Welt dreht wich um Liebe
    see   Liebesmelodie
Gap, The
    Graham   149, (249)
Garbo, Greta
    Agate (b)   (131)
    Sarris (a)   139-40
    Weinberg   (191), (231)
Garden of Allah, The (Richard
    Boleslavsky)
    Graham   125-26
Garden of Delights, The (Carlos
    Saura)
    Kael (a)   263-64
Garden of the Finzi-Continis,
    The
    Kael (a)   363-66
Gardner, Ava
    Reed (c)   66-75
Garis, Robert (quoted)
    Kauffmann (a)   8-9
Garland, Judy
    Sarris (b)   269-71
Gaslight (George Cukor)
    Kael (d)   267
Gaslight (Thorold Dickinson)
    Durgnat   183-85
Gate of Hell, The
    Kael (d)   267-68
    Young   52-55
Gate of Lilacs   see   Gates of
    Paris
Gates of Paris
    Kael (c)   (290)
Gates of the Night
    Weinberg   224
Gauguin (Alain Resnais)
    Durgnat   123
Gauloises Bleues, Les
    Reed (a)   181
Gay Desperado, The
    Ferguson   157-58
    Graham   116-17
Geduld, Harry M.   Film Makers
    on Film Making

Young 323
Geheimnisse des Orients
  see Secrets of the
  Orient
Geheimnisse einer Seele see
  Secrets of a Soul
General Died at Dawn, The
  Ferguson 150-52
  Graham 112-13
General John Regan (Harold Shaw)
  Agate (a) 21
General Line, The
  Sarris (b) (88)
  Warshow (281)
Generale della Rovere, Il
  Kael (d) 268-70
Generals Without Buttons
  Ferguson 216-17
Generation, A
  Kauffmann (b) (355)
Generation of Conquerors see
  Revolutionists
Genevieve
  Kael (d) 270
Genius in the Family see So
  Goes My Love
Genou de Claire, Le see
  Clair's Knee
Genroku Chushingura see Chu-
  shingura (Hiroshi Inagaki)
Gentle Creature see Femme
  Douce, Une
Gentle Sex
  Lejeune 95-96
Gentleman Jim
  Lejeune 101
Gentleman of Paris
  Weinberg 312-13
Gentleman's Agreement (Elia
  Kazan)
  Brown (a) 50-56
  Brown (c) (253)
  Winnington 119-20
Geometry Lesson, A
  Durgnat 129
George Eastman House
  Adler 335-38
Georgy Girl
  Crist 214
  Kael (d) 22-23
  Reed (a) 334-35
  Sarris (b) 186-88
  Simon (c) 257

GERMAN FILMS
  Sarris (b) 141-42
GERMAN FILMS (1920's)
  Durgnat 89-90, 94
GERMAN FILMS (pre-1940)
  Pechter 304
  Sarris (b) 104
  Young xii, 143
GERMAN FILMS (post-1945)
  Young 143
Germany Awake!
  Sarris (a) 372-73
Germany Year Zero
  Brown (c) 277-81
  Winnington 110-11
Germi, Pietro
  Kauffmann (b) 168
Gert, Valeska
  Weinberg (151)
Gertrud
  Crist (210)
  Sarris (a) 251-52
  Sontag (b) (103), (105), (108)
Geschichten aus dem Wiener
  Wald see Tales from the Vi-
  enna Woods
Gestapo see Night Train
Get Off My Back see Synanon
Getting Straight
  Kael (a) 149-50
  Kauffman (a) 261-63
  Reed (a) 286-88
  Schickel 303-05
  Simon (b) 126-27
Ghost Goes West, The
  Graham 40-41
  Kael (d) 270
  Van Doren 311-14
Giant
  Alpert 141-44
  Farber 22-23, (114)
Giant of Metropolis
  Durgnat 252-54, 266
Giardina dei Finzi-Contini see
  Garden of the Finzi-Continis
Gidget
  Pechter 7-8
Gift see Venom
Gift Horse see Glory at Sea
Gift of Gab, The
  Graham (101)
Gigante di metropolis see Giant
  of Metropolis

Gilda
    Alpert 199-200
    Lejeune 180-81
    Winnington 53
Gilman, Richard (quoted)
    Kauffmann (a) 128
Gimme Shelter
    Kael (a) 206-11
    Schickel 334-37
Girl Crazy (Norman Taurog)
    Agee 64
Girl Friends see Amiche
Girl-Getters, The
    Simon (c) 223-26
Girl in Black, A
    Kael (d) 270-71
Girl in Distress see Jeannie
    (Harold French)
Girl in the Mist
    Kael (d) 271
Girl Must Live, A
    Agate (b) 168-70
Girl Number 217
    Agee 177
Girl on a Motorcycle, The
    Kael (b) (210-11)
    Simon (b) 319-21
Girl on the Canal, The
    Lejeune 156
Girl Rosemary, The see Rose-
    mary
Girl Was Young, The
    Van Doren 356
Girl with a Suitcase, The see
    Ragazza con la valigia, La
Girl with Green Eyes, The (Des-
    mond Davis)
    Crist (89)
    Farber 182
Girls' Dormitory
    Graham 124
Girls He Left Behind see
    Gang's All Here (Busby Berk-
    eley)
Girls' School (John Brahm)
    Ferguson 239-40
Gish, Lillian
    Agate (b) 196
    Kael (b) 46
    Pechter (305)
Giulietta degli spiriti see Juliet
    of the Spirits
Glamor for Sale

    Agee (145)
Glamorous Night
    Graham 149-50
Glass Bottom Boat, The
    Crist (209)
Glorious Smell-O-Vision
    Alpert 178-81
Glory at Sea
    Weinberg (196), (246)
Go-Between
    Kael (a) (292), (363-64)
Go West (Edward Buzzell)
    Ferguson 336-37
Go West, Young Man (Henry
    Hathaway)
    Graham 124
God Is My Co-Pilot
    Agee 153
Godard, Jean-Luc
    Adler 152-55, 296-99
    Farber 259-68
    Kael (b) (8), 142-44
    Kael (d) 14-17
    Pechter 242-53, 311-12, 314-
    15
    Reed (c) 177-79
    Sarris (b) (51), 99-100
    Simon (b) (8-9), (22), 167,
    (276), (290), (410)
    Simon (c) 272-96
    Sontag (a) (182-83), (245)
    Sontag (b) (104), (140-41),
    147-49
    Young 280-81, 343
Goddess, The
    Kael (d) 271-73
Godfather, The
    Kael (a) 420-26
Gods at Play see Amphitryon
God's Country and the Woman
    (William Keighley)
    Graham 154-55
God's Little Acre
    Kauffmann (b) 76-79
Goin' Down the Road
    Kael (a) 171-72
Going Home
    Kael (a) 353-54
Going My Way
    Agee 92, (138), 346-48
    Lejeune 126-27
Going to Work in the Morning in
    Brooklyn

Reed (a) 142-43
Gold Diggers of 1933
  Kael (d) 273
Gold of Naples
  Young 97-99
Gold Rush, The
  Agee (23), 337-38
  Kael (d) 273
Golden Age of Comedy, The
  Kael (d) 273-74
Golden Age of Primitive Flemish
  Painters, The
  Young 74-75
Golden Boy
  Graham 255
Golden Coach, The
  Kael (c) 101-04
Golden Earrings
  Agee (295)
  Winnington 81
Golden Fern, The
  Young 226-27
Golden Helmet see Casque d'Or
Golden Marie see Casque d'Or
Goldfinger
  Crist (97)
  Kael (d) 8
Goldstein, Leonard
  Alpert 87-88
Goldwyn, Samuel
  Macdonald 128-30
Goldwyn Follies, The
  Ferguson (216)
Golem, The (Julien Duvivier)
  Ferguson (174)
  Graham 145
  Weinberg 65-67
Golem, The (Paul Wegener)
  Durgnat 92
Gondole aux chimères, La see
  Phantom Gondola, The
Gone Are the Days
  Kauffmann (b) 62
Gone with the Wind
  Agate (a) 207-09
  Crist (189)
  Durgnat (77)
  Ferguson 280-81, 297-98
  Lejeune 18-83
  Macdonald 477-78
Good Earth, The
  Agate (a) 180-82
  Ferguson 167-69

Graham 140-41
Good Fairy, The
  Ferguson 67
Good News (Charles Walters)
  Agee 295
Good Old Soak
  Lejeune 25
Good, the Bad and the Ugly, The
  Kael (b) 53-54
  Kael (d) 23-24
  Sarris (a) 388-89
Good Times, Wonderful Times
  (Lionel Rogosin)
  Young 343-44
Goodbye, Columbus
  Gilliatt 253-56
  Kael (a) (4), 260
  Kauffmann (a) 154-57
  Pechter (98)
  Reed (a) 164-67, 172-73
  Sarris (a) 431-34
  Sarris (b) (107)
  Simon (b) 322-23
Goodbye, Mr. Chips (Herbert
  Ross)
  Kael (a) 37-41
  Reed (a) 257-58
  Simon (b) 332-333
Goodbye Mr. Chips (Sam Wood)
  Ferguson 255-56
  Graham 227-28
  Kael (d) 275
Goode, James. The Misfits
  Sarris (a) 172-74
Gordon, Ruth
  Reed (b) 22-29
Gorky Trilogy see Childhood
  of Maxim-Gorky
Gospel According to St. Matthew,
  The
  Crist 218
  Kauffmann (b) 30
  Macdonald 437-40
  Sarris (a) (245)
  Schickel 58-61
  Simon (b) (372)
Goto, Island of Love
  Simon (b) 387
Gotterdammerung (Luchino Vis-
  conti) see Damned
Gottesman, Ronald, ed. Focus
  on Kane
  Sarris (b) 116-17

Goudal, Jetta
  Weinberg 218
Goupi mains rouges see It Hap-
  pened at the Inn
Government Girl
  Agee 62
Goya (Black and Berg)
  Young 71
Graduate, The
  Adler 40-43, (207)
  Crist 258-59
  Farber 189, 195-99
  Kael (b) 125-27
  Kauffmann (a) (24), 36-46,
    201, (276-77)
  Pechter (98)
  Schickel 160-62
  Simon (b) 103-06
  Young 394
Graham Sutherland
  Durgnat 120
Grand amour de Beethoven, Le
  see Life and Loves of Bee-
  thoven
Grand Hotel
  Crist (135-38)
  Kael (d) 275
Grand Illusion, The see Grande
  Illusion, La
Grand Maneuvers
  Young 80
Grand Meaulnes see Wanderer
Grand Prix
  Crist (216)
  Kael (d) 9-10
  Reed (a) 379-80
Grande aurora, La see Great
  Dawn, The
Grande guerra, La see Great
  War, The
Grande Illusion, La
  Ferguson 236-37
  Kael (c) 108-111
  Kauffmann (b) 3-5
  Weinberg 79-83, (212)
Grandma's Boy
  Agee 11, (228)
Granitsa see Frontier
Grant, Cary
  Alpert 4, 31
Grapes of Wrath
  Ferguson 9, 282-85
  Kael (c) (289)

Kael (d) 275-76
  Young (90-92)
Grass Whistle see Wheat
  Whistle
Grasshopper, The
  Kauffmann (a) (277)
  Reed (a) 290-91
Graves, Charles (quoted)
  Weinberg 253
Great Adventure, The (Arne Suck-
  sdorff)
  Kael (d) (276)
  Young (52), 249-51
Great American Broadcast, The
  Ferguson 366-67
Great Barrier, The
  Graham 132
Great Dawn, The
  Agee 277
Great Dictator, The
  Ferguson 314-16
  Kauffmann (b) 162-64
  Lejeune 54-56
  Sarris (a) 124-28
  Warshow 210
  Weinberg 95-99
Great Expectations (David Lean)
  Agee 266-68, (289)
  Durgnat (100)
  Kael (d) 276
  Winnington 73-74
Great God Gold, The
  Graham 16
Great Guy
  Graham 137-38
  Van Doren 348-49
Great McGinty, The
  Ferguson 310-11
Great Man, The
  Kael (d) 277
Great Moment (Preston Sturges)
  Weinberg 191
Great War, The
  Young 133-34
Great White Hope, The
  Kael (a) 158-61
  Sarris (b) 245-52
Great Ziegfeld, The
  Ferguson 131-32
  Graham 100-01
Greatest Love, The
  Sarris (a) 36-38
Greatest Story Ever Told, The

Crist 103-06
Kauffmann (b) 28-29
Macdonald 430-37
Simon (c) 150-53
Greed
    Agee (143)
    Macdonald (4), (11), 129
    Weinberg 71-72, 128-36,
        220-21
Green Berets, The
    Adler 177-78, 188-90
Green Carnation see Trials of
    Oscar Wilde
Green Grass of Wyoming
    Agee (306)
Green Man, The
    Kael (d) 277
Green Pastures, The
    Graham 121-22
Green Years, The
    Agee 197-98
Greene, Graham
    Graham 1-4, 276-77
Greene, Graham (quoted)
    Young 404
Greengage Summer see Loss
    of Innocence
Greenwich Village Story (Jack O'-
    Connell)
    Crist 18-19
    Simon (c) 72-73
Greetings
    Kael (b) (206)
    Kauffmann (a) 133-34
    Reed (a) 141-42
    Sheed 232-34
    Simon (b) 110-111
Grido, Il
    Kauffmann (b) 311-12
    Macdonald (463)
Grierson, John
    Durgnat (63)
    Graham 40
    Sarris (b) 102
Griffith, Andy
    Farber 119-20
Griffith, David Wark
    Agate (a) (80)
    Agee 313-18, 396-98
    Kael (b) 42-47
    Kael (c) (341)
    Macdonald 70-73, 76-78,
        105-05, (446-47)

Pechter 283, 296-97, 300
Sarris (b) 16-17, 44, (88),
    139-41
Simon (c) 8
Sontag (a) 242-43
Young 15-21
Grip of Fear, The see Experi-
    ment in Terror
Group, The
    Crist 174-76
    Kael (d) 67-100
    Sarris (a) 245-48
    Simon (c) 218-19
Groupies, The
    Kael (a) 197-99
    Sarris (b) 253-55
G'schichten aus dem Wiener Wald
    see Tales from the Vienna
    Woods
Guadalcanal Diary
    Agee 59
Guernica
    Durgnat 20-21, 123
Guerra Americana, La see
    American War, The
Guerre des Boutons, La see
    War of the Buttons, The
Guerre des Gosses, La see
    Generals without Buttons
Guerre est finie, La
    Crist 184, 224-25, 258
    Kael (d) 162-66
    Kauffmann (a) (188)
    Reed (a) 373-74
    Sarris (a) 285-87
    Schickel 95-97
    Sheed 189-90
    Simon (b) 67-70
Guess Who's Coming to Dinner?
    Adler 65-66, (211-12)
    Crist 254-55
Guest, The
    Gilliatt 109-10
    Kauffmann (b) 213-15
    Sarris (a) 118-19
Guiles, Fred L. Norma Jean
    Sarris (a) 452-54
Gun Crazy
    Pechter (89)
Gunfighter, The (Henry King)
    Macdonald 453, 485
    Warshow 144-47
Gunga Din

Ferguson 246-47
Kael (d) 278
Gunn
  Sarris (a) 298-99
Guns in the Afternoon see Ride
  the High Country
Guns of the Trees
  Macdonald 317-19
  Weinberg 200-01, 245
Guv'nor, The
  Graham 42
Guy Named Joe, A
  Agee 69, 89-90
Guys and Dolls
  Sarris (a) 17-19
Gycklarnas afton see Naked Night
Gypsy Moths, The
  Farber 219

-H-

Hadaka no shima see Island
Haesearts, Paul
  Durgnat 129
Hail, Hero!
  Kael (a) 42
  Reed (a) (255)
Hail the Conquering Hero
  Agate (b) 255-56
  Agee 114-17, 352-53
  Farber 56
  Winnington 25
Hairy Ape, The
  Agee 98
Half a Sixpence
  Adler 51-52
Hall, Ben M. The Best Remain-
  ing Seats
  Macdonald 450-51
Hallelujah
  Agate (b) 28-30
Hallelujah, I'm a Bum
  Weinberg (318)
Hallelujah, I'm a Tramp see
  Hallelujah, I'm a Bum
Hallelujah the Hills
  Kauffmann (b) 161
  Macdonald 328-30
  Weinberg 219-20, 228-30
Hamlet (Alexander Korda)
  Agate (a) 165-66
Hamlet (Grigori Kozintsev)

Macdonald 271-73
Hamlet (Laurence Olivier)
  Agee 388-96
  Brown (c) 145-53
  Durgnat (49)
  Kael (c) 280
  Winnington 112-14
Hamlet (Tony Richardson)
Hand on the Gun, The see
  Mano sul fucile, Il
Hands Across the Table
  Ferguson 101-02
Hands of a Stranger see Hands
  of Orlac
Hands of Orlac
  Graham 11
Hands on the City see Mani
  sulla città
Hands over the City see Mani
  sulla città
Handsome Serge see Beau Serge
Handy Andy
  Ferguson (45)
Hang 'Em High
  Sarris (a) 390
Hanging Tree, The
  Kauffmann (b) 142-43
Hangmen Also Die
  Agee 35
  Lejeune 97-98
Hangover Square
  Agate (a) 271-73
  Agee (140)
  Winnington 33
Hannibal Brooks
  Reed (a) 179
Hanoi: Tuesday, December 13
  Adler 352
Happening, The
  Reed (a) 375
Happiest Days of Your Life, The
  Kael (d) 278
  Lejeune 100
  Winnington 11, 13
Happy Ending, The
  Reed (a) 260-65
Happy Knowledge see Gai Sav-
  ior
Happy Land
  Agee 63, (67), 89
Här här du ditt liv see Here Is
  Your Life
Harakiri see Seppuku

Hard Contract
  Reed (a) 236-37
  Simon (b) 354-55
Hard Day's Night, A
  Crist (90)
  Gilliatt 213-15
  Macdonald 400-01
  Sarris (a) 160-63
  Simon (c) 182
Hard Way, The
  Agee 27-28, (66)
Hardy, Oliver see Laurel and
  Hardy
Hari-Kari (Nicolas Farkas) see
  Thunder in the East
Harlot
  Macdonald 42-44
Harlow
  Crist 129-31
  Kael (d) 278-79
  Simon (c) 173-74
Harlow, Jean
  Crist 79-80
  Sarris (a) 149-54
Harp of Burma, The see Bur-
  mese Harp
Harper
  Crist 179-80, 215
  Kael (d) 279
  Reed (a) 348-49
  Schickel 51-53
Harris, Julie
  Simon (c) 300
Harrison, George Bagshawe
  Agate (a) 151-53
Hart, William S.
  Agee 228
  Sarris (b) 210
Harvest
  Ferguson 267-68
  Kael (d) 279-80
  Weinberg 83-86
Harvey Girls, The
  Winnington 49-50
Hatari!
  Kael (c) (297)
  Weinberg 194-95, 219
Hatful of Rain
  Alpert 159-60
Hatimonhi see Dreamer
Haunted Honeymoon
  Ferguson 344
Haunting, The

Kael (c) (10-13)
Have You Heard of the San Fran-
  cisco Mime Troupe?
  Adler 186-87
Haviland, Olivia de
  Farber 84-85
Having a Wild Weekend
  Kael (d) 280
Having Wonderful Crime
  Agee (145)
Hawaii
  Crist 187-88
  Kael (d) 135-36
  Reed (a) 333-34
  Sarris (b) 177-79
Hawks, Howard
  Durgnat 82-84
  Farber 12, 14-17, 22-23, 25-
    30
  Kael (c) 304-05, 318-19
  Sarris (b) 44
  Young (93)
Hawks and the Sparrows, The
  Simon (c) 251-52
Häxan
  Sontag (b) (140)
Hazard
  Agee (306)
He see This Strange Passion
He Who Gets Slapped
  Simon (b) 392
Head
  Adler 284-85
  Kael (b) 185-86
Head over Heels (Sonnie Hale)
  see Head over Heels in Love
Head over Heels in Love
  Graham 139
Heads Up (Victor Shertzinger)
  Agate (b) (54)
Health of a Nation
  Graham 224
Heart Is a Lonely Hunter, The
  Adler 198-200, (213)
  Reed (a) 349-52
  Reed (b) 93-101
  Simon (b) 41-42
Heart of a Mother, The see
  Sons and Mothers
Heart of Spain
  Van Doren 373
Heat's On, The
  Agee 64

Heaven Can Wait
  Agee 49-50
Hecht, Harold
  Alpert 32-35, 39
Heir to Jenghis-Khan see Storm
  over Asia
Hell in the Pacific
  Kael (b) 271-72
  Reed (a) 217
Hellfighters, The
  Reed (a) 145-47, 217
Hello, Dolly!
  Kael (a) 80-85
  Simon (b) 333-34, 402
Hello Down There
  Reed (a) 227
Hellzapoppin!
  Agee 335-36
Help!
  Farber 160
  Kael (d) 116-17
  Macdonald 403-06
  Sarris (a) 205-07
  Simon (c) (182)
Henry V (Laurence Olivier)
  Agee 207-12, 235-36, 361-66
  Lejeune 134-35
Hepburn, Katharine
  Agate (b) 178-79
  Durgnat 141
  Farber 4
  Kael (b) 176-78
Her Arnes pengar see Sir
  Arne's Treasure (Gustave Mo-
  lander)
Her Highness and the Bell-Boy
  Agee (176)
Her Jungle Love
  Lejeune 38-41
Her Kind of Man
  Agee 203
Hercules Conquers Atlantis
  Durgnat 252-54, 267
Here Come the Waves
  Agee 135
Here Comes the Navy
  Ferguson (5-6), 43
Here Is a Man see All That
  Money Can Buy
Here Is Your Life
  Kauffmann (a) 130-32, (179)
  Simon (b) 299
  Young 298-300

Here We Go Round the Mulberry
  Bush
  Adler 67-68
  Kael (b) 63-65
  Simon (b) 139
Here's Your Life see Here Is
  Your Life
Heroin Gang see Sol Madrid
Herr Arne's Treasure see Sir
  Arne's Treasure (Gustav Mo-
  lander)
Herrscher, Der
  Graham 151
Heston, Charlton
  Durgnat 44
Hi Diddle Diddle
  Agate (b) 239
Hi, Mom!
  Gilliatt 225-26
  Simon (b) 124
Hidden Fortress, The
  Kauffmann (b) 378
  Macdonald 420
  Young 115-21
High and Low
  Crist 36-39
  Kauffmann (b) 383-85
  Young 223
High Command, The
  Graham 157
High Cost of Loving, The
  Kael (d) (277)
High Noon
  Kael (d) 280-81
  Warshow 148-49
High School
  Kael (a) 20-24
  Schickel 256-58
High Sierra
  Faber (3)
  Ferguson 338-39
  Kael (c) (293-94)
  Sarris (b) 53
High, Wide and Handsome
  Graham 163-64
Higher and Higher
  Agee 68
Hill, The
  Simon (c) 190-91
Hippie Revolt, The
  Sheed 212-13
Hired Killer, The
  Young 136-37

Hiroshima, Mon Amour
  Alpert 211-13
  Durgnat (21), (108), 160-64
  Kael (c) 31-35
  Macdonald (xiv), 366-68, 472
  Pechter 67-76
  Simon (b) (185)
  Simon (c) (161)
  Young 144, 189-91
His Affair see This Is My Af-
  fair (William Seiter)
His Butler's Sister
  Lejeune 108-09
His Girl Friday
  Ferguson 281
  Kael (d) 281
  Sarris (b) (59)
His Kind of Woman
  Farber 58
Histoire immortelle, L' see
  Immortal Story
Histoires extraordinaires see
  Spirits of the Dead
HISTORICAL FILMS
  Lejeune 60-61
HISTORIOGRAPHY see HISTORY
  OF THE CINEMA; DISCUSSIONS
  OF
HISTORY IN FILMS
  Graham 74
  Macdonald 484
History Is Made at Night
  Van Doren 361-62
HISTORY OF THE CINEMA (see
  also AMERICAN FILMS;
  FRENCH FILMS, etc.)
  Ferguson 4
  Kael (b) 3-4, 103
  Macdonald xvii-xviii
  Sarris (b) 137-43
  Sontag (a) 244
  Weinberg 16-17, 21-22
HISTORY OF THE CINEMA (be-
  ginnings)
  Weinberg 283
HISTORY OF THE CINEMA
  (1930's)
  Pechter 308
HISTORY OF THE CINEMA
  (1940's)
  Farber 143-44
  Sarris (b) 21-37
HISTORY OF THE CINEMA

(1950's)
  Farber 143-44
  Young 273-76
HISTORY OF THE CINEMA
  (1960's)
  Crist 263-71
  Farber 143-44, 188-89
  Macdonald 174
  Pechter ix
  Young 273-76
HISTORY OF THE CINEMA, DIS-
  CUSSIONS OF
  Kauffmann (b) 402
  Pechter 293-94, 296, 312-13
  Sarris (b) 26-27
HISTORY OF THE CINEMA, HIS-
  TORIOGRAPHY see HISTORY
  OF THE CINEMA, DISCUS-
  SION OF
Hitchcock, Alfred
  Alpert 31, 168-77
  Durgnat 85-86
  Farber 165-66, 208
  Ferguson (6), (304)
  Kael (c) 297-98
  Kael (d) 75, (150)
  Kauffmann (a) (40), (46)
  Macdonald (475-76)
  Pechter 177-78
  Sarris (a) 333-36
  Sarris (b) (26), (36), (48),
    (54-55)
  Van Doren 355
  Weinberg 221
  Young (19)
Hitler Gang, The
  Agee 92
Hobson's Choice (David Lean)
  Kael (d) 282
  Weinberg (215)
Hoffman, Dustin
  Kael (a) 349
Hog Wild
  Farber (136)
Hohe Schule
  Graham 53-54
Hold Me While I'm Naked
  Farber 248-49
Holden, William
  Alpert 29
  Durgnat 139
Hole see Night Watch (Jacques
  Becker)

Hole (Kaneto Shindo) see Oni-
  baba
Holiday in Spain see Scent of
  Mystery
Holland, Norman
  Pechter 37-39
HOLLYWOOD (see also AMER-
  ICAN FILMS; INDUSTRY,
  FILM)
  Adler 262-63
  Agate (a) 45
  Agate (b) 130-32
  Agee 150, 155, 188, (190),
    237-39, 289-90
  Alpert 11-14, 23-25
  Durgnat 61-62, 64
  Farber 54-57, 61-63
  Ferguson 39, 55, 135-36,
    174, 180, 238-39, 422-58
  Kael (a) 238
  Kael (b) 93-94
  Kael (c) 35-36
  Kael (d) 12-14
  Macdonald 38
  Pechter 3-4, 160, 268
  Sarris (b) 25, (47), 79
  Schickel 20, 35
  Simon (b) 307-08
Hollywood Canteen
  Agee (136)
  Winnington 36
HOLLYWOOD IN FILMS
  Crist 72
"HOLLYWOOD TEN"
  Agee 285-87
  Winnington 85
Holy Matrimony
  Agate (b) 236-37
Hombre
  Reed (a) 336-37
Home Before Dark
  Kael (d) 282
Home for Life
  Kael (a) (207)
Home from the Hill
  Macdonald (459)
Home in Indiana
  Agee 101
Home of the Brave
  Brown (c) 251-54
  Farber 68-70
Homer
  Reed (a) 306-07

Homme au chapeau rond, L'
  see Eternal Husband, The
Homme de nulle part, Le see
  Late Mathias Pascal, The
  (Pierre Chenal)
Homme de Rio, L' see That
  Man from Rio
Homme du Jour, L'
  Graham 196-97
Homme et une femme, Un see
  Man and a Woman, A
Homme qui cherche la verité, L'
  see Man Who Seeks the
  Truth, The
Honeymoon (Leo McCarey) see
  Once Upon a Honeymoon
Honeymoon Killers, The
  Kael (a) 105-07
Hoodlum Priest, The
  Kael (c) (134)
Hop Pickers, The
  Kauffmann (b) 399
Hope, Bob
  Agee 18-19
Hora e vez de Augusto Matraga,
  A see Time and Hour of
  Augusto Matrage, The
Hori ma panenko see Fireman's
  Ball
Horror Chamber of Dr. Faustus,
  The
  Durgnat 38
  Kael (c) 7
HORROR FILMS
  Adler 115
  Crist 82, 177
  Durgnat 37, 94-95, 106
  Kael (c) 6, 11-13
  Simon (b) 403-06
  Sontag (a) (215-16)
  Young 329
Horse's Mouth, The (Ronald Ne-
  ame)
  Kael (d) 282
  Kauffmann (b) 45-47
Hortobagy
  Graham 124-25
  Lejeune 147
Hose, Die see Royal Scandal,
  A (Hans Behrendt)
Hospital, The (Arthur Hiller)
  Kael (a) 378-79
Hospital (Frederick Wiseman)

Kael (a) 101-02
Hostages (Raymond Bernard)
  see Mayor's Dilemma
Hostages (Frank Tuttle)
  Agee 54
  Lejeune 131-32
Hot Millions
  Gilliatt 252-53
  Schickel 205-08
Hot Rock, The
  Kael (a) 401-03
Hotel
  Reed (a) 362-63
Hotel Berlin
  Agee 149
Hôtel du Nord
  Graham 229-30
Hotel Imperial (Robert Florey)
  Graham 213-14
Houen zo see Steady
Hound of the Baskervilles, The
  (Sidney Lanfield)
  Ferguson 259
  Graham 231, 234
Hour of the Furnaces, The
  Kael (a) 257-59
Hour of the Wolf, The
  Adler 111-12, 116-17
  Farber 213-15
  Kauffmann (a) 62-65
  Schickel 175-79
  Sheed 216-18
  Simon (b) (225), 230-33
Hours of Love, The
  Sarris (a) 211-12
House of Greed, The
  Ferguson 45
House of Lovers see Lovers
  of Paris
House on 92nd Street, The
  Agee 177
HOUSE UN-AMER. ACTIVITIES
  see "HOLLYWOOD TEN"
Houseman, John (quoted)
  Sarris (b) 114-15
Housing Problems
  Ferguson 207
  Graham 108
Houston, Penelope
  Durgnat 70
Houston, Penelope (quoted)
  Kauffmann (b) 420
Hoven zo see Steady

How Green Was My Valley
  Ferguson 396-98
  Sarris (b) (132)
How I Won the War
  Farber 200-04
  Kauffman (a) 30-34, (68),
    (128), 206
  Sheed 204-06
  Simon (b) 342-46
How to Murder Your Wife
  Macdonald 161-62
  Simon (c) 146-48
How to Save a Marriage--and
  Ruin Your Life?
  Kael (b) 18-24
How to Steal a Diamond in Four
  Easy Lessons see Hot Rock
How to Succeed in Business With-
  out Really Trying
  Crist 236
Howard, Leslie
  Lejeune 96-97
Howe, James Wong
  Ferguson (447-48)
Huckleberry Finn see Adven-
  ture of Huckleberry Finn, The
  (Richard Thorpe)
Hucksters, The
  Agee 270
Hud
  Crist 6-9
  Kael (c) 79-94
  Kauffmann (b) 159-61
  Macdonald 299-301
  Sarris (a) 90-91
  Simon (c) 81
Hudson's Bay
  Ferguson 329-30
Huff, Theodore (quoted)
  Macdonald 104-06
Hugo and Josefin
  Farber 240
Hugs and Kisses
  Adler 213-15
  Farber 226-27
  Gilliatt 216-17
  Sarris (a) (316)
  Simon (b) 376
Human Beast, The
  Agate (a) 231-33
  Durgnat (34)
  Ferguson 290-91
  Graham 220

Sontag (b) (106)
Human Comedy, The
    Agate (b) 225-26
    Agee 30-33, 36
    Lejeune 93-94
Human Relations see RoGoPag
Humanism, Victory of the Spirit
    Young 75-76
Hunchback of Notre Dame, The
    (William Dieterle)
    Ferguson 282
    Graham 271
HUNGARIAN FILMS (mid-1960's)
    Kauffmann (b) 405
Hunger
    Adler 208-09
    Kauffmann (a) 100-02
    Simon (c) (254-55)
Hunt, The
    Schickel 112-14
    Simon (c) 250-51
Hunter, Ross
    Alpert 78-96
Hurdes see Land without
    Bread
Hurry Sundown
    Crist (xvii-xviii), 232-33
    Reed (a) 376-78
    Reed (c) 146-51
Husbands
    Kael (a) 222-24
Hussey, Olivia
    Reed (b) 273-86
Hustler, The
    Crist (138-39), 165-66
    Kauffmann (b) 56-58
Huston, John
    Agee 320-31, 400-01
    Alpert 147-50
    Farber 32-34
    Kael (c) 298-300
    Pechter 8
    Sarris (b) 121-22
Hyman, Kenneth
    Schickel 211-12
Hymn of the Nations
    Agee 200

-I-

I, a Woman
    Crist (266)

I Am a Fugitive from a Chain
    Gang
    Kael (d) 283
I Am Curious (Blue)
    Kauffmann (a) 150
    Reed (a) 291
    Simon (b) 144
    Young 309-10
I Am Curious (Yellow)
    Kael (a) (18)
    Kauffmann (a) 147-50
    Reed (a) 311-16
    Sarris (b) 106-07
    Simon (b) 132-34, 143-45
I, Claudius
    Farber 243-44
    Simon (b) 393-94
    Weinberg 254, 275, (342)
I Could Go On Singing
    Simon (c) 55
I Cover the Waterfront
    Graham 198
I Dream Too Much
    Graham 53
I Even Met Happy Gypsies
    Adler 88-89
I Know Where I'm Going
    Agee 274
    Lejeune 159-60
I Live in Grosvenor Square see
    Yank in London
I Love You, Alice B. Toklas!
    Kael (b) 158
    Reed (a) 205
I Married Adventure
    Ferguson 306
I Met a Murderer
    Agee 150-51
I Met Him in Paris
    Ferguson 181
I Never Sang for My Father
    Kael (a) 169-71
    Reed (a) 291-93
I Remember Mama
    Agee (300), 384-86
I See a Dark Stranger see Ad-
    ventures
I Shot Jesse James
    Farber 56
I Stand Condemned see Mos-
    cow Nights (Anthony Asquith)
I Walk Alone
    Agee 295

Sarris (b) 75-76
I Walk the Line
    Kael (a) 199-200
I Want to Live!
    Kael (d) (50)
I Want You
    Warshow 182-88
I Wanted Wings
    Agate (b) 185-87
Ice
    Kael (a) 163-68
Ice Station Zebra
    Adler 323
    Kael (b) 222-23
Iceman Cometh, The (Sidney Lu-
    met)
    Kael (d) 85-86
Ichikawa, Kon (quoted)
    Weinberg 288-89
Ideal Husband, An
    Agee 294
Idiot, The (Alan Bridges)
    Young 354-56
Idiot, The (Georges Lampin)
    Agee (300)
Idiot's Delight
    Ferguson 247-48
    Graham 214-15
Ieri, oggi, domani see Yester-
    day, Today and Tomorrow
If...
    Kael (b) 279-86
    Kauffmann (a) 134-37
    Pechter 99-100
    Schickel 220-22
    Simon (b) 109-110
    Young 350-51
If It's Tuesday This Must Be
    Belgium
    Reed (a) 177
If Winter Comes (Victor Saville)
    Agee (295)
If You Could Only Cook
    Graham 65
Ignace
    Graham 245-46
Ikiru
    Farber 144, 151-52
    Kauffmann (b) 374-76
I'll Take Romance
    Lejeune 34
I'll Tell the World (Edward
    Sedgwick)

Ferguson 34-35
Illegals, The
    Agee 312
    Warshow 243-49
Illiac Passion, The
    Adler 119-20
Illicit Interlude see Summer
    Interlude
Illustrated Man, The
    Reed (a) 162-63
Ils etaient neuf célibataires see
    Nine Bachelors
I'm All Right, Jack
    Kael (c) 64-65
    Kauffmann (b) 51-53
Image of Love
    Durgnat 129-30
Imitation of Life (Douglas Sirk)
    Alpert 80, 92-93
    Durgnat 80
Immoral Mr. Teas, The
    Kael (a) (58)
    Simon (b) 154-55
Immortal Battalion see Way
    Ahead
Immortal Story, The
    Adler 242
    Kauffmann (a) 146-47
    Reed (a) 221
Immortelle, L'
    Sontag (b) (135)
Impatient Years, The
    Agee 114
Imperfect Lady, The (Tim Whel-
    an)
    Graham 50
Impossible Years, The
    Adler 308-09
Imposter, The (Julien Duvivier)
    Agee 83
Imposter, The (Tatsuo Osone)
    Young (55), (57)
In a Lonely Place
    Farber (5)
In Cold Blood
    Adler (3), 27-30
    Crist 259
    Farber (195-99)
    Macdonald (12-13), 46-52
    Sarris (a) 328-30
    Sheed 209-11
    Simon (b) 171-73
    Young 389-90

In jenen Tagen see In Those
  Days
In Name Only
  Ferguson (269)
In the Heat of the Night
  Adler 64-65
  Crist 259
  Kael (b) 109-10
  Sarris (a) 306-09
  Schickel 123-25
  Young 388-89
In the Street
  Farber 45-46
In the Year of the Pig
  Kael (a) 42-45
  Kauffmann (a) 218-19
In Those Days
  Young 143-44
In Which We Serve
  Agate (b) 215-16
  Agee 23-24
  Lejeune 79-80
Inadmissible Evidence
  Kauffmann (a) 91-93
Incendiary Blonde
  Agee 168-69
Indagine su un cittadino al sopra
  di ogni sospetto see Investi-
  gation of a Private Citizen
INDEPENDENT FILMS (see also
  INDUSTRY, FILM)
  Alpert 13-14
  Pechter 263
  Schickel 337
  Weinberg 151
INDIAN CINEMA
  Kael (c) 252
Indian Village
  Young 251
INDIANS (AMERICAN) IN FILMS
  (see also WESTERNS)
  Kael (d) 38
Indisk by see Indian Village
Industrial Britain
  Durgnat (90)
Industrial Symphony
  Ferguson 132-33
INDUSTRY, FILM (see also
  HOLLYWOOD; INDEPENDENT
  FILMS)
  Adler 262-63
  Agee 150, 190, 308-09
  Alpert 8-25

Ferguson 180, 214, 336,
  458
  Kael (a) 238
  Kael (b) 179
  Kael (d) 3-4
  Pechter 8
  Sarris (b) 96
  Winnington 7
Infidelity (Philippe DeBroca)
  see Five-Day Lover, The
Informer, The (John Ford)
  Ferguson 79-80
  Graham 26
  Young 91-92
Innocents, The
  Kael (c) 163-72
  Kauffmann (b) 107-08
Innocents of Paris
  Agate (b) 23-25
Inside Daisy Clover
  Farber 184
  Kael (d) 283
Inside Nazi Germany, 1938
  Ferguson 211-12
  Van Doren 389-91
Inside North Vietnam
  Kauffmann (a) (57)
Inspector Clouseau
  Adler 196-97
  Gilliatt 245-47
Inspector Hornleigh
  Graham 211-12
Interlude
  Simon (b) 314
Intermezzo (Gregory Ratoff)
  Graham 265-66
International Art Film Festival,
  New York, 3rd, 1957.
  Young 68-76
International Children's Film
  Festival see New York In-
  ternational Children's Film
  Festival
International Festival of Ani-
  mated Film see Internation-
  al Tournée of Animation.
International Film Festival...
  see also:
  Internat'l Art F... F...; In-
  ternat'l Tournée...; Karlovy-
  Vary Internat'l F... F...;
  New York F... F...; New
  York Internat'l Children's F...

F...; Montreal Internat'l F...
F...; San Sebastian Internat'l
F... F...
International Film Festival,
Cannes, 14th, 1961
Macdonald 467-69
International Film Festival,
Cannes, 21st, 1968
Adler 152-55
Young 327
International Film Festival,
Cannes, 23d, 1970
Reed (a) 393-410
International Film Festival, Mar
del Plata, 2d, 1960.
Macdonald 465-67
International Film Festival, Ven-
ice, 24th, 1963
Young 217-27
International Film Festival, Ven-
ice, 29th, 1968
Adler 229-38
International Tournée of Anima-
tion, New York, November,
1968
Sarris (b) 197
Interns, The
Sarris (a) 48
Intimate Lighting
Gilliatt 338-39
Kauffmann (a) 222-23
Simon (c) 253
Intolerance
Agate (a) (17-18)
Durgnat 59
Kael (a) (320)
Kael (b) 420-45
Sarris (b) 217-19
Van Doren 324-25
Weinberg (259)
Young 15-21
Intruder in the Dust
Kael (d) 283-86
Invaders, The (Michael Powell)
Agate (a) 244
Invasion of the Body Snatchers
Kael (d) 286
Invention of Destruction see
Deadly Invention
Investigation of a Citizen Above
Suspicion see Investigation
of a Private Citizen
Investigation of a Private Citizen

Kael (a) 220-22
Reed (a) 396
Ipcress File
Crist 150
Farber 165
Sarris (a) 210-11
Irene (Herbert Wilcox)
Agate (a) 213-14
IRISH FILMS
Kauffmann (b) 218
Irma la Douce
Gilliatt 264-65
Iron Curtain, The
Agee (306)
Iron Major, The
Agee 61
Is Everybody Happy?
Winnington 70
Is Paris Burning?
Crist 197-200, 210
Simon (c) 256-57
Is There Sex After Death?
Kael (a) 324-26
Isabel
Reed (a) 387-88
Simon (b) 292
Isadora see Loves of Isadora
Isaksson, Ulla (quoted)
Pechter 143-44
Island, The (Kaneto Shindo)
Kael (d) 286-87
Kauffmann (b) 386-87
Young 208-09
Isle of Spice
Agate (b) 116-17
Isle of the Dead
Agee 175
It Happened at the Inn
Agee 189
It Happened Here
Simon (c) 242-44
It Happened in Brooklyn
Agee 247
It Happened in Spain
Weinberg 319-20
It Happened One Night
Agate (a) 123
Ferguson 18-19, 23, 33-34
It Happened One Summer see
State Fair (Walter Lang)
It Happened Tomorrow
Agee 92, 346
It Started in Naples

Kauffmann (b) 53-55
ITALIAN FILMS (early 1910's)
   Young (17)
ITALIAN FILMS (post-1945)
   Alpert 182-83
   Young 4-5, 61
ITALIAN FILMS (early 1960's)
   Kauffmann (b) 340
   Sarris (a) 29-33
   Young 126-37, 228-39
Italian Straw Hat, The
   Kael (d) 287
Italiano Brava Gente
   Crist 169-70
It's a Gift
   Ferguson (66)
   Gilliatt 258-59
It's a Mad, Mad, Mad, Mad
   World
   Crist 30-33
   Gilliatt 160-62
   Macdonald 161, 163, 166
It's a Wonderful Life
   Agee 233-34
   Weinberg 108
It's a Wonderful World (W. S.
   Van Dyke)
   Ferguson 257
It's All True (Orson Welles)
   Weinberg (175)
It's Always Fair Weather
   Kael (d) 287-88
It's in the Bag
   Agee 157-58
It's Love I'm After see Awful
   Truth (Leo McCarey)
It's Love I'm After (Archie
   Mayo)
   Kael (d) 288
It's My Life see My Life to
   Live
Itto
   Van Doren (323)
Iunost' poeta see Young Push-
   kin
Ivan the Terrible (Sergei Eisen-
   stein)
   Agee 248-50, 369-70
   Durgnat (32), (36-37), (52-
      53)
   Kael (d) 288-89
   Kauffmann (b) 20-22
   Macdonald 256-64

Young 153-54
I've Always Loved You
   Winnington 49
Ivy
   Agee 271

                    -J-

Jack of All Trades
   Graham 56
Jalshagar see Music Room
Jamaica Inn
   Agate (b) 163-65
   Ferguson 270
   Graham 222-23
Jamming the Blues
   Agee 131
Jane Eyre (Robert Stevenson)
   Agate (b) 242-43
   Agee 76-77
   Weinberg (105)
Jannings, Emil
   Durgnat 91
   Reed (a) (404)
Janosik
   Graham 87
   Van Doren 349-50, 407
Janov, Arthur. The Primal
   Scream
   Sarris (b) 15
Janus Films
   Kauffmann (b) 337
JAPANESE FILMS
   Young 99-103
JAPANESE FILMS (post-1945)
   Young 5-7, 51-58, (277),
      311
Jardin de las delicias see
   Garden of Delights (Carols
   Saura)
Jazz Comedy
   Graham 23-24
Jealousy (Gustav Machaty)
   Agee 169
Jealousy, Italian Style see
   Pizza Triangle
Jeannie (Harold French)
   Agate (b) 188-89
   Agee 58
Jeg--en kvinde see I, a Woman

Jenny (Grace Bloomefield)
  Reed (a) 268
Jenny Lamour
  Agee 300
  Sarris (b) (88)
  Winnington 96
Jessica
  Sarris (a) 48-49
Jeu de Massacre
  Young 336-37
Jeux de l'amour see Love
  Game
Jeux interdits see Forbidden
  Games
Jew Süss (Veit Harlan)
  Weinberg (260)
Jew Süss (Lothar Mendes)
  Agate (b) 104-06
  Weinberg (260)
JEWS IN FILMS
  Kael (a) 345
  Sarris (a) 394-95
JEWS IN FILMS (World War II)
  Crist 161
Jezebel
  Kael (d) 289-90
  Van Doren 395-96
Jigokumon see Gate of Hell
Jimmy the Gent
  Ferguson 36-37
Jinrui gaku myumon see Por-
  nographer
Joan Miró Makes a Colored Print
  see Miró
Joan of Arc (Carl Dreyer) see
  Passion of Joan of Arc, The
Joan of Arc (Gustav Ucicky)
  Graham 29
Joan of Paris
  Lejeune 76
Joan of the Angels? see Mother
  Joan of the Angels
Joanna (Michael Sarne)
  Adler 301-03, 310-12
  Kael (b) 193-95
  Kauffmann (a) (134)
  Reed (a) 205
  Simon (b) 297-98
Job, The see Sound of Trum-
  pets, The
Joe
  Kael (a) 151-53
  Schickel 324-27

Simon (b) 99-101
John and Mary
  Kael (a) 72-73
John F. Kennedy: Years of
  Lightning...
  Reed (a) 346-47
  Schickel 66-70
Johnny Apollo
  Lejeune 53-54
Johnny Come Lately
  Agate (a) 250-51
  Agee 58-59
Johnny Guitar
  Durgnat (15), 186-98
Johnny in the Clouds
  Lejeune 150-52
Johnny Vagabond see Johnny
  Come Lately
Joi-uchi see Rebellion
Joke, The
  Gilliatt 133-36
  Kauffmann (a) 260-61
Joker, The
  Kauffmann (b) 234-35
Joli Mai, Le
  Simon (c) (85)
Jolson Story, The
  Agee 227
  Winnington 71
Jones, Jennifer
  Durgnat 169
Jour de fête, La see Big Day,
  The
Jour se leve see Daybreak
Journal d'un curé de campagne
  see Diary of a Country Priest
Journal d'une femme de chambre
  see Diary of a Chambermaid
  (Luis Buñuel)
Journey for Margaret
  Agee 27
Journey into Fear
  Agate (b) 237-38
  Agee 29, (45)
Journey to Italy see Strangers
  (Roberto Rossellini)
Journey's End (James Whale)
  Agate (a) 62-67
Joyless Street see Streets of
  Sorrow (Georg Pabst)
Juarez
  Ferguson 254-55
  Graham 254-55

Judas Was a Woman see Hu-
    man Beast, The
Judex (George Franju)
    Sarris (a) (245)
    Weinberg 270-71
Judex (Louis Feuillade)
    Weinberg 270-71
Judgment at Nuremberg
    Alpert 235
    Kael (d) 208-09
    Kauffmann (b) 12-14
Judith
    Crist 163-64
Juduska golovev see House of
    Greed
Juke Girl
    Lejeune 78
Jules and Jim
    Durgnat 28
    Farber 153
    Kael (c) 216-222
    Kauffmann (b) 226-30
    Macdonald 376-80
    Reed 110
    Sarris (a) 42-44
    Sontag (b) (140), (147), (149)
    Young 174-76
Juliet of the Spirits
    Crist 139-41, 149
    Farber 166-68
    Kael (b) (100)
    Kauffmann (b) 325-29
    Macdonald 351-54
    Sarris (a) 215-19
    Simon (b) (372)
    Simon (c) 193-98
Julius Caesar (Joseph L. Man-
    kiewicz)
    Alpert 153-54, 242-43
    Kael (d) (198)
Julotta see Christmas Morn
July 14 see Fourteenth of July
June 13th
    Agee (34)
Junge Törless, Der see Young
    Torless
Jungfrukallan see Virgin Spring
Jungle Princess, The
    Graham 126-27
    Lejeune 21-22
Juno and the Paycock
    Agate (a) 59-61
Junost' Maksima see Youth of

Maxim
Justice Is Coming
    Agate (b) 250-51
    Winnington 22-23
Justine
    Simon (b) 48-51

-K-

Kabinett des Dr. Caligari see
    Cabinet of Dr. Caligari, The
Kael, Pauline
    Durgnat (152), (154)
    Kael (b) vii-viii
    Kael (c) 4-6, 228-334
    Sarris (b) 55-56, 111-36
    Simon (b) 10-22
Kael, Pauline. "Fantasies of the
    Art House Audience"
    Durgnat 156-65
Kael, Pauline. Going Steady
    Simon (b) 17-22
Kael, Pauline. I Lost It at the
    Movies
    Macdonald 470-74
    Simon (b) 13-14
Kael, Pauline. Kiss Kiss Bang
    Bang
    Simon (b) 14-17
Kagi
    Kael (c) 160-63
Kaja, ubit cú te see Kaya, I'll
    Kill You
Kakushi toride no san-akunin see
    Hidden Fortress
Kamera Unit (Poland)
    Kauffmann 404-05
Kameradschaft
    Agate (a) 108-10
    Durgnat (50)
    Ferguson (8), 262-63
    Kael (d) 290
    Weinberg 40-42
Kanal
    Kauffmann (b) 355
    Simon (b) (166)
    Simon (c) 21-22
Kanchenjungha
    Schickel 77-80
Karamasov see Mörder Dimitri
    Karamazov
Käre John see Dear John

Kärlek 65 see Love '65
Karlovy-Vary International Film
    Festival, 14th, 1964
    Kauffmann (b) 399-401
Karlson, Phil
    Farber 23
Katia
    Graham 201, 203
Katz und Maus see Cat and
    Mouse (H. Pohland)
Kauffmann, Stanley
    Kauffmann (a) xiii-xiv
    Kauffmann (b) ix-x
Kaya, I'll Kill You
    Adler 263-64
Kazan, Elia
    Alpert (23), 133-37
Keaton, Buster
    Agee (8), 14-17
    Farber 175-76
    Gilliatt 45-54
    Reed (c) 120-23
    Sarris (b) 93, 165-69
    Simon (c) 187
Keaton, Buster (quoted)
    Macdonald 405
Keep an Eye on Amelia see
    Oh, Amelia
Keep Your Powder Dry
    Winnington 36
Keighley, William
    Farber 13
Kelland, Clarence Budington
    Kael (c) 294-95
Kelman, Ken
    Kauffmann (b) 424
Kennedy, John Fitzgerald
    Sarris (a) 51-53
Kentucky
    Graham 210
Kermesse Héroique, La
    Ferguson 153-54
    Graham 111
    Kael (d) 244-45
    Van Doren 341-42
Kerr, Walter
    Alpert 233, 235, 243
Key Largo
    Agee 312
Keys of the Kingdom, The
    Agee 134-35
    Lejeune 141-43
Khartoum

Schickel 54-57
Kid, The (Charles Chaplin)
Kid for Two Farthings, A
    Kael (d) 290-91
Kid from Brooklyn, The
    Agee 202
Kid from Spain, The
    Agate (b) 82
Kid Galahad (Michael Curtiz)
    Ferguson 181-82
Kidnapped (Alfred Werker)
    Graham 197
Kids in the Shoe, The
    Ferguson (85)
Killer (Claude Charbrol) see
    This Man Must Die
Killer McCoy
    Agee (300)
Killers, The (Robert Siodmak)
    Agee 217
    Kael (d) 291
    Winnington 71
Killing, The
    Kael (d) 291
Killing Game see Jeu de Mas-
    sacre
Killing of Sister George, The
    Adler 319-20
    Kael (b) 206-08
    Reed (a) 208-10
    Sarris (a) 416-17
    Sarris (b) (106)
    Simon (b) 43-44
Kimiko
    Van Doren 360-61
Kind Hearts and Coronets
    Kael (d) 292
Kind of Loving, A
    Kauffmann (b) 200-03
    Young 167-68
King, Henry
    Macdonald 86-88, (105)
    Sarris (b) 38-39
King and Country
    Farber 184-85
    Macdonald 396-97
King in New York, A
    Weinberg (164)
King Kong
    Agate (a) (117)
    Agate (b) 88-90
King Lavra and the Barber
    Crist (113)

King Lear (Peter Brook)
  Kael (a) 354-57
King of Burlesque
  Ferguson 122
King of Hearts
  Gilliatt 222
King of Kings (Nicholas Ray)
  Macdonald 427-30
King Solomon's Mines (Robert
  Stevenson)
  Graham 161
King Steps Out, The
  Graham 108
Kingdoms of This World
  Young 72
King's Ransom
  Crist 36-39
Kings Row
  Agate (a) 247-48
  Ferguson 415-16
KINO PRAVDA see CINEMA
  VERITE
Kipps (Carol Reed)
  Agate (a) 220-21
  Ferguson 393-94
Kiri no naka no shojo see Girl
  in the Mist
Kiss and Tell
  Agee 177-78
Kiss Me Deadly
  Durgnat (76)
  Sontag (b) 161
Kiss Me, Stupid
  Crist 95-97
  Macdonald 163-64
Kiss of Death
  Agee 274-75, 376-77
  Warshow (129)
Kiss the Other Sheik
  Adler 197-98
Kitchen, The
  Kauffmann (b) 198-200
Kite from the Other Side of the
  World
  Crist 113-14
KITSCH see AESTHETICS
Kitty Foyle
  Ferguson 334
Kliou the Killer see Kliou the
  Tiger
Kliou the Tiger
  Graham 65-66
Klondike Annie

Graham 75-76
Klute
  Kael (a) 280-82
Kluven värld see Divided World
Knack, The
  Crist 124-26
  Kael (d) 116-17
  Kauffmann (b) 215-17
  Macdonald 401-03
Knave of Hearts
  Kael (d) 311-12
  Simon (c) 184
Knife in the Water
  Crist (34)
  Kauffmann (b) 358-60
  Simon (c) 95-96
  Weinberg 231-32
  Young 366-68
Knight Without Armour
  Graham 170-71
Knight, Arthur (quoted)
  Kael (d) 206
Knight, Shirley
  Reed (c) 101-06
Knock on Wood
  Kael (d) 292
Knute Rockne--All American
  Ferguson 334
Kolii Rebellion see Mass Strug-
  gle
Koliivshchina see Mass Struggle
Koncert za mašinsku pusku see
  Concerto for Sub-Machine Gun
Konez Sankt-Peterburga see
  Petersburg Nights
Kongress tanzt see Congress
  Dances
Korda, Alexander
  Agate (a) 165-66
  Graham 2
Korda, Zoltan
  Farber 13
Koritsi me ta mavra see Girl
  in Black
Koumiko Mystery, The
  Kael (d) 292-93
  Weinberg (272-73)
Kracauer, Siegfried
  Pechter (280), (310)
Kracauer, Siegfried. Theory of
  Film
  Kael (c) 269-92
Kramer, Stanley

Kael (d) 203-14
Sarris (a) (378)
Sarris (b) (60)
Kremlin Letter, The
Kael (a) 104-05
Reed (a) 275
Krestiane see Peasants
Kribbebijter, Die
Graham 95
Ku Kan
Ferguson 382-83
Kubrick, Stanley
Alpert 132
Pechter 8
Külvárosi legenda see Love in the Suburbs
Kukan see Ku Kan
Kulesov, Lev
Pechter 301
Sarris (b) 89, 239
Kumonosujo see Throne of Blood
Kurosawa, Akira
Kauffmann (a) 44
Kauffmann (b) 385
Macdonald 481-83
Weinberg (241)
Young 285-86, 291-92
Kutuzov see 1812 (Vladimir Petrov)
Kvarteret korpen see Raven's End
Kvinnors väntan see Secrets of a Woman
Kwaidan
Weinberg 273

-L-

L. S. Lowry
Durgnat 127-28
L-Shaped Room, The
Durgnat (39)
Labarthe, Andre S. (quoted)
Simon (b) 8
Laburnum Grove
Graham 90-91
Ladies' Man, The (Jerry Lewis)
Durgnat 101
Ladies' Man (Lothar Mendes)
Sarris (b) 128-29
Ladies of the Bois de Boulogne
see Dames du Bois de Boulogne
Ladies of the Park see Dames du Bois de Boulogne
Ladri di biciclette see Bicycle Thief
Lady and the Monster, The
Agee 93
Lady Eve, The
Farber (180)
Ferguson 347-48
Lady from Constantinople, The
Simon (b) 386
Lady from Shanghai, The
Durgnat (226)
Weinberg (158), (280)
Winnington 102-03
Lady Hamilton see That Hamilton Woman
Lady in the Dark
Agee 82
Lejeune 119-20
Weinberg 105
Lady in the Lake
Weinberg 107
Lady in the Morgue
Ferguson 221-22
Lady Is Willing, The (Gilbert Miller)
Ferguson 44
Lady Macbeth of Minsk
Young 212-13
Lady Surrenders, A (Leslie Arliss)
Lejeune 130-31
Winnington 40, 42
Lady Takes a Chance, A
Agee 53-54, (67)
Lady Vanishes, The
Ferguson 237-38
Kael (d) 293
Sarris (a) 212-13
Lady with a Dog, The
Kauffmann (b) 364-66
Macdonald 270-71
Weinberg 200
Young 123
Lady with Red Hair, The
Agate (a) 225-27
Lady with the Little Dog see Lady with a Dog, The
Ladybug Ladybug
Simon (c) 104-05

Ladykillers, The
  Kael (d) 293
Lambert, Gavin
  Durgnat 62
Lancaster, Burt
  Alpert 31-39
Land We Love, The
  Macdonald 460-61
Land without Bread
  Graham 179
Landlord, The
  Kauffmann (a) (277)
Landru
  Kauffmann (b) 254-56
  Sarris (a) 86-87
  Simon (b) (10)
  Simon (c) 63-64
Landsbykirken see Danish Par-
  ish Churches (Carl Dreyer)
Lang, Fritz
  Durgnat (85), 92-93, 104
  Ferguson 374-78
  Kael (c) 299-300
  Pechter 304
  Weinberg (150-51), 233, (239),
    284-86
Lang, Fritz (quoted)
  Durgnat 41
  Weinberg 9-11, 252
Langdon, Harry
  Agee (8), 12-14
  Gilliatt 127-42
Langer, Gilda
  Weinberg 221-22
Langlois, Henri
  Adler 152, 255-58, 330
Lansbury, Angela
  Reed (c) 114-19
Larceny, Inc.
  Agate (b) 208-09
Lash of the Czar, The
  Macdonald (65), (67)
Lash of the Penitentes, The
  Agee (145)
Lasky jedne plavovlasky see
  Loves of a Blonde
Lassie Come Home
  Agee 54
  Winnington 16
Last Card, The
  Agee (228)
Last Chance, The (Leopold Lind-
  berg)

Agee 180-81
Lejeune 171-72
Last Command, The (Josef von
  Sternberg)
  Weinberg 232
Last Day of Summer
  Young (171)
Last Holiday, The
  Kael (d) 293-94
Last Laugh, The
  Durgnat 91
  Macdonald (5), (14)
  Weinberg (107), (178)
Last Love
  Graham 35
Last Movie, The
  Kael (a) 297-99
Last Night, The
  Ferguson 177-78
Last of the Mobile Hot Shots, The
  Reed (a) 270
Last of the Mohicans, The
  (George Seitz)
  Agate (b) 133-34
  Van Doren 340
Last Outpost (Louis Gasnier)
  Graham 37-38
Last Picture Show, The
  Kael (a) 293-97
Last Summer
  Kauffmann (a) 177-79
  Pechter 98-99
  Reed (a) 228-30
  Sarris (a) 450-51
  Simon (b) 113-15
Last Ten Days, The
  Kael (d) 294
  Weinberg 337
  Young 81
Last Train from Madrid, The
  Graham 154
Last Valley, The
  Kael (a) 248-50
Last Will of Dr. Mabuse, The
  Weinberg 101-03, (150)
Last Year at Marienbad
  Alpert 213-16
  Durgnat (39), 110-11
  Kael (c) (21), (181-82), 186-
    93
  Kauffmann (b) 246-51
  Macdonald xv, 369-72, (472)
  Pechter 59-76

Sontag (b) (123-25), (133), (135)
Weinberg (203)
Young 187-88, 191-93, (327)
Late Mathias Pascal, The (Pierre Chenal)
Van Doren 379-80
Laughter
Agate (b) 49
Weinberg 317-18
Laughter in Paradise
Kael (d) 294
Laughter in the Dark
Gilliatt 86-88
Reed (a) 179-80
Sarris (a) 436-41
Simon (b) 47-48
Laughton, Charles
Agate (b) (131)
Lejeune 17
Weinberg (241)
Laura
Kael (c) (298)
Laurel and Hardy (comedy team)
Agee (6), (8), (18)
Lavender Hill Mob, The
Kael (d) 295
Law and Order
Kael (a) 20, (207)
Lawrence of Arabia
Farber 146, 150, 152-53
Kael (d) 136
Kauffmann (b) 24-27
Sarris (a) 65-67
Simon (c) 42-45
Weinberg (212)
Lawson, John H. Film, the Creative Process
Young 327-28
Lazarillo
Simon (c) 64-65
Lean, David
Kael (d) (132)
Lean, David (quoted)
Winnington 7-8
Learning Tree, The
Kauffmann (a) 202-03
Reed (a) 238-39
Leather Boys, The
Farber 182-83
Sarris (a) 231-34
Schickel 43-45
Leáud, Jean-Pierre

Farber 225
Leave Her to Heaven
Agee 360
Lejeune 173-74
Lebenszeichen see Signs of Life
Leda
Durgnat 102
Weinberg 172-74
Left-Handed Gun, The
Alpert (55)
Durgnat (39)
Kael (d) 60
Legend of Lylah Clare, The
Adler 215-16
Legend of Prague, The see Golem (Julien Duvivier)
Legion of Decency (see also CENSORSHIP)
Alpert 217-18
Kael (d) 96
Legion of Honor see Un de la Légion
Lejeune, Caroline A.
Lejeune 11-13
Lejeune, Caroline (quoted)
Agate (b) 147
Graham 39
Lektion i karlek see Lesson in Love
Lenauer, Jean
Ferguson 219
LENGTH see VERSIONS, ABBREVIATED
Lenin in October
Graham 206-07
Macdonald 226-28
Leo the Last
Reed (a) 396-97
Leopard, The
Kauffmann (b) 330-32
Macdonald 345-47
Sarris (a) 92-93
Leopard Man, The
Farber 49-50
Lermontov
Winnington 37, 39
LeRoy, Mervyn
Macdonald 97-100
Lesson in Love, A
Kauffmann (b) 275-76
Lester, Richard
Farber 160-64

Young 281-82
Let 'Em Have It
   Ferguson 82
Let It Be
   Simon (b) 127-29
Let There Be Light
   Agee (200), 236
Let's Make Love
   Kauffmann (b) 53-55
Letter, The (William Wyler)
   Agate (a) 221-22
   Kael (d) 295-96
Letter from an Unknown Woman
   Kael (d) 296
Letter That Was Not Sent, The
   Weinberg (199)
Letzte akt, Der see Last Ten
   Days, The
Letzte Chance, Die see Last
   Chance, The (Leopold Lindt-
   berg)
Letzte liebe see Last Love
Letzte mann, Der see Last
   Laugh, The
Leuchter des Kaisers see Em-
   peror's Candlesticks
Levant, Oscar
   Weinberg 214
Levine, Joe
   Macdonald 130-32
Lewis, Joseph
   Sarris (b) 29
Lewton, Val
   Farber 47-50, 55
Lezione di geometria see Geom-
   etry Lesson
Liaisons Dangereuses, Les
   Kael (c) (43)
   Kael (d) 296-97
Libeled Lady
   Ferguson 161
Libertine, The
   Simon (b) (150)
LIBRARIES, FILM (see also
   ARCHIVES, FILM)
   Sarris (b) 21
Liebe de Jeanne Ney, Die
   see Love of Jeanne Ney, The
Liebesmelodie
   Graham 64-65
Life (magazine)
   Schickel 5, 17-18, 22-23, 30
Life and Death of Colonel Blimp,

The see Colonel Blimp
Life and Loves of Beethoven,
   The
   Agate (a) 199-201
   Graham 230
Life Begins at 8:30
   Agee (24)
Life Begins for Andy Hardy
   Ferguson 388-89
Life Begins Tomorrow
   Weinberg (175)
Life Dances On see Carnet de
   Bal, Un
Life Is Beautiful see Simple
   Case
Life Is Very Good see Simple
   Case
Life of Emile Zola, The
   Agate (b) 144-47
   Ferguson (10), 188-90
   Graham 177
   Van Doren 370-71
Life of Oharu
   Sarris (a) 138-39
Life Upside Down
   Gilliatt 113-14
   Kauffmann (b) 267-69
   Macdonald (411)
   Simon (c) 178-80
Life with Father
   Agee 272
Lifeboat
   Agee 71-72
Light in the Piazza
   Sarris (a) 50
Light of Heart see Life Begins
   at 8:30
Light That Failed, The (William
   Wellman)
   Graham 262, 264
LIGHTING
   Durgnat 49, 53-55, 95-96
Lights of Variety see Variety
   Lights
Lights Out in Europe
   Ferguson 296-97
Lily of Killarney see Bride of
   the Lake
Limelight (Charles Chaplin)
   Pechter 284
   Sarris (a) 164-67
   Warshow 225-39
   Young 31-33

Limelight (Herbert Wilcox)
　Agate (a) 171-73
Lindgren, Ernest. Art of the
　Film
　Sarris (a) 174-75
Lion Has Wings, The
　Graham 249-50
Lion Hunters, The
　Simon (b) 282
Lion in Winter, The
　Adler 279-81
　Kael (b) 174-76
　Reed (a) 202
　Schickel 213-16
　Simon (b) 347-50
Lions Love
　Kael (a) 30-31
　Simon (b) 386
Lisbon Story, The
　Lejeune 177
List of Adrian Messenger, The
　Kael (d) 297-98
Listen to Britain
　Agee (65-66)
LITERARY ADAPTATIONS see
　ADAPTATIONS
LITERATURE AND THE CINE-
　MA
　Durgnat 178-81, 236-38
　Ferguson 3-4, 9, 11, 69
　Kael (a) 235-38
　Macdonald 366, 445-46
　Sarris (a) (363-64)
　Sontag (b) 155-59
Little and Big
　Adler 19
Little Big Horn
　Farber 58
Little Big Man
　Kael (a) 212-16
Little Caesar
　Macdonald 98-99
Little Fauss and Big Halsy
　Kael (a) 173-74
　Reed (a) 302
　Schickel 331-33
Little Foxes, The
　Durgnat (29-30), (41)
　Ferguson 13-17, 383-85, (394)
Little Friend
　Ferguson 50
Little Fugitive, The
　Alpert 200
Little Man, What Now?

Ferguson 38
Little Match Girl, The
　Simon (c) 261
Little Miss Marker
　Ferguson 38
Little Murders
　Kael (a) 253-57
Little Road see Pather Pan-
　chali
Little Soldier, The
　Simon (c) 183-84
Little Tough Guy
　Graham 198-99
Little Women (George Cukor)
　Agate (b) 103-04
Littlest Rebel, The
　Graham 78
Lives of a Bengal Lancer, The
　Agate (a) 129-31
　Ferguson 65-66
Living see Ikiru
Living Dangerously
　Graham 88-89
Living One's Life
　Durgnat 128
Lizards, The
　Durgnat 107
Lizzani, Carlo
　Young 234
Ljubavni slucaj, tragedija
　sluzbenice PTT see Affair
　of the Heart
Lloyd, Harold
　Agee (8), 10-12, 17
　Gilliatt 157-58
　Sarris (b) 263-64
Lloyds of London
　Graham 149
LOCATION (see also SETS)
　Alpert 17-20
　Farber 20-21
Lodger, The (John Brahm)
　Agee 77
　Lejeune 109
　Weinberg (105)
Loin de Vietnam see Far from
　Vietnam
Lola Montès
　Crist (189)
　Farber 230
　Gilliatt 297-303
　Kauffmann (a) 160-64
　Sarris (b) 153-56
　Simon (b) 352-54

Simon (c) 86
Lolita
  Kael (c) 203-09
  Kauffmann (b) 111-13
  Macdonald 287-89
  Sarris (a) 60-61
London Town
  Winnington 64, 66
Lone Ranger, The (serial, William Witney)
  Graham 221-22, 225
Loneliness of the Long Distance Runner, The
  Farber 137
  Kael (c) 256-61
  Kauffmann (b) 188-89
  Macdonald 389-91
Lonely Are the Brave
  Kael (d) 40
Lonely Boy
  Kael (a) (109)
Lonely Woman, The see Strangers (Roberto Rossellini)
Lonesome Cowboys
  Reed (a) 194
  Schickel 229-32
Long Ago, Tomorrow
  Kael (a) 321-24
Long Day's Dying, The
  Adler 161-62, (166-67)
  Young 345-46
Long Day's Journey into Night
  Kael (d) 298
  Kauffmann (b) 74-76
  Macdonald 130-32
  Simon (c) 41-42
Long Night, The
  Agee 273
Long Ships, The
  Crist 74-75
Long Voyage Home, The
  Durgnat (79)
  Ferguson 313-14
  Young 92
Look After Amelia see Oh, Amelia
Look Back in Anger
  Kael (c) 67-70
  Kauffmann (b) 179-83
Look Up and Laugh
  Graham 12
Looking Glass War, The
  Kael (a) 117-19

Lord Jim (Richard Brooks)
  Simon (c) 153
Lord Love a Duck
  Kael (d) 298-99
  Reed (a) 347-48
  Sarris (a) 241-43
  Simon (c) 222-23
Lord of the Flies, The
  Crist (40)
  Kauffmann (b) 122
Lords of the Forest see Masters of the Congo Jungle
Lorentz, Pare
  Weinberg (239)
Lorna Doone (Basil Dean)
  Agate (b) 109-111
Los Angeles, California
  Kael (c) 3-5
Losey, Joseph
  Reed (b) 141-46
  Simon (b) 407-08
  Young 223-24
Loss of Innocence
  Sarris (a) 49
Lost Angel
  Agee 70-71
  Winnington 16, 18
Lost Boundaries
  Brown (c) 255-60
LOST FILMS
  Weinberg 11, 256, 306
Lost Horizon, The (Frank Capra)
  Agate (a) 183-85
  Ferguson 169
  Graham 145, 148
Lost in a Harem
  Agee 130
Lost Weekend, The
  Agee 182-84
Lot in Sodom
  Ferguson 32-33
  Weinberg 52, 201, 209-10, 343
Lotna
  Sarris (a) (251)
Loudest Whisper, The see Children's Hour, The
Louis, Joe
  Ferguson 140-43
Louise
  Graham 228
Louisiana Purchase
  Ferguson 407-08

Louisiana Story
   Kael (c) (276)
   Young 23-25
Loups entre eux, Les see Sequel to Second Bureau
Love Affair (Leo McCarey)
Love Affair (Dusan Makavejev) see Affair of the Heart, An
Love Affair ... or, The Case of the Missing Switchboard Operator see Affair of the Heart, An
Love and Larceny
   Weinberg 217
Love and the Frenchwoman
   Weinberg (175)
Love at Twenty
   Crist (33)
   Simon (c) 51-55
   Weinberg 217
Love Dossier see Affair of the Heart, An
Love Eternal see Eternal Return
Love from a Stranger (Rowland Lee)
   Van Doren 362-63
Love Game, The
   Kauffmann (b) 233
Love in the Suburbs
   Simon (c) 84
Love Is a Funny Thing
   Reed (a) 322-23
Love Letters (William Dieterle)
   Agee 176
Love Me Forever
   Ferguson 83-84
   Graham 20
Love Me Tonight
   Weinberg (253)
Love of Jeanne Ney, The
   Van Doren 352-53
   Weinberg 50-51
Love on the Dole (John Baxter)
   Agate (b) 183-84
Love '65
   Young 282-83
Love Story (Leslie Arliss) see Lady Surrenders, A
Love Story (Arthur Hiller)
   Kael (a) 216-20
   Schickel (22-23)
Love with a Proper Stranger

Crist 50-51
Loved One, The
   Kael (d) 299-301
   Kauffmann (b) 126-27
Lovely Is the Summer Night
   Young 141
Lover Boy see Knave of Hearts
Lover Come Back (Delbert Mann)
   Kael (c) (233)
   Macdonald 111-13
Lovers, The (Louis Mallé)
   Alpert 203-04, 229
   Kauffmann (b) 222-23
Lovers and Thieves
   Kael (d) 301-02
Lovers, Happy Lovers see Knave of Hearts
Lovers of Paris
   Kael (d) 333
Lover's Return, A
   Agee 294
Loves of a Blonde
   Crist 214
   Simon (c) 254-54
Loves of Ariane see Ariane
Loves of Isadora, The
   Kauffmann (a) 164-68
   Reed (a) 175-77
   Simon (b) 356
   Young 349
Loving
   Kael (a) 119-22
   Reed (a) 266-68
Loving Couples
   Reed (a) 328
LOW BUDGET FILMS
   Crist 16-19
Lower Depths, The (Akira Kurosawa)
   Kauffmann (b) 378-79
Lower Depths, The (Jean Renoir)
   Ferguson 193-95
   Gilliatt 13-15
   Graham 184
   Kael (d) 302
   Van Doren 371-73
Loy, Myrna
   Reed (b) 45-51
Loyval Forty-Seven Ronin see Chushingura (Hiroshi Inagaki)

Lubitsch, Ernst
  Agee (26)
  Macdonald 82-85, (105)
  Pechter 306-07
  Weinberg (37), (324)
Lucas, Eduard V.
  Agate (a) 43-45
Luci del varieta see Variety
  Lights
Lucia
  Adler 347-48
Luck of Ginger Coffey, The
  Kael (a) (119)
  Kauffmann (b) 128-29
Lucky Partners
  Ferguson 309-10
Lueurs
  Durgnat (97-98)
Lumet, Sydney
  Kael (d) 70-71, 75, 81-99
Lumière brothers
  Pechter 294-95
Lunch on the Grass see Dé-
  jeuner sur l'herbe, Le
Luntz, Eddie
  Reed (a) 401
Lupino, Ida
  Farber 3
Lust for Life
  Sarris (b) 42-43
Luv
  Crist 245-46
  Gilliatt 79-81

-M-

M
  Durgnat 232
  Kael (d) 302-03
M*A*S*H
  Kael (a) 92-95
  Kauffmann (a) 229-31
  Reed (a) 273-74
  Schickel 283-85
  Simon (b) 303-05
Ma Nuit Chez Maud
  Farber 241-42
  Gilliatt 54-57
  Reed (a) 275
  Schickel 306-08
  Simon (b) 392-93
Macbeth (Roman Polanski)

Kael (a) 399-401
Macbeth (Orson Welles)
  Pechter 170-71
McBride, Joseph
  Sarris (b) 114-15
McBride, Joseph. Persistence of
  Vision
  Sarris (b) 114
McCabe & Mrs. Miller
  Kael (a) 277-80
McClintock!
  Crist (35)
Macomber Affair, The
  Agee (273)
McCullers, Carson
  Reed (c) 38-43
Macdonald, Dwight
  Kael (c) (24)
  Macdonald 74-78, 473-74
  Schickel 23
  Simon (b) 410-14
Macdonald, Dwight (quoted)
  Sarris (b) 83-84
  Simon (a) 11
Macdonald, Dwight. Dwight Mac-
  donald on Movies
  Simon (b) 410-14
McLaren, Norman
  Weinberg 180-81, 197
McLuhan, Marshall
  Sarris (a) (257-58)
Mad at the World
  Kael (c) (60)
Mad Emperor, The
  Ferguson 352
Mad Love (Robert Wiene) see
  Hands of Orlac
Mad Miss Manton, The
  Ferguson 239
Mad Room, The
  Reed (a) 180-81
Madame Curie
  Agate (a) 255-57
  Agee (64), 68
  Lejeune 110-11
Madame de... see Earrings
  of Madame de...
Madame Pimpernel see Paris
  Underground
Madame X (David Lowell Rich)
  Kael (d) 121-23
  Sarris (a) 256-59
Mädchen Johanna, Das see

Joan of Arc (Gustav Ucicky)
Mädchen Rosemarie, Das see
  Rosemary
Made for Each Other
  Kael (a) (369-73)
Made in USA
  Farber 228-29
  Simon (b) (380)
Mademoiselle
  Crist 211
Mademoiselle Docteur (Edmond
  Greville)
  Graham 186
Mademoiselle Fifi
  Agee 129
Mademoiselle France see Re-
  union in France
Mademoiselle Gobette
  Kael (d) 303
Madigan
  Sarris (a) 352-53
Madmen of Europe see English-
  man's Home (Albert de Cour-
  ville)
Madwoman of Chaillot, The
  Kael (a) 25-26
  Reed (a) 245-47
  Simon (b) 51-52
Maedchen in Uniform
  Kael (d) 303
Mafioso
  Crist 89
Magasiskola see Falcons
Magic Bullet see Dr. Ehrlich's
  Magic Bullet
Magic Christian, The
  Kael (a) 123
  Reed (a) 283
Magic Garden of Stanley Sweet-
  heart, The
  Kauffmann (a) (277)
  Simon (b) 124-26
Magician, The (Ingmar Bergman)
  Alpert 75-76
  Kael (d) 303-04
  Kauffmann (b) 273-75
  Pechter 134-42
  Weinberg (177)
Magnificent Ambersons, The
  Durgnat (29)
  Kael (d) 304
  Lejeune 89-90
  Pechter 167, 169

Weinberg (158)
  Young 407-08
Magnificent Flirt
  Weinberg 315
Magnificent Obsession (Douglas
  Sirk)
  Alpert 89-90
Magnificent Seven, The (Akira
  Kurosawa) see Seven Samu-
  rai, The
Magus, The
  Adler 315-16, (318)
  Reed (a) 206-07
  Simon (b) 351-52
Mahanagar see Big City
Maid of Salem
  Graham 136-37
Majesty of Wood, The
  Young 73-74
Major Barbara
  Ferguson 365-66
Make Mine Music
  Agee 198-99
  Lejeune 185-87
  Winnington 59
Make Way for Tomorrow
  Graham 150-51
Male Hunt
  Simon (c) 162
Malraux, André
  Sarris (b) (88)
Maltese Bippy, The
  Gilliatt 257
Maltese Falcon, The (John Hus-
  ton)
  Ferguson 390
  Kael (c) (299)
  Kael (d) 305
  Macdonald 453-54
Mamma Roma
  Young 235
Mamoulian, Rouben
  Macdonald 80-82
Man, The
  Young (224)
Man About Town
  Agee (282), (289)
Man and a Woman, A
  Crist 218
  Kael (d) 126
  Schickel (84), 90
  Simon (c) 239-42
  Young 306-07

Man Called Adam, A
    Crist (209)
Man Called Horse, A
    Young 398-99
Man Escaped, A
    Kael (d) 305-06
    Sontag (a) (201)
    Sontag (b) (181)
    Young 106-07
Man for All Seasons, A
    Crist 203-05, 213
    Kael (d) 154-55
    Sarris (a) 277-80
    Simon (b) (372-73)
    Simon (c) 262-63
    Young 317
Man from the Diners' Club, The
    Gilliatt 168-69
Man Hunt (Fritz Lang)
    Ferguson (361), 371-73
Man in Grey, The
    Agate (b) 230-31
Man in Half Moon Street, The
    Agee 131
Man in the White Suit
    Kael (d) 306
Man in the Wilderness
    Kael (a) 357-59
Man Is Ten Feet Tall see
    Edge of the City
Man of Aran
    Agate (a) 121-23
    Ferguson 54-55
    Graham 29-30
    Kael (d) 306-07
Man of Conquest
    Ferguson 259
Man of Evil
    Lejeune 118-19
Man of the Hour, The see
    Homme du Jour, L'
Man of the World
    Sarris (b) 127-28
Man on the Flying Trapeze, The
    Ferguson 88
Man Power see Manpower
Man They Could Not Arrest, The
    Agate (a) 104-05
Man to Remember, A
    Ferguson (370-71)
Man Who Broke the Bank at
    Monte Carlo, The
    Graham 50

Man Who Came Back, The (Jean
    Renoir) see Swamp Water
Man Who Came Back, The
    (Raoul Walsh)
    Agate (b) 45-46
Man Who Came to Dinner, The
    Ferguson 408-09
Man Who Cheated Himself, The
    Farber 60
Man Who Could Work Miracles,
    The
    Graham 97-98
Man Who Knew Too Much, The
    (Alfred Hitchcock, 1935)
    Weinberg 38
Man Who Seeks the Truth, The
    Ferguson 390-91
Man Who Shot Liberty Valance,
    The
    Farber 136, (147)
    Kael (d) 42
    Pechter 226-34
    Sarris (b) 147-52
Man with a Million, The
    Kael (d) 307
Man with the Camera, The
    Sontag (b) (140), (158)
Man with the Golden Arm, The
    Sarris (b) 46-47
Man with the Green Carnation,
    The see Trials of Oscar
    Wilde, The
Man with the X-Ray Eyes, The
    Durgnat 101
Man with Two Faces, The
    Ferguson (46)
Man Within, The see Smug-
    glers
Manchurian Candidate, The
    Farber (150-51), 152-54
    Kael (b) 95
Mandabi
    Simon (b) 393
Mani sulla Città, Le
    Young (220)
Mankiewicz, Herman J.
    Sarris (b) 114, 119, 123-31
Mankiewicz, Joseph L.
    Alpert 150-56
    Sarris (b) 118, 132
    Weinberg 219
Mann, Anthony
    Farber 13, 16-17

MANNERS AND MORALS see
  SOCIETY AND FILMS
Människor i stad see Rhythm of
  a City
Mano sul Fucile, La
  Young 237-38
Manpower
  Agate (b) 202-03
Man's Favorite Sport?
  Sarris (a) 128-29
Man's Hope
  Agee 239-42, 288
Mar del Plata Film Festival see
  International Film Festival,
  Mar del Plata
Marat/Sade
  Crist 230-31
  Reed (a) 363-65
  Simon (b) 26-28
  Sontage (b) (122)
March of Time, The (series)
  Graham 34-35
Marchand d'Amour
  Graham 101
Mare see Sea
Mare Nostrum
  Weinberg 280
Maria Bashkirtseff
  Graham 105
Marie
  Weinberg 239
Marie Antoinette (W. S. van Dyke)
  Agate (a) 195-96
  Ferguson 231
Marie, Légende Hongroise see
  Marie
Marie Nover see Marie
Marie Walewska see Conquest
  (Clarence Brown)
Mariée était en noir, La see
  Bride Wore Black, The
Marilyn
  Gilliatt 33-34
  Kauffmann (b) 55-56
  Simon (c) 69
Marine Raiders
  Agee 103
Marinetti, Filippo T.
  Sontag (b) 118
Mark, The
  Kael (c) 155-59
Mark of Zorro, The (Fred Niblo)
  Weinberg (211)

Marked Woman
  Graham 166
  Kael (d) 307-08
  Van Doren 363
Marnie
  Crist (80-81)
  Sarris (a) 141-44
Marooned
  Kael (a) 86
Marquis d'Eon see Spy of Ma-
  dame Pompadour, The
Marriage, Italian Style
  Kauffmann (b) 297-99
  Simon (c) 141-43
Marriage of Corbal, The
  Graham 78-80
Married Couple, A
  Kael (a) 107-111
  Kauffmann (a) 226-27
Married Woman, A
  Kauffmann (a) (12)
  Kauffmann (b) 244-46
  Simon (c) 180-82
Marseillaise, La
  Weinberg 87-90
Marsh, Mae
  Kael (b) 46
Marty
  Alpert 33
Martyred Love see Martyrs of
  Love
Martyrs of Love
  Reed (a) 145
Marvin, Lee
  Crist 146
Marx Brothers (comedy team)
  Agate (b) (178)
  Agee (18)
  Lejeune 168-69
Marx Brothers at the Circus,
  The
  Graham 257
Marx Brothers Go West, The
  see Go West (Edward Ruzzell)
Marx, Harpo
  Van Doren 368-69
Mary of Scotland
  Ferguson 146-48
Mary Poppins
  Crist (90), (112)
Maschera del demonio, La see
  Black Sunday (Mario Bava)
Masculine Feminine

Kael (b) (4)
Kael (d) 127-30
MASH see M*A*A*S*H
Mask (Max Ophuls) see Plai-
  sir
Mask of the Demon, The see
  Black Sunday (Mario Bava)
Maskerade see Masquerade in
  Vienna
Mason, James
  Reed (c) 129-33
Masquerade in Mexico
  Agate (b) 266-67
Masquerade in Vienna
  Weinberg 62-65
Mass Struggle
  Ferguson 51
Masters of the Congo Jungle
  Kael (d) (181)
Mat' see Mother (Vsevolod
  Pudovkin)
Mata Hari
  Weinberg 219
Maternelle, La
  Ferguson 99-100
  Van Doren 302-04
Matka Joanna see Mother Joan
  of the Angels
Matrimonio all'Italiana see
  Marriage Italian Style
Mattatore, Il see Love and
  Larceny
Matter of Dignity, A
  Young 124-25
Matter of Innocence, A
  Adler 54-55
  Kael (b) 54
Matter of Life and Death, A
  see Stairway to Heaven
Mauvais Coups, Les
  Crist (34)
  Young 255-58
Maxim Gorky Trilogy
  Macdonald 451-53
  Winnington 15, 18-19
Mayer, Carl
  Weinberg 222
Mayerling (Anatole Litvak)
  Ferguson 195
  Graham 113, 115
Mayerling (Terence Young)
  Kael (b) 268-71
  Reed (a) 147, 213-14

Mayor's Dilemma, The
  Graham 234-35
Mazurka
  Graham 130-31
Me see Naked Childhood
Medal for Benny, A
  Agee (169)
Medea
  Reed (a) (281),   321-22
Medium, The
  Kael (c) (286)
  Kael (d) 308
Medium Cool
  Kauffmann (a) 192-96
  Pechter 102-03
  Reed (a) 241-43
  Schickel 247-49
  Simon (b) (66), 76-81, (401)
Meet John Doe
  Ferguson 349-51
Meet Me in St. Louis
  Agee 126-28, 356-57
  Winnington 33
Meet Whiplash Willie see For-
  tune Cookie
Mein Kampf
  Macdonald 447-49
Mekas, Jonas
  Kael (c) 314-17
  Macdonald 327
  Sontag (a) (227)
Méliès, Georges
  Pechter 295
  Sontag (b) 101
Melody Time
  Agee (306)
Member of the Wedding, The
  Alpert 159
  Kael (d) 308-09
Memorandum
  Simon (b) (382)
Memorias de subdesarrollo see
  Memories of Underdevelop-
  ment
Memories of Underdevelopment
  Adler 349
Memory Expert, The see Man
  on the Flying Trapeze, The
Memphis Belle
  Agee 88-89
Men, The (Fred Zinnemann)
  Farber (62)
Men in Danger

Graham 223
MEN IN FILMS
Crist 179
Kael (a) 174, (348), 350
Sarris (a) 67
Men in White
Ferguson 39-40
Men of the Sea see Midship-
man Easy (Carol Reed)
Men with Wings
Graham 205
Ménilmontant
Kael (c) (291)
Mennesker mødes og sød musik
opstår i hjert see People
meet and sweet music fills
the heart
Menschen am Sonntag see
People on Sunday
Menschen am Wege see Three
Loves (Wilhelm Dieterle)
Menzel, Jiri
Kauffmann (a) (33-34)
Menzies, William Cameron
Durgnat 77
Mercouri, Melina
Reed (c) 140-45
Merlusse
Ferguson 218-19
Graham 62
Merrie Melodies (series)
Farber 51-53
Merry Go Round, The (Erich von
Stroheim)
Weinberg 50, 165-68
Merry Widow, The (Erich von
Stroheim)
Weinberg 49, 55-56, (177),
(262)
Merry Wisdom see Gai Savoir
Meshes of the Afternoon
Agee 191
METAPHOR see EDITING
Metropolis
Kael (c) (284-85)
Kael (d) 309-10
Macdonald (4)
METTEUR-EN-SCENE see DI-
RECTORS
Metzergerstein see Spirits of
the Dead
MEXICAN FILMS
Weinberg 261

Meyerhold, Vsevolod
Sontag (b) 115, 118
Michael Strogoff (George Nich-
olls Jr.) see Soldier and
the Lady, The
Michelangelo (Curt Oertel) see
Titan: The Story of Michel-
angelo
Michelson, Annette (quoted)
Young 324-27
Mickey Mouse
Reed (b) 248-49
Mickey One
Crist 149
Middle of the Night
Kauffmann (b) 95-97
Midnight Cowboy
Kael (a) 4
Kauffmann (a) 170-74
Reed (a) 185-87
Reed (b) 251-59
Sarris (a) 441-45
Schickel 237-39
Simon (b) 357-60, 401-02
Midshipman Easy (Carol Reed)
Graham 42
Midsummer Night's Dream, A
(Dieterle and Reinhardt)
Agate (a) 152-54
Agate (b) 122-24
Ferguson 97-98
Graham 28-29
Van Doren 299-302
Midsummer Night's Dream, A
(Dan Eriksen)
Kael (b) 70-71
Mikhael
Sarris (a) (234)
Milczaca guiazda see First
Spaceship on Venus, The
Mildred Pierce
Agee 176
Milestone, Lewis
Macdonald 98-103
Milky Way, The
Ferguson 119-20
Graham 58-59
Kael (a) 102-03
Kauffmann (a) 231-35
Simon (b) 197-202
Million, Le (René Clair)
Agate (a) 98-99
Million Dollar Legs (Edw. Cline)

Gilliatt   259-60
Million Pound Note, The   see
    Man with a Million, The
Millions Like Us   see   Happiest
    Days of Your Life, The
Mills, Hayley
    Reed (c)   158-63
Milne, Tom.   Losey on Losey
    Simon (b)   407-08
Mimi
    Graham   10-11
Mine Own Executioneer
    Winnington   88-89
Minelli, Vincente
    Agee   358-59
    Durgnat   55
    Sarris (b)   (51)
Mir vhodjasccemu   see   Peace
    to He Who Enters
Miracle (Robert Rossellini)   see
    Ways of Love
Miracle in Milan
    Kael (d)   310
Miracle of Morgan's Creek, The
    Agee   73-76, 342-43
    Weinberg   105
Miracle of the Bells, The
    Agee   (301
Miracle on 34th Street
    Agee   274
Miracolo a Milano   see   Miracle
    in Milan
Mirages de Paris
    Ferguson   27-28
Miró
    Young   70-71
Mischief-Makers, The
    Kael (d)   310-11
MISE-EN-SCENE   see   DIRECT-
    ING
Misérables, Les (Richard Boles-
    lavsky)
    Agate (a)   144-45
    Ferguson   77-78
Misère au Borinage, La   see
    Borinage
Misfits, The
    Gilliatt   31-32
    Kael (c)   (37-38)
    Kauffmann (b)   99-102, (104)
    Macdonald   285-86
    Sarris (a)   172-74
    Weinberg   (257), (259)

Miss Julie
    Young   (190)
Miss London, Ltd.
    Lejeune   91
Mission to Moscow
    Agee   37-39
Mississippi Mermaid, The
    Kauffmann (a)   255-56
    Simon (b)   219-221
Mr. and Mrs. Smith
    Ferguson   343
Mr. Arkadin
    Durgnat (112)
    Macdonald   296-97
    Sarris (a)   63-65
    Weinberg   136-39, (153-54),
        206, 241
Mr. Belvedere Goes to College
    Brown (c)   137-42
Mr. Blanding Builds His Dream
    House
    Agee   (301)
Mister Buddwing
    Crist   192, 212
Mr. Deeds Goes to Town
    Ferguson   127-28
    Graham   96-97
    Van Doren   331-32
    Weinberg   53
Mr. Hobo   see   Guv'nor
Mr. Hulot's Holiday
    Kael (d)   312-13
Mr. Skeffington
    Agee   95-96
    Winnington   39
Mr. Smith Goes to Washington
    Ferguson   273-74
    Graham   260-61
Misteri di Roma, Gli   see   Mys-
    teries of Rome
Misterio di Atlantide, Il   see
    Giant of Metropolis
Mistons   see   Mischief-Makers,
    The
Mistral
    Weinberg   203
Mistress   see   Älskarinnan
Mitchum, Robert
    Durgnat   144-45
Mitry, Jean
    Sarris (b)   89
Mitt hem är Copacabana   see
    My Home Is Copacabana

Mizoguchi, Kenji
  Sarris (b) 60, 85
Moby Dick (John Huston)
  Sarris (b) 42-43
Model Shop
  Farber 5
  Kael (b) 263-67
  Reed (a) 147-49
Modern Times
  Agate (a) 163-65
  Ferguson 117-18
  Graham 51-53
  Van Doren 314-16, 325-26
  Warshow 209
  Weinberg 177
Modesty Blaise
  Crist (209)
  Reed (b) 144-46
Moi universitet' see Maxim
  Gorky Trilogy
Mole, The see Topo, El
Mollet, Luc
  Simon (b) (8)
Molly and Me (Lewis Seiler)
  Agee 158
Molly Maguires, The
  Kael (a) 103-04
  Reed (a) 275
Moment of Truth
  Kael (d) 118-20
Mon Oncle
  Gilliatt 5-9
  Kael (d) 311
  Kauffmann (b) 42-44
Monde de Paul Delvaux, Le
  Durgnat 122
Monde va nous prendre pour des
  sauvages, Le
  Durgnat 127
Mondo Cane
  Simon (c) 59-60
Mondo Nouveau see Young
  World
Mondo nuovo see RoGoPag
Monica and Martin
  Graham 186
Monkey in Winter
  Weinberg 212
Monroe, Marilyn
  Alpert 163-67
  Crist 78-79
  Gilliatt 32-33
  Kael (c) 37

Sarris (a) 452-54
Sarris (b) 76-78
Weinberg 187, 194
Young 330
Monsieur Beaucaire (George Mar-
  shall)
  Agee 216
Monsieur Ripois see Knave of
  Hearts
Monsieur Verdoux
  Agee 250-62, (282), 288,
    370-72
  Brown (a) 107-13
  Crist 76-77
  Kauffmann 256-58
  Macdonald (7), 116-25
  Sarris (a) 144-49
  Sarris (b) (256-57)
  Weinberg (227), 248
  Winnington 86, 88
Monsieur Vincent
  Kael (d) 312
Monster of Fate, The see
  Golem, The (Paul Wegener)
MONTAGE
  Agate (b) 236
  Macdonald xviii-xix, 187,
    200, 251-52
  Pechter 114-15, 118-19
  Sarris (b) 57-58, 83-85, 87-
    89, 138-39
  Warshow 272
Montague, Charles Eduard (quot-
  ed)
  Agate (b) 185-86
Monte Walsh
  Kael (a) 162
  Reed (a) 301-02
Monterey Pop
  Adler 330-32
Montreal International Film Fes-
  tival, 1962
  Weinberg 180-83
Montreal International Film Fes-
  tival, 1965
  Weinberg 255
Moon and Sixpence, The
  Agate (b) 220-22
Moon Is Down, The
  Agate (a) 244-45
  Agee 35-36
Moon over Miami
  Agate (b) 195

Moonbird
  Adler (293)
Moon's Our Home, The
  Graham 83-84
Moore, Grace
  Ferguson 83-84
MORALITY see CENSORSHIP
Morals of Marcus, The
  Weinberg 52-53
Moravia, Alberto (quoted)
  Sarris (a) 183-84
  Sarris (b) 133
Mörder Dimitri Karamazov, Der
  Weinberg 245
Mörder sind unter uns, Die
  see Murderers Among Us
More
  Farber 219
  Simon (b) 117-18
More the Merrier, The
  Agee 42, (67)
Moreau, Jeanne
  Farber 3, (144), (153), (180)
  Kauffmann (b) 407
  Macdonald (111)
Morgan!
  Kael (d) 20-22
  Macdonald 406-11
  Sarris (b) 186-88
  Schickel 74-76
  Simon (c) 219-222
Morituri
  Kael (d) 194
Morocco
  Kael (b) 113
Mort du cygne, La
  Winnington 45
Mort en ce Jardin, La
  Durgnat (64)
Moscow Nights (Anthony Asquith)
  Graham 35-36
Mosjoukine, Ivan
  Durgnat (46-47)
Moss Rose
  Agee 271
Most, The
  Kael (a) (109-110)
Mother (Vsevolod Pudovkin)
  Ferguson 37-38
  Kael (d) 312
Mother Jeanne of the Angels see
  Mother Joan of the Angels
Mother Joan of the Angels

Kauffmann (b) 356-58
  Weinberg (192)
  Young 213-14
Mother, 1905 see Mother
  (Vsevolod Pudovkin)
Mouchette
  Farber 231-32
  Sontag (b) 181
  Young 334-35
Moulin Rouge
  Alpert 148-49
  Durgnat (116)
  Kael (c) (298-99)
Mourir d'aimer see To Die of
  Love
Mourlet, Michel
  Sarris (b) 84-85
Mourning Becomes Electra
  Agee (295), 382-83
Move Over, Darling
  Simon (c) 101-02
MOVEMENT see
  EDITING
Movie (magazine, London)
  Durgnat 65-66
  Kael (c) 310
MOVIEGOING see AUDIENCES
Moving Target see Harper
Mozda Diogen see Diogenes
  Perhaps
Mučedníci lasky see Martyrs
  of Love
Muerte en esta jardin, La see
  Mort en ce Jardin, La
Mumford, Lewis (quoted)
  Kauffmann (b) 18-19
Munk, Andrzej
  Gilliatt 96
Muraglia cinese see Behind the
  Great Wall
Murder in Thornton Square see
  Gaslight (George Cukor)
Murder in Trinidad
  Ferguson 40
Murder Man, The
  Graham 16
Murder, My Sweet
  Agee 131
  Kael (d) 313
Murder on the Blackboard
  Ferguson 40
Murderer Dimitri Karamasoff,
  The see Mörder Dimitri

Karamazov, Der
Murderers Among Us
　　Winnington　110
Murderers' Row
　　Crist　211
Muriel
　　Crist　(33-34)
　　Durgnat　110
　　Kauffmann　(b)　251-52
　　Macdonald　(475)
　　Sarris　(a)　102-07
　　Simon　(c)　85-86
　　Sontag　(a)　232-41
　　Sontag　(b)　(123), (149), (158)
　　Weinberg　225-26
Murmur of the Heart, A
　　Kael　(a)　305-10
Murnau, Friedrich W.
　　Pechter　304
　　Sarris　(a)　(351)
　　Weinberg　118-24, 207
Musashi miyamoto　see　Samurai
Museum of Modern Art, New
　　York, N.Y.
　　Farber　208
MUSEUMS AND THE CINEMA
　　Sarris　(b)　91-92
MUSIC, FILM
　　Agate　(a)　30, 38-39
　　Agee　164
　　Durgnat　31-32, 118
　　Farber　215-16
　　Ferguson　456
Music for Millions
　　Agee　(135-36)
　　Lejeune　144-45
Music in Darkness　see　Night Is
　　My Future
MUSIC IN FILMS (see also
　　MUSIC, FILM)
　　Lejeune　125
Music in the Dark　see　Night Is
　　My Future
MUSIC IN THEATERS
　　Agate　(a)　(27)
　　Agate　(b)　14-15, 100-01
　　Durgnat　(32)
Music Lovers, The
　　Kael　(a)　238-43
Music Room, The (Satyajit Ray)
　　Kael　(c)　251
　　Kauffmann　(b)　372-73
　　Simon　(c)　88-90

MUSICALS
　　Adler　71-74
　　Agate　(a)　265-66
　　Agate　(b)　180
　　Ferguson　85, 94-95
　　Kael　(a)　84
　　Kael　(b)　100
　　Kael　(c)　277-80
　　Kael　(d)　234
　　Sarris　(a)　367
　　Sarris　(b)　30
　　Simon　(b)　328
　　Weinberg　59
Musiker i mörker　see　Night Is
　　My Future
Mutiny on the Bounty (Frank
　　Lloyd)
　　Agate　(a)　125, 157-63
　　Ferguson　103-05
　　Van Doren　306-07
My Apprenticeship　see　Maxim
　　Gorky Trilogy
My Darling Clementine
　　Durgnat　102
　　Warshow　149
　　Weinberg　108
　　Young　(89-90)
My Fair Lady
　　Crist　(112)
　　Kauffmann　(b)　41-42
　　Sarris　(a)　175-81
My Favorite Wife
　　Ferguson　302
My First Love　see　She Was
　　Like a Wild Chrysanthemum
My Heart Goes Crazy　see　Lon-
　　don Town
My Home Is Copacabana
　　Young　271-72
My Hustler
　　Sarris　(a)　302
My iz Kronstadta　see　We from
　　Kronstadt
My Life Is Mine　see　Fire with-
　　in
My Life to Live
　　Kael　(c)　(15)
　　Kauffmann　241-42
　　Sarris　(a)　96-97
　　Simon　(c)　73-74
　　Sontag　(a)　196-208, (235),
　　　(241)
　　Weinberg　219-20

My Life with Caroline
    Ferguson (361)
My Little Chickadee
    Agate (b) 177
    Kael (d) 313-14
My Man Godfrey (Gregory La
    Cava)
    Graham 104, 106
My Name Is Ivan
    Kael (c) (15)
My Name Is Julia Ross
    Agee 181
My Night at Maud's see Ma
    Nuit Chez Maud
My Son John
    Warshow 163-71
My Uncle, Mr. Hulot see Mon
    Oncle
My Universities see Maxim
    Gorky Trilogy
Myortvetz see Death
Myra Breckinridge
    Reed (a) 263
    Simon (b) 151-53
Mystère Kuomiko, Le see
    Koumiko Mystery, The
Mystère Picasso, Le
    Durgnat 125-26
    Kael (d) 315
Mysteries of Rome
    Young 221-22
Mystery of the Wax Museum,
    The
    Agate (a) 117-19

                    -N-

Nachalo see Début
Nachts, wenn der Teufel kam
    see Devil Strikes at Night,
    The
Naked Autumn see Mauvais
    Coups, Les
Naked Childhood
    Adler 253-54
    Reed (a) 280
Naked City, The
    Agee (301)
Naked Island, The see Island,
    (Kaneto Shindo)
Naked Night, The
    Durgnat (64), (92)

    Kael (d) 315
    Simon (a) 29-30, 32
    Simon (c) 35-37
    Young 82-83
Naked Truth (Mario Zampi) see
    Your Past Is Showing
Nana (Jean Renoir)
    Durgnat 91
    Sontag (b) (103)
Nanook of the North
    Agee (228)
    Kael (d) 316
    Sarris (b) 101-02
Napoleon
    Simon (b) 381
Nassreddin v Buhare see Ad-
    ventures in Bokhara
Nathan, George Jean
    Agate (b) 196
National Catholic Office for Mo-
    tion Pictures see Legion of
    Decency
National Student Film Awards,
    1966
    Simon (c) 260-61
National Velvet
    Agee 132-34
    Kael (d) 316
Nattens vän see Lovely Is the
    Summer Night
Nattlek see Night Games
Nattvardsgasterna see Winter
    Light
Nave bianca, La see White
    Ship, The
Navigator, The
    Agee 18-19
    Weinberg (160)
Nazarin
    Adler 179-80
Neal, Patricia
    Reed (b) 79-85
Negatives
    Reed (a) 380-82
    Simon (b) 316-17
Negri, Pola
    Agate (a) 54-56
Negro Soldier, The
    Agee 79-80
NEGROES IN FILMS see
    BLACKS IN FILMS
Neko to shozo to futari no onna
    see Cat and Two Women, A

Nelson Touch, The see Cor-
    vette K-225
Nero
    Agate (a) 19-20
Nevada Smith
    Kael (d) (39-40)
Never Bet the Devil Your Head
    see Spirits of the Dead
Never Give a Sucker an Even
    Break
    Agee 334-35
    Ferguson 395-96
Never on Sunday
    Alpert 21
    Crist (270)
    Simon (a) 35
Never Say Die (Elliott Nugent)
    Graham 210
New Adventure of Lemmy Cau-
    tion, A see Alphaville
NEW AMERICAN CINEMA (see
    also EXPERIMENTAL FILMS;
    UNDERGROUND FILMS)
    Kael (c) 18-19
    Kauffmann (b) 423-26
    Macdonald 39
    Young 322-27
New Angels, The
    Young 234-35
New Cinema Playhouse (Theatre,
    New York City)
    Farber 246
New Earth
    Ferguson 125-26
    Van Doren 335-36
New Empire (theater, London)
    Agate (b) 14-15
New Gulliver, The
    Ferguson 102
    Graham 120-21
    Van Doren 304-06
New Kind of Love, A
    Crist 29-30
New Leaf, A
    Kael (a) 269
New Lot, The
    Lejeune 136
New Orleans (Arthur Lubin)
    Agee 271
New Republic (magazine)
    Kauffmann (b) ix-x
NEW WAVE see NOUVELLE
    VAGUE

New Year's Eve
    Agate (a) 81
New York Film Critic's Circle
    Best Picture of the Year,
    1968
    Schickel 215-16
New York Film Festival, 1st,
    1963
    Kauffmann (b) 396-98
    Simon (c) 83-87
New York Film Festival, 3rd,
    1965
    Kauffmann (b) 408-12
    Simon (c) 182-89
New York Film Festival, 4th,
    1966
    Simon (c) 248-55
New York Film Festival, 5th,
    1967
    Farber   225-29
    Sarris (a) 314-18
    Simon (b) 373-82
New York Film Festival, 6th,
    1968
    Farber   230-40
New York Film Festival, 7th,
    1969
    Farber   241-45
    Simon (b) 382-98
New York Herald Tribune
    Crist xiii-xix
NEW YORK IN FILMS
    Crist 48-51
    Kael (a) 313-15
New York International Chil-
    dren's Film Festival, 1st,
    1965
    Crist 111
New York Society of Film Crit-
    ics
    Adler xxv
New York Times
    Adler xiii-xxiv
    Reed (a) 387
New York World Journal Tribune
    see New York Herald Tribune
New Yorker (magazine)
    Kael (b) vii
Newman, Paul
    Reed (b) 132-40
NEWSREELS
    Agee 99-100, 151-52, 161-
    62

Graham 242-43, 258
Ni Liv see Nine Lives
Nice Girl?
  Ferguson 354-55
Nice Girl Like Me, A
  Reed (a) 238
Nicholas and Alexandra
  Kael (a) 366-69
Nichols, Mike
  Reed (c) 44-54
  Sarris (a) (364)
Nicht Versöhnt see Unrecon-
  ciled
Nicoll, Allardyce
  Sontag (b) 106
Niebelungen, Die (Fritz Lang)
  Durgnat 104
  Weinberg 254
Nieuwe Gronden see New Earth
Night see Notte, La
Night and Fog
  Macdonald 448
  Sarris (a) (102-03)
  Sarris (b) (62)
Night and the City
  Kael (d) 316
Night at the Opera, A
  Agate (a) 266
  Ferguson 105-07
  Kael (d) 317
  Lejeune 165-66
  Sarris (b) 131
  Van Doren 309-11
Night Games
  Kael (d) 103-04
  Reed (a) 361-62
  Young 295-96
Night in Casablanca, A
  Agee 201
  Winnington 59-60
Night Is My Future
  Macdonald (463)
Night Journey in Russia, 1943
  see In Those Days
Night Mail
  Ferguson 208
  Graham 60
Night Must Fall (Karel Reisz)
  Crist 58-60
Night Must Fall (Richard Thorpe)
  Ferguson 178-80
  Graham 154
  Van Doren 364-65

Night of the Following Day, The
  Kael (b) 277-78
Night of the Hunter, The
  Kael (d) 317
  Pechter 273
Night of the Jester, The see
  Naked Night
Night Out, A (Charles Chaplin)
  Agee 9-10
Night People
  Kael (c) 319-22, (323-26),
  (329-31)
Night They Raided Minsky's, The
  Kael (b) 237-39
Night Train
  Ferguson 332-33
Night Train to Munich see
  Night Train
Night Watch (Jacques Becker)
  Sarris (a) 136-37
  Sontag (a) 183
  Young 145-46
Nightmare Alley
  Agee 280-81, 381
Nights of Cabiria
  Kael (d) 318
  Sarris (a) 23-29
Nightwatch (Jacques Becker)
  see Night Watch
Nikdo se nebude smát see No-
  body Laughs Last
Nils Holgerssons underbara Resa
  see Wonderful Adventures of
  Nils, The
Nine Bachelors
  Agate (b) 173-75
Nine Days a Queen see Tudor
  Rose
Nine Days of One Year
  Macdonald 273-76
Nine Hours to Rama
  Simon (c) 61
Nine Lives
  Young 105-06
1905 [nineteen five] see Mother
  (Vsevolod Pudovkin)
Ningen see Man
Ninotchka
  Agate (a) 202-04
  Ferguson 274-75
  Graham 271-72
  Kael (d) 318
Ninth Circle, The

Kauffmann (b) 360-61
Nitchevo
  Graham 179
Nizhny, Vladimir. Lessons with
  Eisenstein
  Macdonald 264-65
No Greater Love (Frederick Erm-
  ler)
  Agee 81
No Love for Johnny
  Young (138)
No More Excuses
  Adler 194
  Gilliatt 123-25
No Relations see Sans Famille
No Way Out
  Alpert 3
  Farber 62-63
No Way to Treat a Lady
  Kael (b) 74-75
Noa Noa
  Pechter 270-71
Noah's Ark (Michael Curtiz)
  Agate (a) 40-42
Nobi see Fires on the Plain
Noblesse du bois, La see
  Majesty of Wood, The
Nobody Laughs Last
  Gilliatt 129-30
  Simon (b) 281-82
Nobody Waved Goodbye
  Crist 110-11, 150
  Young 265-66
Nogiku no gotku kumi narik see
  She Was Like a Wild Chrys-
  anthemum
Noia see Empty Canvas
NON-AMERICAN WESTERNS
  Adler 238-40
None but the Lonely Heart
  Agee 128
  Warshow 128
NONFICTION FILMS
  Agee 58
  Ferguson 219-20
  Kauffmann (a) 226
NONPROFESSIONAL FILMS see
  INDEPENDENT FILMS
NONPROFESSIONAL ACTORS
  AND ACTRESSES see AC-
  TORS AND ACTRESSES
Normal Love
  Simon (c) 145

North by Northwest
  Alpert 169-71
  Durgnat (233), (235)
  Kael (c) (294)
  Kael (d) 318-19
  Pechter 175-76
North Star, The (Lewis Mile-
  stone)
  Agate (b) 241-42
  Agee 57-58, (60)
  Winnington 16
North to Alaska
  Kael (c) (297)
Northern Pursuit
  Lejeune 113
Northwest Mounted Police
  Ferguson 331
Northwest Passage
  Ferguson 287-88
Norwood
  Reed (a) 289-90
Nosferatu
  Kael (d) 319
  Weinberg (160)
Not as a Stranger
  Kael (d) 204-05
Not on Your Life!
  Kauffmann (b) 353-54
  Young 226
Not to Mention All These Women
  see All These Women
Notes on the Port of St. Francis
  Weinberg 283-84
Nothing but a Man
  Crist 100-01
  Kauffmann (b) 167-68
  Simon (c) 143-45
Nothing but the Best
  Crist 77-78
  Sarris (a) 154-56
Nothing Sacred
  Kael (d) 319-20
  Van Doren 381-83
Notorious
  Agee 213-14
  Kael (d) 320
Notorious Cleopatra, The
  Reed (a) 397
Notorious Gentleman, The (Sid-
  ney Gilliat)
  Agee 219-22
  Lejeune 163-65
  Winnington 45

Notre Dame, Cathédrale de Paris
    Durgnat   130
Notte, La
    Alpert   190
    Durgnat   109, (233), (235)
    Farber   137-38
    Kael (c)   179-86, (188), 192-
      95
    Kauffmann (b)   302-07
    Macdonald   333-37
    Young   157-61, 194
Notti bianche, Le   see   White
    Nights
Nought for Behavior   see   Zero
    de conduite
Nous sommes tous des assassins
    see   We Are All Assassins
Nouveau monde   see   RoGoPag
Nouvelle terre   see   New Earth
NOUVELLE VAGUE
    Alpert   196-216
    Kauffmann (b)   224-26, 252
    Young   253-56
Novak, Kim
    Durgnat   166-68
NOVELS INTO FILMS   see
    ADAPTATIONS
Novyi Gulliver   see   New Gulli-
    ver
Now I'll Tell
    Ferguson   38
Now, Voyager
    Agate (b)   238-39
    Lejeune   102-03
Nowell-Smith, Geoffry.   Luchino
    Visconti
    Simon (b)   408-10
Noz w wodzie   see   Knife in the
    Water
Nozo no Yureisen
    Young   (101)
Nugent, Frank (quoted)
    Sarris (b)   130
Number One
    Reed (a)   182
Nun, The   see   Religieuse, La
Nunca Pasa Nada
    Young   225-26
Nun's Story, The
    Alpert   160
    Kauffmann (b)   49-51
Nuovi angeli, I   see   New Angels,
    The

Nurse Edith Cavell
    Graham   247-48
Nutrition
    Graham   108-09
Nutty Professor, The
    Kael (c)   (26)

-O-

Obchod na korze   see   Shop on
    Main Street, The
Objective Burma!
    Agee   144-45
OBSCENITY   see   CENSORSHIP
Occupational Risks   see   Risques
    du Métier, Les
Occupe-Toi d'Amélie   see   Oh,
    Amelia
October
    Durgnat   (50)
    Graham   61-62
    Young   (150)
Odd Couple, The
    Adler   135-36
    Kauffmann (a)   75-77
Odd Man Out   (Carol Reed)
    Kael (d)   321
    Winnington   78-79
Odd Obsession, The   see   Kagi
Oedipus Rex   (Tyrone Guthrie)
    Kael (d)   321-22
Oeil pour oeil   see   Eye for an
    Eye, An
Of a Thousand Delights   see
    Sandra
Of Human Bondage   (John Crom-
    well)
    Ferguson   41
Of Human Bondage   (Kenneth
    Hughes)
    Simon (c)   185
Of Human Hearts
    Van Doren   391-92
Of Mice and Men
    Ferguson   285-86
Oggi, domani e dopo domani   see
    Kiss the Other Sheik
Ogi, Masahiro
    Crist   36-37
Oh, Amelia
    Kael (d)   320-21
Oh Dad, Poor Dad...

Reed (a) 366-67
Oh! What a Lovely War
    Kael (a) 14-17
    Reed (a) 248-49
    Schickel 263-65
    Simon (b) 394-95
Oil for the Lamps of China
    Graham 36
Oklahoma
    Alpert 159
Oklahoma Kid, The (Lloyd Bacon)
    Graham 221
Old Acquaintance
    Agee 60
    Lejeune 132-33
Old and New see General Line
Old Maid, The
    Ferguson 269
    Graham 264
Old Man and the Sea, The
    Kauffmann (b) 87-90
Oldest Profession, The see
    Anticipation
Ole Dole Doff
    Young 331-33
Oliver!
    Adler 334
    Kael (b) 200-05
    Reed (a) 213
    Sarris (a) 422-23
    Simon (b) 329-30
Oliver Twist (David Lean)
    Brown (c) 269-74
    Kael (d) 322
    Winnington 120, 122
Olivier, Laurence
    Agee 366-67
    Farber 3
    Young 58
Olvidados, Los
    Kael (a) (376)
    Kael (d) 322-23
    Young (328)
Olympia, Festival of the Nations
    Kael (d) 323
    Winnington 99-100
Olympiad (Riefenstahl) see
    Olympia, Festival of the Nations
Olympische Spiele, 1936 see
    Olympia, Festival of the Nations

On a Clear Day You Can See
    Forever
    Reed (a) 288-89
    Simon (b) 334-35
On Approval (Clive Brook)
    Agee (140-41)
    Kael (d) 323-24
On Her Majesty's Secret Service
    Kael (a) 85-86
On Nothing Days
    Farber 252
On the Avenue
    Graham 157, 160
On the Beach
    Durgnat (64)
    Kael (d) 206-07
    Kauffmann (b) 10-12
On the Bowery
    Kael (d) 324
On the Night of the Fire
    Graham 255-56
On the Waterfront
    Alpert (137)
    Durgnat (64), 74, (102), (265)
    Kael (c) 46-55, (60)
On Wings of Song see Love Me
    Forever
On Your Toes (Ray Enright)
    Graham 273
Ona zaschishchavet rodinu see
    No Greater Love (Frederick Ermler)
Once in the Glorious West
    Sarris (b) 204-07
    Young 396-97
Once to Every Woman
    Ferguson (39-40)
Once Upon a Honeymoon
    Reed (a) 323
Once Upon a Time (Alexander Hall)
    Agee 105
Once Upon a Time in the West
    see Once in the Glorious West
One A.M. (Charles Chaplin)
    Agee 9
One A.M. (Jean-Luc Godard)
    see One American Movie
One Against Seven see Counter-Attack

One American Movie
  Adler 296-99
One and Only Genuine Original
  Family Band, The
  Adler 90-91
One Day of War
  Agate (a) 239-41
One-Eyed Boy see Roots, The
One-Eyed Jacks
  Alpert 55-59
  Kauffmann (b) 34-37
  Sarris (b) (50)
One Fine Day
  Simon (b) (395)
One Foot in Heaven
  Agate (b) 205
  Lejeune 74-75
One for the Book see Voice of
  the Turtle
One Minute to Zero
  Durgnat (265)
One Night in Lisbon
  Lejeune 61-62
One Plus One see Sympathy for
  the Devil
One New York Night see Trunk
  Mystery
One Night of Love
  Ferguson 49
One Parallel Movie see One
  American Movie
One Perfect Movie see One
  American Movie
One Plus One see Sympathy for
  the Devil
One Potato, Two Potato
  Crist 99-100
One Rainy Afternoon
  Graham 86
One Romantic Night
  Agate (b) 39-40
One Summer of Happiness see
  Lovely Is the Summer Night
One, Two, Three
  Kael (c) 150-55
  Kauffmann (b) 150
  Simon (a) 22
One Way Ticket
  Graham 65
One Wish Too Many
  Crist 113
Onibaba
  Simon (c) 149-50

Only Angels Have Wings
  Farber (145)
  Ferguson 256
  Graham 247
Only Game in Town, The
  Kael (a) 122-23
  Reed (a) 276-78
Only Two Can Play
  Gilliatt 206-08
Open City
  Agee 192-96, 198, 236-37
  Kael (d) 324
Operation Abolition
  Kauffmann (b) 391-94
Operation Correction
  Kauffmann (b) (395)
Operation San Gennaro see
  Treasure of San Gennaro, The
Ophuls, Max
  Durgnat 28, 55-57
  Sarris (a) (74)
  Young (407)
Orage see Storm (Marc Allé-
  gret)
Oratorio for Prague
  Adler 260-61
ORCHESTRAS see MUSIC IN
  THEATERS
Orchids and Ermine
  Kael (d) 325
Ordet
  Kael (d) 325-26
Orfeu Negro see Black Orpheus
Organizer, The
  Crist 70-72, 89
  Kauffmann (a) (208)
  Kauffmann (b) 340-42
  Macdonald 360-63
  Simon (b) (66)
  Simon (c) 126-27
  Young 235-36
ORGANS
  Agate (b) 14-15
Orgueilleux, Les see Proud and
  the Beautiful, The
Orlacs Hände see Hands of Or-
  lac
Orphée
  Durgnat 54, (103), 239-46
  Kael (c) (286)
  Kael (d) 326-27
  Sontag (a) (197)
Orribile segreto del dottor Hitch-

cock, L' see Terror of
Dr. Hitchcock, The
Oscar, The
    Crist 171-73
    Farber 184
    Kael (d) (134-35)
Oscar Wilde
    Kauffmann (b) 194-96
    Weinberg 157
OSCARS, 1948
    Sarris (b) 33
OSCARS, 1967
    Simon (b) 396-73
OSCARS, 1968
    Reed (b) 54-62
OSCARS, 1969
    Simon (b) 398-402
OSCARS, 1971
    Sarris (b) 121
Osmy dzien tygodnia see
    Eighth Day of the Week
Ossessione, L'
    Macdonald 342
    Sontag (b) (174)
Ostatni dzien lata see Last
    Day of Summer
Ostre sledovane vlaky see
    Closely Watched Trains
Otages, Les see Mayor's Di-
    lemma, The
Othello (David MacKane)
    Agate (b) 278-79
Othello (Laurence Olivier)
    Crist 168-69
    Kael (d) 173-75
    Sarris (a) 235-41
    Simon (c) 210-14
Othello (Orson Welles)
    Pechter 171
    Young 409-11
Other One, The
    Sarris (a) 316-17
    Simon (b) 381
Our Daily Bread (King Vidor)
    Durgnat (57)
    Ferguson 44-45
Our Hearts Were Growing Up
    Lejeune 179
Our Heritage see This England
Our Man Flint
    Crist 215-16
Our Man in Havana
    Kael (d) 327

Weinberg (160)
Our Mother's House
    Crist 247-48
Our Neighbors, the Carters
    Graham 258
Our Town
    Ferguson 300-02
Our Vines Have Tender Grapes
    Agee 176
    Lejeune 163-64
Ourselves Alone
    Graham 90-91
Out in the World see Maxim
    Gorky Trilogy
Out of a Chinese Painting-Brush
    Durgnat 125
Out of It
    Reed (a) 275-76
Out of the Fog (Anatole Litvak)
    Ferguson 446-50
Out of the Past (Jacques Tour-
    neur)
    Agee (301), 384
    Winnington 92-93
Outback
    Kael (a) 415-417
Outcast of the Islands, An
    Kael (d) 327-28
Outcry, The see Grido, Il
Outsider, The (Paul Stein)
    Agate (b) 161-62
Outsider, The (Luchino Visconti)
    see Stranger, The
Outsiders, The (Jean-Luc God-
    ard)
    Farber 188-89
    Kael (d) 112-15
    Simon (c) 146
Over 21
    Agee 170
Overlanders, The
    Winnington 66-67
Overtaken on the Road see
    Easy Life, The
Owl and the Pussycat, The
    Kael (a) 183-85
Ox-Bow Incident, The
    Agee (42), 44, 66
    Kale (d) 328
    Warshow (142), 147
Ozu, Yasujiro
    Sontag (a) (180), (194)

Sontag (b) (105)

-P-

P. M.
  Adler 341
Pabst, Georg
  Macdonald (255)
  Pechter 304
  Weinberg 39-45, (150)
Pabst, Georg (quoted)
  Durgnat 33
Paddy
  Simon (b) 121-24
Padre e a môça, O   see Priest
  and the Girl, The
Pagador de Promessas, O
  Weinberg 189
Page, Geraldine
  Simon (c) 300
Paint Your Wagon
  Kael (a) 26-30
  Reed (a) 256-57
  Reed (b) 166-73, 206-09
  Simon (b) 330-32
Painted Boats   see Girl on the
  Canal, The
PAINTING AND THE CINEMA
  (see also ART, FILMS ON)
  Durgnat 115
Paisan
  Agee 301
  Pechter 278-79
  Simon (b) (166)
  Warshow 251-59
Pal Joey
  Durgnat (53)
Palace of Angels
  Reed (a) 402
Paleface, The
  Agee 18
Palm Beach Story, The
  Agate (b) 210
Palooka
  Ferguson (33)
Pan
  Young 201-03
Pan-Americana
  Agee 146-47
Pandora's Box
  Weinberg 51, 204
Panic   see Panique

Panic in the Streets
  Alpert 134-35
Panic in the Year Zero
  Sarris (a) (50)
Panique
  Kael (d) 328
Panofsky, Erwin
  Alpert 247
  Macdonald (xix), (27)
  Pechter (310)
  Sarris (b) (76), (79)
  Sontag (b) (99), 103-04, 107-
    08, 110-11, (114), (116),
    (119)
Panofksky Erwin (quoted)
  Kael (b) 189
  Weinberg 194
Papas, Irene
  Reed (b) 125-31
Paper Lion
  Simon (b) 317
Paradine Case, The
  Agee 295
Paradise Lagoon
  Kael (d) 328-29
Paranoia   see Kiss the Other
  Sheik
Parapluies de Cherbourg, Les
  see Umbrellas of Cherbourg,
  The
Parent Trap, The
  Kael (c) (232-33)
Parents Terribles, Les   see
  Storm Within, The
Paris Blues
  Kauffmann (b) 58
Paris Commune
  Macdonald 222-23
Paris Exposition, 1900
  Crist 264-65
Paris in Spring   see Paris Love
  Song
Paris Love Song
  Graham 7
Paris qui dort   see Crazy Ray,
  The
Paris Seen by Six   see Six in
  Paris
Paris Underground
  Agee 178
Paris vu par six   see Six in
  Paris
Parker, Tyler

Pechter 282
Parnell
  Graham 155-56
Parson's Widow, The
  Sarris (b) (57)
Partie de campagne, Une see
  Day in the Country, A
Party and the Guests, The see
  Report on the Party and the
  Guests
Party Girl
  Simon (b) (8)
Passage to Marseille
  Agee 80
Passager de la pluie see
  Stranger in the Rain
Passages from James Joyce's
  Finnegans Wake
  Kauffmann (a) 26-28
  Macdonald 461-62
Passing of the Third Floor Back,
  The
  Graham 33-34
  Van Doren 330-31
Passion (Ingmar Bergman) see
  Passion of Anna, The
Passion de Jeanne d'Arc, La
  see Passion of Joan of Arc,
  The
Passion of Anna, The
  Gilliatt 353-60
  Kauffmann (a) 267-71
  Reed (a) 401-02
  Schickel 314-16
  Simon (b) (225), 239-46
Passion of Joan of Arc, The
  Durgnat 25, (36), 47-48, 51,
    (90)
  Kael (d) 329
  Weinberg 27-29, 243, (273)
  Young 44-50
Passport to Fame see Whole
  Town's Talking, The (John
  Ford)
Passport to Pimlico
  Kael (d) 330
Pat and Mike
  Kael (d) 330
Pasteur
  Ferguson 291-92
Pather Panchali
  Kauffmann (b) 367
  Young 95-96

Patriote, Le see Mad Emper-
  or, The
Patterns
  Farber (122)
Patterns of Power see Patterns
Patton
  Kael (a) 97-100
  Kauffmann (a) 235-38
  Reed (a) 271-73
  Schickel 286-88
  Simon (b) 93-95
Paty jexde je strach see Fifth
  Horseman Is Fear, The
Paw see Pan
Pawnbroker, The
  Crist 109-110
  Kael (d) 161
  Kauffmann (b) 129-32
  Macdonald 136-37
  Sarris (a) 200-01
  Simon (c) 159-61
Peace Film, The
  Graham (69)
Peace to He Who Enters
  Weinberg 189
Peace to the Newcomer see
  Peace to He Who Enters
Peace to Whom Enters see
  Peace to He Who Enters
Pearl, The
  Agee 301
Pearls of the Crown, The
  Ferguson 221
  Graham 175
  Van Doren 400-01
Peasants
  Ferguson 10, 92-93
Peau douce see Soft Skin
Peeping Tom
  Durgnat (98)
Peg of Old Drury
  Graham 20
Pendulum
  Reed (a) 160-61
Penny Serenade
  Agate (a) 224
  Ferguson 360-61
Penthouse, The (Peter Collinson)
  Crist 247, (270)
  Sheed 196
  Young 346
People Against O'Hara, The
  Farber 59

People Meet and Sweet Music
  Fills the Heart
  Reed (a) 184-85
People of the Cumberland, The
  Van Doren 404
People on Sunday
  Kauffmann (b) (151)
People Will Talk (Joseph L.
  Mankiewicz)
  Farber 73
People's Avengers, The
  Agee 102-03
Pépé le Moko
  Agate (a) 219
  Ferguson 342
  Graham 144-45
  Weinberg 100-01
Peppard, George
  Reed (c) 181-86
Perfect Friday
  Kael (a) 193
Perfect Gentleman, The see
  Imperfect Lady, The (Tim
  Whelan)
Perfect Strangers (Alexander
  Korda) see Vacation from
  Marriage
Perfido Incanto
  Durgnat (103)
Performance
  Sarris (b) (62)
  Simon (b) 363-67
Perils of Pauline, The
  Agee 270
PERIOD FILMS see HISTORI-
  CAL FILMS
Period of Adjustment
  Kauffmann (b) (60)
Perles de la couronne, Les see
  Pearls of the Crown, The
Perlman, William J. The
  Movies on Trial
  Van Doren 408-11
Persecution and Assassination of
  Jean-Paul Marat... see
  Marat/Sade
Persona
  Crist 234-35
  Farber 190, 195-98
  Kael (d) 171-72
  Kauffmann (a) 13-18
  Sarris (a) 289-92, 403
  Sarris (b) (62)

Schickel 178-79
Sheed 191-94
Simon (b) (166), 225-29,
  (399)
Sontag (b) 123-45, (158)
Young 296-98
Personal Column (Robert Siod-
  mak)
  Ferguson 343-44
  Graham 268
Personality Parade
  Graham 179-80
Persons in Hiding
  Graham 210
Peter and Paula see Black
  Peter
Peter the First (Vladimir Petrov)
  Graham 230-31
  Macdonald 224-26
Peterburgskaya noch see Pet-
  ersburg Nights
Petersburg Nights
  Ferguson 51
  Graham 6-7
  Warshow 271
  Weinberg 52, (292)
Petit Soldat, Le see Little
  Soldier, The
Petr see Peter the First
Petrified Forest, The
  Graham 89-90
Petulia
  Adler 168-69, 182-83, 327-
  28
  Gilliatt 125-27
  Kael (b) 117-21
  Kauffmann (a) 87-91
  Sarris (a) 367-70
  Schickel 187-90
  Simon (b) 346-47
Phaedra
  Crist (34)
  Macdonald 293-95, (463)
  Simon (a) (11), 34-38
Phantom Goldola, The
  Graham 87
Phantom Lady, The
  Agee 77-78
Phantom Light, The
  Graham 7
Phantom of the Opera, The
  (Arthur Lubin)
  Agate (a) 252-54

Phantom of the Opera, The (Rupert Julian)
  Kael (d) 330-31
Philadelphia Story, The
  Agate (b) 179-80
  Ferguson 324-25
  Gilliatt 72-73
  Sarris (b) (63)
Philip
  Reed (a) 225-26
Philips Radio see Industrial Symphony
PHOTOGRAPHY AND THE CINEMA
  Durgnat 98
  Weinberg 195
  Young 49-50
Piccadilly
  Agate (a) 82
  Agate (b) 16-18
Picasso (Sergio Amidei)
  Durgnat 122
Picasso Mystery, The see Mystère Picasso, Le
Pickpocket, The
  Kauffmann (b) 259-60
  Sontag (b) 180-81
Pickwick Papers, The (Noel Langley)
  Kael (d) 331
Picnic
  Alpert 248
  Durgnat 28
Picnic on the Grass, The see Déjeuner sur l'herbe, Le
Picture of Dorian Gray, The (Albert Lewin)
  Agee 147-49
  Kael (d) 146
  Lejeune 148-50
Pied Piper, The
  Agate (b) 219
Pièges see Personal Column
Pierre and Paul
  Farber 244
Pierrot le Fou
  Kauffmann (a) 138-40
  Reed (a) 219-20
  Sarris (a) 423-27
  Simon (b) (167)
Pigpen
  Simon (b) 388
Pillow Talk

Alpert 83, 95
Pillow to Post
  Agee 359-60
Pink Panther, The
  Gilliatt 250-52
  Kael (c) (25)
Pinocchio
  Agate (a) 205-06
  Ferguson 289-90
  Lejeune 172-73
Piotr see Peter the First
Pirate, The
  Agee 306-07
Pittsburgh
  Agate (b) 223-24
Pizza Triangle, The
  Kael (a) 193-95
Place for Lovers, A
  Farber 219
  Reed (a) 239-40
Place in the Sun, A
  Alpert 138-40
  Farber 74-75, (82)
  Kael (d) 331-32
Place to Stand, A
  Crist (257)
Plainsman, The
  Graham 131-32
Plaisir, Le
  Kael (c) (298)
  Weinberg 154
Planet of the Apes
  Adler 37-38
  Kael (b) 36-38
  Schickel 180-81
Planet of the Dead see First Spaceship on Venus, The
Playboy of the Western World, The (Brian D. Hurst)
  Kauffmann (b) 218-19
PLAYS INTO FILMS see ADAPTATIONS
PLOTS, DISCUSSION OF
  Adler 237, 317-18
  Crist 19-21
  Durgnat 174-75, 178-81, 197-99
  Kael (c) 8-9, 20, 44-46, 136-37
  Kauffmann (a) (163)
  Lejeune 73, 92-93, 157-58
  Sontag (a) 182-83
  Sontag (b) 116, 134-35,

(139), 157-58, 179-80
Plough and the Stars, The
   Agate (a) 177-80
   Van Doren 351-52
Plow That Broke the Plains, The
   Ferguson 145-46
Pluck of the Irish, The see
   Great Guy
Plus belles escroqueries du
   monde, Les
   Weinberg (241)
Plus vieux métier du monde, Le
   see Anticipation
Pogador Promesa [sic] see
   Pagador de Promessas, O
Point Blank
   Farber 157-59
   Pechter 85-86
   Sarris 320-21
   Schickel 145-48
Point of Order!
   Crist (68)
   Kauffmann (b) 395
   Sarris (a) 116-17
Poison Pen (Paul S. Stein)
Poitier, Sidney
   Adler 211
Pojken i trädet see Boy in the
   Tree, The
Pokolenie pobeditelej see Rev-
   olutionists
Polanski, Roman
   Young 107
POLISH FILMS (late 1950's)
   Young 170-72
POLISH FILMS (mid-1960's)
   Kauffmann (b) 404-05
POLITICS AND THE CINEMA
   (see also POLITICS IN FILMS;
   PROPAGANDA FILMS; SOCI-
   ETY IN FILMS)
   Adler 237-38
   Crist 66-69
   Kauffmann (b) 426
   Schickel 33
   Van Doren 323-24
   Weinberg 154
POLITICS IN FILMS
   Durgnat 261-62, 268-70
   Kael (c) 326-46
   Sarris (b) 34-35
   Simon (b) 66
   Weinberg 45

Polonsky, Abraham
   Pechter 147-61
Pommer, Erich
   Weinberg (239)
Pookie see Sterile Cuckoo,
   The
Poor Cow
   Adler 30-31
   Kael (b) 25-28
   Reed (b) 266-70
   Simon (b) 290-91
Poor Outlaws see Round Up
   (Miklos Jancso)
Pop Goes the Easel
   Durgnat 128-29
Popcorn
   Kael (a) 58-59
Popi
   Reed (a) 226
Popiol i diamant see Ashes
   and Diamonds
Poppy (A. E. Sutherland)
   Graham 87-88
Por primera vez see For the
   First Time
Pornographer, The
   Young 311-12
PORNOGRAPHY IN FILMS see
   EROTICISM IN FILMS
Port of Shadows
   Ferguson 275-77
   Kael (c) (298)
   Kael (d) 332
Porte des lilas, La see Gates
   of Paris
Portes de la nuit, Les see
   Gates of the Night
Portrait of a Woman
   Lejeune 175-76
Portrait of Jason
   Crist 268-69
   Sarris (a) 317
   Simon (b) (382)
Positif (magazine)
   Durgnat 67
Possessed (Curtis Bernhardt)
   Agee 372-73
   Winnington 90
Postman Always Rings Twice,
   The
   Agee 199
   Kael (d) 332-33
   Winnington 50

Postmaster see Two Daughters
Posto, Il see Sound of Trum-
  pets, The
Pot Bouille see Lovers of
  Paris
Pot Luck
  Graham 65
Potemkin
  Agee (341)
  Durgnat (103)
  Kael (c) (276)
  Kael (d) 333-34
  Macdonald (4), (11), (13)
  Warshow 270-71
  Weinberg (161), (199), (210-
    12), (244), (292)
  Young (19), (150)
Potomok Chingis-Khan see
  Storm over Asia
Pound
  Gilliatt 196-97
Pour la suite du monde
  Young 263-65
Powder River
  Warshow (149)
Powell, Dilys (quoted)
  Agate (b) 255
Power, The (Byron Haskin)
  Adler 70-71
Power (Lothar Mendes) see
  Jew Süss
Powers Girl, The
  Agee 27
Practially Yours
  Agee 154
Prästänken see Parson's
  Widow, The
Prawdziwy koniec wielkiel wojny
  see Real End of the Great
  War, The
Prelude to War
  Agee 40-41, (66)
  Winnington 32
Preminger, Otto
  Durgnat 84-85
  Kael (c) 306
  Kauffmann (b) 170-76
  Pechter (8)
  Reed (c) 146-51
Presenting Lily Mars
  Lejeune 93
PRESERVATION OF FILMS
  Adler 257

Sarris (b) 91-94
Weinberg 216-17, 256
Presidentessa, La see Made-
  moiselle Gobette
President's Analyst, The
  Crist 260-61
Press for Time
  Gilliatt 164-66
PRESS RELEASES see ADVER-
  TISING FOR FILMS
Pretty Poison
  Kael (b) 168-70
  Reed (a) 388-89
  Simon (b) 295-96
  Young 393
Price, James (quoted)
  Pechter 224
Pride and the Passion, The
  Durgnat 227-28
Pride of the Marines, The (Del-
  mer Daves)
  Agee 175
Priest and the Girl, The
  Young 363-64
Prima della rivoluzione see
  Before the Revolution
Prime Minister, The
  Agate (a) 215-17
Prime of Miss Jean Brodie, The
  Kael (b) 286-88
  Kauffmann (a) 140-42
  Reed (a) 149-51, 217-18
  Simon (b) 46-47
Primrose Path, The (La Cava)
  Ferguson 294-95
Prince and the Showgirl, The
  Kael (d) 334
Princess O'Rourke
  Agee 61
Princess Sen
  Young 99-100
Prisoner, The
  Kael (a) (203)
Prisoner of Corbal, The see
  Marriage of Corbal, The
Prisoner of Shark Island, The
  Ferguson 8-9, 121-22
  Van Doren 317-19
Prisoner of Zenda, The (John
  Cromwell)
  Ferguson 195-96
Prisonnière, La
  Simon (b) 145

PRIVATE COLLECTIONS OF
   FILMS
   Sarris (b) 91-92
Private Life of Don Juan, The
   Ferguson 63-64
Private Life of Henry VIII, The
   Agate (b) 98-100
Private Life of Sherlock Holmes,
   The
   Kael (a) 186-87
Private Navy of Sgt. O'Farrell,
   The
   Adler 141-42
Private Property
   Alpert 224-25
   Macdonald 320-22
Private Scandal (Ralph Murphy)
   Ferguson 43-44
Private Worlds
   Ferguson 70-71
Privilege
   Young (312), 316
Prize, The
   Kael (c) (26)
Procès de Jeanne d'Arc, Le see
   Trial of Joan of Arc, The
Prodigal, The
   Kael (c) 60
PRODUCERS
   Agate (a) 8
   Alpert 14, 26-39
   Ferguson 437-39, 443-45
   Schickel 212
Producers, The
   Adler 86-87, 99-100, 194
   Kael (b) 66-68
PRODUCTION see FILM MAK-
   ING
PRODUCTION CODE
   Alpert 21, 218-19, 226, 228
Professional Soldier, The
   Graham 76
Professionals, The
   Kael (d) 334
Professor Mamlock
   Ferguson 242-43
   Graham 240-41
PROJECTION (see also WIDE-
   SCREEN SYSTEMS)
   Agee (b)
   Ferguson 306-07, 352-57
   Sontag (b) 111
Promise, The see Pagador de

Promessas, O
Promise at Dawn
   Kael (a) 245-48
Promise Her Anything
   Reed (a) 349
Promised Payment, The see
   Pagador de Promessas, O
Promoter, The
   Kael (d) 335
PROMOTION see ADVERTIS-
   ING FOR FILMS
PROPAGANDA FILMS (see also
   PROPAGANDA IN FILMS)
   Agee 161-62
   Ferguson 29-30, 59-60
PROPAGANDA IN FILMS (see
   also PROPAGANDA FILMS)
   Kael (c) 330-42
Prostoi sluchai see Simple
   Case, A
Proud and the Beautiful, The
   Kael (d) 335
   Young 80
Proud Valley
   Graham 275
Prowler, The
   Farber 59
Prudence and the Pill
   Adler 151, 193-94
   Gilliatt 192-93
Psychiatry in Action
   Agee (58)
Psycho
   Alpert (31), 175-77, 223
   Durgnat 208-20
   Farber 209-10
   Kael (b) (88)
   Kauffmann (b) (278)
   Macdonald 50-51
   Pechter 180-83
   Sarris (b) (54)
Psych-Out
   Adler 95-96
Public Enemy
   Durgnat (83)
   Ferguson (7)
   Macdonald 454-56
Public Hero No. 1
   Ferguson 82
   Graham 8
PUBLIC MORALS see CENSOR-
   SHIP
Public Nuisance Number One

Graham 57
PUBLICITY see ADVERTISING
FOR FILMS
Pudovkin, Vsevelod
  Agate (a) (44-45)
  Macdonald (71)
  Pechter 301-03
  Sarris (b) 141
  Weinberg 115-18
Pudovkin, Vsevelod. Film Act-
ing
  Agate (a) 154-57
Pugni in tasca, I see Fist in
His Pocket
Pull My Daisy
  Macdonald 310-11
  Pechter 10-12
Pumpkin Eater, The
  Macdonald 399-400
  Reed (a) 341-44
Puritain, Le see Puritan, The
Puritan, The
  Kael (d) 335
Purple Heart, The
  Agee 80
  Weinberg 104
Pursuit of the Graf Spee, The
  Kauffmann (b) 7
Puss och kram see Hugs and
Kisses
Putney Swope
  Gilliatt 268-72
  Kauffmann (a) 189-90
  Schickel 250-52
  Simon (b) 301
Puzzle of a Downfall Child
  Kael (a) 250-53
Pygmalion
  Agate (a) 260-62
  Alpert 249
  Ferguson 243-44
Pyotr see Peter the First

-Q-

Q Planes see Clouds over
Europe
Quackser Fortune Has a Cousin
in the Bronx
  Reed (a) 296
Quai des brumes see Port of
Shadows

Quai des orfèvres see Jenny
Lamour
Quality Street (George Stevens)
  Kael (d) 336
Quare Fellow, The
  Kauffmann (b) 219-20
Quatorze Juillet, Le see Four-
teenth of July, The
Quatre cents coups, Les see
400 [four hundred] Blows, The
Quattro passi fra le nuvole see
Four Steps in the Clouds
Que la bête meure see This
Man Must Die
Que Viva Mexico see Time in
Sun
Queen, The
  Adler 175-76, 181-82
  Sarris (a) 383-86
  Simon (b) 73
Queen Christina
  Ferguson 29
Queen Kelly
  Pechter 298
  Weinberg (164), 168-72, 191,
    223-24
Queen of Destiny see Sixty
Glorious Years
Queen of Sheba, The (J. Gordon
Edwards)
  Agate (a) (17-18)
Queen of Spades, The
  Young 28-30
Queens, The
  Adler 75-76
  Sarris (a) (384)
Queimada see Burn!
Quiet American, The
  Alpert 155-6
  Kael (d) 336
Quiet Man, The (John Ford)
  Farber 108-09
Quiet Place in the Country, A
  Reed (a) 296-98
Quiet Wedding
  Ferguson 409
Quigley, Isobel (quoted)
  Young 372
Quiller Memorandum,
The
  Kael (d) 10-11
  Reed (a) 363

-R-

R. P. M.
 Kael (a) 150
 Reed (a) 307
R34
 Farber 254-55
Rachel, Rachel
 Adler 220-21
 Reed (a) 370-73
 Reed (b) 134-36
 Schickel 198-200
 Simon (b) 317-18
Rack, The (Arnold Laven)
 Farber 118
Radnitz, Robert
 Crist (112), (114)
Raduga see Rainbow, The
Raffles (D'Arrast and Fitzmaur-
ice)
 Agate (a) 74-75
Ragazza con la valigia, La
 Young 134-35
Rage in Heaven
 Ferguson 351-52
Raices see Roots
Raider, The (British Royal Navy)
 Agee 222-24, 237
 Winnington 28-29
Rain (Joris Ivens)
 Ferguson 124-25
Rain People, The
 Farber 219-20
 Kauffmann (a) 202
 Pechter 105-08
 Reed (a) 243-44
Rainbow, The (Mark Donskoy)
 Agee 123-26
Rainmaker, The (Joseph Anthony)
 Kael (d) 336-37
Raisin in the Sun, A
 Kauffmann (b) 151-53
Rake's Progress, A see No-
 torious Gentleman, The (Sid-
ney Gilliat)
Ramparts We Watch, The
 Ferguson 305-06, 307
Ramsaye, Terry
 Ferguson 219
Ramsaye, Terry. A Million and
 One Nights
 Ferguson 443

Random Harvest
 Agee (24)
Rank, Joseph Arthur
 Winnington 62, 94-95
Rashomon
 Kael (d) 337
 Macdonald (463-64)
 Sarris (b) 112
 Young 52-58
Raskolnikoff
 Durgnat 103
Rat, The (Jack Raymond)
 Lejeune 34-35
Rat Life and Diet in North Amer-
ica
 Farber 253-54
RATINGS FOR FILMS
 Alpert 231
 Crist 180-83, 250-51
 Macdonald (59)
 Simon (b) 135-37
Ravaged Earth
 Agee (24)
Raven, The (Roger Corman)
 Agee 302
Raven's End
 Simon (c) 185
Ray, Satyajit
 Kauffmann (b) 373
 Pechter 254-58
 Young 11
Razor's Edge, The
 Winnington 75
Razumov
 Van Doren 357-59
Razzia
 Kael (d) 337-38
Razzia sur la chnouf see Raz-
zia
Real End of the Great War, The
 Young 110-12, (171), (404)
Real Glory, The
 Graham 262
Reap the Wild Wind
 Agate (b) 201-02
Rebecca
 Ferguson 295
Rebel, The (Robert Day) see
 Call Me Genius
Rebel Son
 Graham 236
Rebel Without a Cause
 Durgnat 72-73

Rebellion
  Simon (b) 381
Rebyata jazz see Jazz Comedy
Red and the White, The
  Farber 233
  Kauffmann (a) 158-59
  Schickel 226-28
  Simon (b) 300-01
  Young 358-61
Red Badge of Courage, The
  Sarris (a) 172-74
Red Balloon, The
  Young (290)
Red Beard
  Kauffmann (a) 132-33
  Simon (c) 188
  Weinberg 273
  Young 302-04
Red Desert, The
  Kael (d) 24
  Kauffmann (b) 313-19, 407
  Macdonald 339-41
  Sarris (a) 189-93
  Simon (c) 154-58
Red Dust
  Weinberg (55
Red House, The
  Agee (274)
Red River
  Farber 19
  Kael (d) 338
Red Salute see Arms and the
  Girl (Sidney Lanfield)
Redgrave, Lynn
  Reed (c) 164-69
Redi, Beryl
  Reed (c) 170-75
Reed, Carol
  Graham 2-4
  Kael (c) (297)
  Young (19)
Reed, Oliver
  Reed (b) 241-46
Reed, Rex
  Reed (c) ix-xii
Reflections in a Golden Eye
  Farber 156-57
  Kael (b) 30, 33-34
  Sarris (a) 321-25
  Sarris (b) (107)
  Simon (b) 34-35
  Young 13-14
Reg Butler

Durgnat 128
Regain, Le see Harvest
Regal Picture Palace (Brixton,
  London)
  Agate (a) 52-53
Regen, Der see Rain (Joris
  Ivens)
Règle du jeu, La see Rules of
  the Game, The
Reifende Jugend, Die
  Graham 45
Reivers, The
  Kael (a) 75-76
Relentless
  Agee (302)
RELIGION AND THE CINEMA
  Weinberg 192
Religieuse, La
  Adler 245-46
  Farber (239)
Reluctant Debutante, The
  Kauffmann (b) 39-40
Remarkable Mr. Kipps, The
  see Kipps
Rembrandt (Alexander Korda)
  Algate (b) 134-36
  Durgnat (49)
  Ferguson (10), 162-64
  Graham 117, 120
  Lejeune 15-17
  Van Doren 347
Remember the Day
  Agate (b) 202
Remontons les Champs-Elysées
  see Champs-Elysées
Renoir, Jean
  Durgnat 48-49
  Gilliatt 303-24
  Kael (a) (238)
  Kael (c) 247-48
  Kael (d) 76, (197)
  Pechter (122), 195-214, 315
  Sarris (a) (380)
  Sarris (b) 60, 86
  Simon (b) 397-98
Renoir, Jean (quoted)
  Weinberg 82-83, 88-89
Repent at Leisure
  Ferguson 355
Report on Italy
  Agee 145
Report on the Party and the
  Guests, A

Adler   244-45, 328
Gilliatt   131-33
Repulsion
    Farber   (181)
    Macdonald   52-55
    Sarris (a)   208-10
    Sarris (b)   62
    Simon (c)   191-92
Requiem for a Heavyweight
    Farber   (137)
Resnais, Alain
    Simon (c)   (128)
    Sontag (b)   (110)
Resnais, Alain (quoted)
    Pechter   71
Rest Is Silence, The
    Kauffmann (b)   346-48
Rest ist Schweigen, Der   see
    Rest Is Silence, The
Return of Frank James, The
    Ferguson   307
Reunion in France
    Lejeune   91-92
REVIEWING   see   CRITICISM
Revolution (Jack O'Connell)
    Adler   203-04
Revolutionary, The (Paul Will-
    iams)
    Reed (a)   294-95
    Simon (b)   96-99
REVOLUTIONARY THEMES
    Weinberg   344
Revolutionists
    Graham   149
    Van Doren   350
Revue du Cinema, La (magazine)
    Durgnat   (43), (66)
Rhapsody Rabbit
    Agee   218-19
RHETORIC   see   AESTHETICS;
    EDITING
Rhodes
    Agate (b)   127-29
    Ferguson   (7),   123-24
    Graham   61-62
    Van Doren   321-23
Rhodes of Africa   see   Rhodes
Rhythm of a City, The
    Young   246-47
Rhythm on the Range
    Graham   93-94
Rich Bride, The
    Graham   236-37

Macdonald   223-24
Richard III (Laurence Olivier)
    Kael (c)   281
Richardson, Samuel
    Sontag (a)   242-43
Richardson, Tony
    Farber   138-39
Richardson, Tony (quoted)
    Sarris (b)   82
    Weinberg   207
Richie, Donald.   The Films of
    Akira Kurosawa
    Macdonald   481-83
Rickshaw Man
    Kael (c)   (290)
Ride the High Country
    Kauffmann (a)   183
Ride the Pink Horse
    Agee   282
Rider in the Rain   see   Stranger
    in the Rain
Rider of the White Horse   see
    Schimmelreiter, Der
Rider on the Rain   see   Stranger
    in the Rain
Riders to the Sea
    Graham   40
Riding High (George Marshall)
    Agee   69-70
Rififi
    Durgnat   224
    Kael (d)   338-39
    Weinberg   (176)
Rififi Spells Trouble   see   Rififi
Ring of Bright Water
    Reed (a)   223-24
Rise of Helga, The   see   Susan
    Lenox: Her Fall and Rise
Rise of Louis XIV, The
    Sarris (a)   314
    Simon (b)   378-79
Risques du métier, Les
    Young   333-34
Rite, The   see   Ritual, The
Riten   see   Ritual, The
Ritual, The
    Farber   244
    Simon (b)   391
River, The (Pare Lorentz)
    Ferguson   203-05
    Van Doren   376-77
River of Unrest   see   Ourselves
    Alone

Ro Go Pag   see   RoGoPag
Road, The   see   Strada, La
Road Back, The
    Ferguson 184
    Graham 172-73
Road to Frisco, The   see   They
    Drive By Night
Road to Glory, The (Howard
    Hawks)
    Van Doren 338-40
Road to Morocco, The
    Agate (b) 216-17
Road to Rio, The
    Agee (295)
Road to Zanzibar, The
    Ferguson 355-57
Roaring Twenties, The
    Farber 122
    Ferguson (7), 277-79
Robbe-Grillet, Alain (quoted)
    Pechter 63-64
Robber Symphony, The
    Graham 76, 78
Robin and the Seven Hoods
    Gilliatt 166-67
Robinson, William R.   Man and
    the Movies
    Young 328-30
Rocco and His Brothers
    Durgnat (64), (102)
    Kauffmann (b) 329-30
    Macdonald (130), 344-45
    Sarris (a) (30-31)
    Young 129-31
Rocha, Glauber
    Young 362
Rocking Horse Winner, The
    Kael (d) 339
Roger Touhy, Gangster
    Agee 97-98
Rogers, Ginger
    Agate (b) 180-81
    Sarris (b) 175-76
RoGoPag
    Simon (c) 85
Roi Pausole, Le
    Weinberg 296
Roma, Città Aperta   see   Open
    City
Roman d'un tricheur   see
    Tricheurs, Les (Marcel
    Carné)
Roman Spring of Mrs. Stone, The

    Kael (c) 139-41
Romeo and Juliet (Renato Castel-
    lani)
    Kael (d) 339-40
Romeo and Juliet (George Cukor)
    Ferguson 148-50
    Graham 109-11
    Van Doren 336-38, 342-43
Romeo and Juliet (Franco Zeffir-
    elli)
    Adler 264-65
    Kael (b) 153-58
    Kauffmann (a) 112-14
    Reed (b) 273-82
    Simon (b) 107-08
Romeo, Julie a Tma   see
    Sweet Light in a Dark Room
Ronde, La
    Simon (b) 391-92
Rondo
    Young 339
Roof, The
    Kauffmann (b) 291-93
Roof Garden, The   see   Terrace,
    The
Room at the Top
    Kael (a) (142)
    Kael (c) 67
    Kauffmann (b) 177-79
Roosevelt Story, The
    Agee 275
Roots
    Weinberg 140-41
    Young 97
Roots of Heaven, The
    Alpert 149-50
    Kauffmann (b) 144-46
Rope
    Sontag (b) (108)
Rose of the Rancho (Marion
    Gering)
    Graham 56
Rose Tattoo, The
    Sarris (a) 19-20
Rosemary
    Kael (d) 340
    Kauffmann (b) 344-46
    Macdonald (280)
Rosemary's Baby
    Adler 170-72, 328
    Gilliatt 104-06
    Kauffmann (a) 83-85
    Sarris (a) 373-76

Simon (b) 181-82
Young (307)
Rosi, Francesco
Young 233-34
Ross, Lillian
Sarris (a) 172-74
Rossellini, Roberto
Alpert 183-84
Sarris (a) 29-33
Sarris (b) (51)
Rotha, Paul (quoted)
Kauffmann (b) 262
Rotha, Paul. The Film Till
Now
Agate (a) 79-82
Sarris (b) 101
Rothstein '64
Durgnat 128
Roud, Richard
Durgnat 70
Sarris (b) (39)
Roud, Richard. Jean-Luc God-
ard
Simon (b) (410)
Young 326
Roue, La
Sarris (b) (52), (88)
Roughly Speaking
Agee 145
Rounders, The
Crist 116
Round-Up, The (Miklós Jancsó)
Farber 5
Kauffmann (a) 168-70
Simon (c) (254)
Young 357-58
Roxie Hart
Agee 336
Kael (d) 341
Royal Family of Broadway, The
Agate (b) 53-54
Royal Hunt of the Sun, The
Kael (a) 24-25
Reed (a) 254
Royal Scandal, A (Otto Premin-
ger)
Agee 154-55
Royal Scandal, A (Hans Behrendt)
Weinberg 50, 224
Royaumes de ce monde, Les
see Kingdoms of This World
Rozmane leto see Capricious
Summer

Ruggles of Red Gap (Leo Mc-
Carey)
Agate (a) 137-40
Ruler, The see Herrscher, Der
Rules of the Game, The
Durgnat (29), (231)
Gilliatt 326-30
Kael (c) 193-94
Kael (d) (141), 341-43
Sarris (b) (51), 112
Simon (a) (17)
Simon (c) 22-24
Weinberg (195)
Run Silent, Run Free see
Philip
RUNNING TIME see VER-
SIONS, ABBREVIATED
Runyon, Damon
Agee 339-40
RUSSIAN FILMS (pre-1940)
Graham (39-40)
Macdonald (70), 182-248
RUSSIAN FILMS (mid-1940's)
Macdonald 258-59
Russian Story, The
Agee 340-41
Ryan's Daughter
Kael (a) 188-93
Schickel 50

-S-

S. A. Mann Brand
Ferguson 38
S.O.S. Mediterranean
Graham 205
S.O.S. Submarine
Young 25
Sabotage (Alfred Hitchcock) see
Woman Alone, The
Saboteur (Alfred Hitchcock)
Kael (c) (294)
Saboteur, The see Morituri
Saboteur: Code Name Morituri,
The see Morituri
Sabrina
Simon (a) 26-27
Safety Last
Agee 11-12, (228)
Saga of Anatahan see Anatahan
Sahara (Zoltan Korda)
Agee 53

Saint Joan
  Alpert 97-104, 108-114
St. Petersburg see Petersburg
  Nights
Salaire de la peur, Le see
  Wages of Fear, The
SALARIES
  Alpert 28-30
Salesman
  Kauffmann (a) 150-54
  Reed (a) 170-72
  Simon (b) 73-76
Salome, Where She Danced
  Agee (188)
  Lejeune 154-56
Salt of Svanetia
  Weinberg (199)
  Young 224
Salt of the Earth
  Kael (c) 331-46
Saludos Amigos
  Agee 29
Salvation Hunters
  Macdonald (4)
Salvatore Giuliano
  Kauffmann (a) (23-24)
Samuels, Charles T.
  Simon (b) (5), (21)
Samurai (Hiroshi Inagaki)
  Young 101
San Diego, I Love You
  Agee (122)
San Pietro
  Agee 162-64, 186
San Sebastian International Film
  Festival, 1966
  Sarris (a) 253-56
Sand Pebbles, The
  Kael (d) 8-9
Sanders, George
  Reed (b) 198-204
Sanders of the River
  Agate (b) 117-19
Sandpiper, The
  Crist (xvii-xviii), 127-29
  Kael (d) 343-44
  Simon (c) 171-73
Sandra
  Macdonald 347-48
  Simon (b) (191)
  Simon (c) 188
Sang d'une poete, Le see Blood
  of a Poet, The

Sanjuro
  Kauffmann (b) 381-82
Sans Famille
  Graham 47
Sans mobile apparent see With-
  out Apparent Motive
Santa Fe Trail, The (Michael
  Curtiz)
  Ferguson 330
Sapphire
  Kael (c) 66
Saratoga
  Graham 163
Saratoga Trunk
  Agate (b) 265-66
  Kael (d) 345
Sarris, Andrew
  Durgnat 145
  Macdonald 154-57, 306
  Sarris (a) 11-16
  Sarris (b) 115-16, 265-66
  Simon (b) (4-13)
Sarris, Andrew (quoted)
  Simon (b) 7, 10-11
Såsom i en spegel see Through
  a Glass Darkly
SATIRE
  Simon (c) 123-24
Saturday Night & Sunday Morning
  Kael (c) 74-77
  Kauffmann (b) 196-98
  Macdonald 388-89
Saturday Review (magazine, London)
  Agate (a) 7
Saturday Review (magazine, N.Y.)
  Alpert 1-4
Satyricon (Federico Fellini) see
  Fellini Satyricon
Saura, Carlos
  Adler 154
Savage Eye, The
  Macdonald 321-22
Savo, Jimmy
  Weinberg 35-36
Savoy Hotel 217
  Graham 107-08
Sawdust and Tinsel see Naked
  Night, The
Scalphunters, The
  Kael (b) 89-90
  Sarris (a) 387-88
Scarface
  Agate (a) 219

Faber 25-29
Sarris (b) 44-45
Warshow 132-33, (137), (140)
Scarlet Daredevil, The
  Agate (a) 31-34
Scarlet Empress, The
  Weinberg (52), (150)
Scarlet Letter, The (Victor
  Sjostrom)
  Kael (d) .345
Scarlet Pimpernel, The (Harold
  Young)
  Ferguson 67
Scarlet Street
  Pechter (197)
Sceicco bianco, Lo see White
  Sheik, The (Federico Fellini)
SCENARIOS see SCRIPTWRIT-
  ING
SCENES
  Farber 120
Scent of Mystery
  Alpert 180
Schickel, Richard
  Schickel 5, 15
Schickel, Richard. Movies
  Macdonald 479-81
Schimmelreiter, Der
  Graham 14
Schlesinger, John
  Sarris (a) 206
Schloss in Flandern, Der see
  Castle in Flanders, A
Schmeling, Max
  Ferguson 140-43
SCIENCE FICTION FILMS
  Durgnat 251-70
  Sontag (a) 209-25
Scorpio Rising
  Simon (c) 203-04
  Sontag (b) (158)
Scott, George C.
  Crist (194)
Scoundrel, The
  Ferguson 78
Screen Actors' Guild
  Ferguson 180
Screen Magazine (U.S. Army)
  Agee 78-79
SCREEN PLAYS see PLOTS,
  DISCUSSION OF; SCRIPT-
  WRITING
SCREEN WRITERS see

SCRIPTWRITING
SCREENS see WIDE-SCREEN
  SYSTEMS
SCRIPTS see SCRIPTWRITING
SCRIPTWRITING
  Agate (a) 80-81
  Alpert 124-29, 245, 247
  Durgnat 260
  Ferguson 34-35, 443-44
  Kael (a) (237-38)
  Kael (b) 9-10, 20-21
  Kael (d) 6-7, 59, 153
  Lejeune 160-61
  Pechter 274
  Sarris (a) 183-84, 361-62
  Sarris (b) 35, 46-47, 122-
    23, 133
  Sontag (b) 110-11
Scrooge (Ronald Neame)
  Kael (a) 196-97
  Reed (a) 305-06
Sculptor's Landscape, A
  Durgnat 120
Sea, The
  Simon (c) (85)
Sea Gull, The (Sydney Lumet)
  Kael (b) 230-36
  Reed (a) 210-12
  Sarris (a) 419-22
  Simon (b) 44-46
Sea Gull, The (Josef von Stern-
  berg)
  Weinberg 248
Sea Wall, The
  Kael (d) 345-46
Sea Wolf, The (Michael Curtiz)
  Agate (b) 197-98
  Ferguson 353-54
Seance on a Wet Afternoon
  Crist 83-84, (90)
Search, The
  Agee 302
Searchers, The
  Sontag (b) (106)
  Young 89
Searching Eye, The
  Kauffmann (b) 166-67
Searching Wind, The
  Agee 206
Sebastian
  Kael (b) 19-24
  Kael (d) 25-26
Seberg, Jean

Alpert 97-123
Reed (b) 166-73
Second Bureau
   Graham 46-47
Second in Command, The
   Pechter 296
Seconds
   Crist 193
Secret Agent, The (Alfred Hitch-
   cock)
   Ferguson 138-40
   Graham 74-75
   Sarris (b) (123)
Secret Beyond the Door, The
   Agee 295
Secret Ceremony
   Adler 286
   Kael (b) 171
   Reed (a) 199-201
   Simon (b) 350-51
Secret Command
   Agee 103
Secret Game see Forbidden
   Games
Secret Heart, The
   Winnington 75-76
Secret Land, The
   Brown (c) 294-300
Secret Life of Walter Mitty, The
   Agee 272
Secret of Santa Vittoria, The
   Kael (a) 34-35
   Reed (a) 260
Secret Passion see Freud
Secret War of Harry Frigg, The
   Adler 61-63
   Kael (b) 56-58
Secrets of a Soul
   Weinberg 213
Secrets of a Woman
   Kauffmann (b) 279-80
Secrets of the Orient
   Weinberg (225)
Sedmikrasky see Daisies, The
Seduced and Abandoned
   Crist 88
See Here, Private Hargrove
   Agee 83
See You at Mao
   Kauffmann (a) 265-66
See You in Hell, Darling see
   American Dream, An
Selznick, David O.

Agee 138
Durgnat 77
Graham 3-4
Senator Was Indiscreet, The
   Agee 295
   Crist (66)
Senhime see Princess Sen
Sennett, Mack
   Agee 4-8, 16
Sensation (Brian D. Hurst)
   Graham 130
Sentimental Journey
   Lejeune 181-82
Separate Tables
   Alpert 34-36
Seppuku
   Young 267
Sept Péchés Capitaux, Les see
   Seven Capital Sins, The
Sequel to Second Bureau, The
   Graham 137
Sequence (magazine)
   Durgnat 62-63, (145)
Sequoia
   Agate (a) 133
Serenade (Harry d'Arrast)
   Weinberg 313
Serengeti Shall Not Die see
   They Must Not Die
Sergeant, The
   Kael (b) 240-42
   Reed (a) 140-41
Sergeant Grischa
   Agate (b) 37
Sergeant York
   Ferguson 385-86
SERIALS
   Kael (d) 7
Servant, The
   Crist 55-58, (89)
   Durgnat (98)
   Sarris (a) 129-31
Service for Ladies (Harry d'Ar-
   rast)
   Weinberg 310-12
SETS (see also LOCATIONS)
   Durgnat 96
   Farber 78
   Ferguson 7, 10, 48, 192,
      446-48, 454-55
   Kael (b) 23
   Sarris (b) 101
   Sontag (b) 102, 106

Set-Up, The (Robert Wise)
　　Farber　65-67
Seven Capital Sins, The
　　Sarris (b)　52-53
Seven Days Ashore
　　Agee　(93)
Seven Days in May
　　Crist　67-68
　　Kael (b)　95
　　Simon (c)　109-111
Seven Samurai, The
　　Durgnat　(60)
　　Kael (c)　119-124
　　Simon (c)　31-33
　　Young　85-86
Seven Sinners (Tay Garnett)
　　Ferguson　320-21
Seven Women
　　Crist　(191), 212
　　Kael (d)
　　Sarris (a)　248-50
Seventh Cross, The
　　Agee　114
Seventh Seal, The
　　Durgnat　247-50
　　Kael (c)　(288)
　　Kael (d)　346
Seventh Veil, The
　　Agate (b)　268-69
　　Kael (d)　346-47
SEX IN FILMS see EROTI-
　　CISM IN FILMS
SEX SYMBOLS see VAMPS
Seyrig, Delphine
　　Farber　4
Shadow of a Doubt (Alfred Hitch-
　　cock)
　　Agee　26, (63), (66)
　　Lejeune　87-89
Shadows (John Cassavetes)
　　Kael (b)　196
　　Macdonald　311-12
　　Pechter　9-10
Shadows of Fear see Thérèse
　　Raquin (Jacques Feyder)
Shadows of Our Forgotten Ances-
　　tors
　　Sontag (b)　(108)
SHAKESPEARE IN FILMS
　　Agate (a)　165-67
　　Alpert　242-43
　　Sarris (a)　240-41
　　Van Doren　293-94

Shakespeare Wallah
　　Crist　215
　　Schickel　71-73
　　Simon (c)　186
　　Sontag (b)　(107)
Shalako
　　Adler　283
　　Reed (a)　204
Shame (Ingmar Bergman)
　　Adler　329-30
　　Farber　222-24
　　Kael (b)　214-21
　　Kauffmann (a)　125-28
　　Simon (b)　(225), 233-38
Shame of a Nation see Scar-
　　face
Shameless Old Lady, The
　　Kael (d)　110-11
Shane
　　Alpert　141
　　Kael (d)　347
　　Warshow　150-51
Shanghai Drama
　　Agee　140
Shanghai Express
　　Kael (b)　113-14
Shanghai Gesture, The
　　Lejeune　75-76
Shapes and Forms--Primitive
　　and Modern Art
　　Durgnat　129
Sharif, Omar
　　Reed (b)　147-51
Shawn, Dick
　　Crist　(194)
Shchors
　　Agee　(341)
She (Robert Day)
　　Durgnat　(253)
She (Irving Pichel)
　　Graham　32
She Defends Her Country see
　　No Greater Love (Ermler)
She Let Him Continue see
　　Pretty Poison
She Loves Me Not
　　Ferguson　49
She Was Like a Wild Chrysanthe-
　　mum
　　Young　373
Sherlock Holmes (Alfred Werker)
　　see Adventure of Sherlock
　　Holmes, The

Sherlock, Junior
  Agee 15-16, (228)
  Macdonald x-xi
Shichinin no samurai see Seven
  Samurai, The
Shine On, Harvest Moon
  Agee (85)
Ship of Fools
  Crist 135-39
  Farber (180-81)
  Kael (d) 209-14
  Simon (c) 174-75
Ships with Wings
  Lejeune 63-65
Shipyard Sally
  Graham 239
Shock (Alfred Werker)
  Lejeune 177
Shock Corridor
  Sarris (a) 94-96
  Simon (b) (12)
Shoes of the Fisherman, The
  Adler 291-92
  Kael (b) 181-83
Shoeshine
  Agee 274, (278-80), 288
  Kael (c) 114-16
Shonen see Boy (Nagisa Oshima)
Shoot the Piano Player
  Kael (c) 210-16
  Kael (d) (54)
  Kauffmann (b) 230-32
  Sarris (a) 62-63
Shop Around the Corner, The
  Ferguson 286
Shop on Main Street, The
  Crist 162-63, 214
  Simon (c) 185-86
Shop on the High Street, The see
  Shop on Main Street, The
Shopworn Angel (H. C. Potter)
  Ferguson 223-24
Shors see Shchors
SHORT FILMS
  Adler 128-30
  Young xv-xvi
Short Is the Summer see Pan
Show Boat (James Whale)
  Graham 82-84
Show Business
  Agee (93)
Show of Shows
  Agate (b) 33-35

Show Them No Mercy
  Ferguson 109
Showman
  Kauffmann (b) 398
Shozo a Cat and Two Women
  see Cat and Two Women, A
Shulman, Irving. Harlow: An
  Intimate Biography
  Crist 79
  Sarris (a) 149-54
Si Paris nous était conté
  Weinberg (276-77)
Siberian Lady Macbeth see
  Lady Macbeth of Minsk
Sibirska Ledi Magbet see Lady
  Macbeth of Minsk
Sicario see Hired Killer, The
Sicilian Clan, The
  Simon (b) 270-71
Siècle d'or, Le see Golden Age
  of Primitive Flemish Painters,
  The
Siegel, Don
  Farber 125-28
Siegel, Louis
  Weinberg 209-10
Sight and Sound (magazine)
  Durgnat (23), 62-66, 75
  Kael (c) (63-64), (271), (310),
    (316)
  Pechter 277-78
Sign of the Cross, The (Cecil B.
  deMille)
  Agate (b) 76-78
Sign of the Ram, The
  Agee (302)
Signora senza camelie, La see
  Camille without Camellias
Signoret, Simone
  Reed (b) 71-78
Signs of Life
  Farber 238-39
  Kael (b) (215)
Silence, The (Ingmar Bergman)
  Crist 46-48
  Kauffmann (b) 286-89, (417)
  Macdonald (53), 416-18
  Simon (c) 107-08
Silence est d'or, Le see Man
  About Town
Silencers, The
  Crist 211
Silent Barrier, The (Milton

Rosmer) see Great Barrier,
  The
SILENT FILMS (see also COME-
  DIES, SILENT)
  Durgnat 46
  Kael (a) 319-21
  Macdonald xviii
  Pechter 300, 302-03, 305-06,
    309
  Sarris (b) 26, 138
  Sontag (a) 200
  Sontag (b) (104)
  Young 122-24
SILENT FILMS, AESTHETICS OF
  see SOUND FILMS
Silent Star, The see First
  Spaceship on Venus, The
Silent Village, The
  Agee 46
Silken Skin, The see Soft Skin,
  The
Silliphant, Stirling
  Kael (a) 151
Silly Symphony (series)
  Ferguson 28
  Lejeune 36-37
Simmons, Jean
  Agee 393-94
Simon, John
  Sarris (b) (123)
  Schickel (28-29)
Simon of the Desert
  Kael (b) 257-62
  Kauffmann (a) 144-46
  Pechter 220
  Reed (a) 220-21
  Simon (c) 251
Simple Case, A
  Agate (a) 155
  Pechter (306)
Sin of Jesus, The
  Macdonald 315-16
Sinatra, Frank
  Durgnat 139-40, 144
Sinbad the Sailor
  Weinberg 107
Since You Went Away
  Agee 106-08, 349-51
  Winnington 29-30
Sing and Like It
  Ferguson 41-42
Sing High, Swing Low
  Ferguson 174-75

Sing You Sinners
  Ferguson 231
Singapore
  Farber (24)
Singin' in the Rain
  Kauffmann (b) (136-37)
Singe en hiver, Le see Mond-
  key in Winter
Singing Nun, The
  Kael (d) 176, 177
  Reed (a) 330
Sins of Lola Montès, The see
  Lola Montès
Sir Arne's Treasure (Gustav Mo-
  lander)
  Young (154)
Sirene de Mississippi, La see
  Mississippi Mermaid
Sirocco see Winter Wind
Siska
  Young 201
Sisters, The (Anatole Litvak)
  Graham 218
Six in Paris
  Simon (c) 186-87
Sixty Glorious Years
  Graham 203
Sjöman, Vilgot. L 136: Dagbok
  med Ingmar Bergman
  Young 287, 290
Skammen see Shame (Ingmar
  Bergman)
Ski Bum, The
  Kael (a) (345)
Skidoo
  Reed (a) 151-53
Skin Game
  Kael (a) 299-300
Skinny and Fatty
  Crist 113
Skolimowski, Jerzy
  Gilliatt 100-01
Skopje 63
  Young 269-70
Sky Above, the Mud Below, The
  Kael (d) 347-48
Sky's the Limit, The (Edward
  Griffith)
  Agee 51
Skyscraper Souls
  Agate (b) 71-72
Slave-Ship
  Graham 162

Slavnosti a hostech, O see Re-
     port on the Party and the
     Guests, A
Sleeping Beauty
     Pechter   (6)
Sleeping Tiger, The
     Durgnat   226-27
Slender Thread, The
     Kael (d)   143-45 ·
Slight Case of Murder, A see
     Daybreak
Slow Rain
     Farber   252-53
Smiles of a Summer Night
     Kael (c)   105-07
     Simon (a) (31), (34)
     Simon (c)   17-18
Smilin' Through (Sidney Franklin)
     Agate (a)   20-21
Smith!
     Reed (a)   226-27
Smugglers, The (Bernard Knowles)
     Agee (302)
Smultronstallet see Wild Straw-
     berries
Snake Pit, The
     Brown (c)   288-93
Snow, Michael
     Farber   256-58
Snow White and the Seven Dwarfs
     Brown (b)   96
     Ferguson   209-11
     Kael (b)   191
     Lejeune   31-33, 35-38
     Van Doren   387-89
Snows of Kilimanjaro, The
     Durgnat   227
So Evil My Love
     Agee   312
So Goes My Love
     Winnington   60
So Long at the Fair
     Sarris (a)   212-13
So Proudly We Hail
     Agee   52-53
     Winnington   11
So This Is New York
     Agee (307)
So This Is Paris (Ernst Lubitsch)
     Weinberg (324)
Soapy Run
     Farber   253
SOCIAL CINEMA see SOCIETY

IN FILMS
SOCIAL CONSCIOUSNESS see
     SOCIETY IN FILMS
SOCIETIES, FILM (see also
     Cinema 16)
     Kauffmann (b)   411-12
     Macdonald   168-71, 312-14
SOCIETY AND THE CINEMA
     (see also POLITICS AND
     CINEMA)
     Adler   143-44
     Durgnat   72
     Farber   113, 116
     Ferguson   3-10, 180
     Kael (b)   124-27
     Kael (d)   4-5
     Kauffmann (b)   420-22, 426-
          28
     Pechter   285
     Sarris (b)   45-46, 58
     Simon (c)   177-78
     Weinberg   20, 59
     Young   328
SOCIETY IN FILMS (see also
     POLITICS AND THE CINEMA)
     Adler   143-44
     Crist   69-70
     Durgnat   61-62
     Ferguson   185, 234-35
     Graham   39
     Kauffmann (a)   34, 37-38,
          201-03, 243-45
     Sarris (a)   372
     Sarris (b)   104
     Simon (a)   17
     Simon (b)   66
     Sontag (b)   102-03
     Young   78, 399
SOCIOLOGY OF THE CINEMA
     Sarris (b)   72-73
Sodrásban see Current
Soft Skin, The
     Kauffmann (b)   232
     Macdonald   380-83
     Simon (c)   128-31
     Sontag (b) (149)
     Young   260-62
Soil see Earth
Sol Madrid
     Adler   173
Sol Svanetia see Salt of Svan-
     etia
Solas, Humberto

Adler 345
Soldier and the Lady, The
    Graham 155
Soldier of Love, The see Fan-
    fan the Tulip
Soldiers, The see Carabiniers,
    Les
Soliti ignoti, I see Big Deal on
    Madonna Street
Solomon and Sheba
    Weinberg 159
Some Came Running
    Kauffmann (b) 47-49
Some Like It Hot (William Wyler)
    Crist (96)
    Kael (d) 348)
    Kauffman (b) 147-51
Something Else
    Sontag (b) (155)
Something for Everyone
    Reed (a) 295-96
    Simon (b) 160-62
Something to Live For
    Farber (78)
Something to Sing About
    Ferguson 199-200
Something Wild
    Macdonald 322-23
    Young 169
Somewhere I'll Find You
    Lejeune 84-85
Sommarnattens leende see
    Smiles of a Summer Night
Son of Dracula
    Durgnat (148)
Son of Mongolia
    Van Doren 343-45
    Graham 199-200
Song of Bernadette, The
    Agate (a) 257-60
    Agee 72-73, (137), 341-42
    Lejeune 114-15
    Weinberg 105
Song of Ceylon
    Graham 25, (108)
    Young (25)
Song of Freedom
    Graham 103
Song of Love (Clarence Brown)
    Agee 281-82
Song of Norway
    Kael (a) 187
Song of Russia

Winnington 18
Song of Scheherazade
    Weinberg 106-07
Song of Songs (Rouben Mamoul-
    ian)
    Agate (b) 95-97
Song of the Islands
    Lejeune 77
Song of the Open Road
    Agee (101)
Song of the South
    Weinberg 107-08
Song to Remember, A
    Agate (a) 266-68
    Agee (140-41)
    Winnington 27
Song without End
    Weinberg 162)
Sons and Lovers
    Kael (c) 72-74
    Kauffmann (b) 97-99
Sons and Mothers
    Simon (b) 382
Sons of Katie Elder, The
    Sarris (a) 208
Sontag, Susan
    Kael (c) (19)
    Pechter 315
Sontag, Susan (quoted)
    Kauffmann (a) 109-10
    Young 324
Sorok pervyi see Forty-First,
    The (Grigori Chukhrai)
Sorpasso, Il see Easy Life,
    The
Sorrow and the Pity, The
    Kael (a) 426-30
SOS Mediterranean see S.O.S.
    Mediterranean
SOS Submarine see S.O.S.
    Submarine
Sound and the Fury, The
    Kauffmann (b) 93-95
Sound Barrier, The see Break-
    ing the Sound Barrier
SOUND FILMS [includes discus-
    sions of sound vs. silent
    films]
    Agate (a) 26-31, 43-45, 57,
        82
    Agate (b) 20-21, 191
    Alpert 234-36
    Durgnat (32)

Ferguson 5
Graham (1)
Macdonald 103, 200-01, 366-67, 374-75
Pechter 306-10
Sarris (b) 26, 84
Sontag (a) 200
Sontag (b) (104), 115
Van Doren 291
Weinberg 256
Young (20), 122-24
Sound of Fury, The see Try and Get Me
Sound of Music, The
  Adler (207)
  Crist 106-09
  Kael (d) 176-78
  Macdonald 39-42
Sound of Trumpets, The
  Crist 28-29, (39)
  Kauffmann (b) 336-37
  Macdonald 354-55, (394)
  Simon (c) 69-72
  Weinberg 189-90
Sous les toits de Paris
  Agate (a) 87, 97-98
South Riding
  Ferguson 232
Southerner, The
  Agee 166-68, (187)
  Winnington 39-40
Southwest to Sonora see Appaloosa
Spaceship Venus Does Not Reply
  see First Spaceship on Venus, The
"SPAGHETTI" WESTERNS see NON-AMERICAN WESTERNS
Spanish Earth
  Ferguson 190-92
Spanish Main, The
  Lejeune 176-77
Spare Time
  Graham 223-24
Sparrows Can't Sing
  Durgnat (108-09)
  Gilliatt 347-49
  Macdonald 393-95
  Simon (c) 82-83
Spartacus
  Kauffmann (b) 23-24
  Pechter 5-6
Specter of the Rose, The

Agee 205
Spectre, The
  Durgnat (45)
Speedway
  Adler 172-73, 182
Spellbound (Alfred Hitchcock)
  Agee 179-80
  Kael (d) 348
Spencer's Mountain
  Crist 3-6
Spies (Fritz Lang)
  Agate (a) 24-25
Spies, Walter
  Weinberg 207
Spione see Spies (Fritz Lang)
Spiral Staircase, The
  Agee 192-93
  Kael (d) 349
Spirit of the People, The see Abe Lincoln in Illinois
Spirits of the Dead
  Kauffmann (a) 196-98
  Sarris (a) 459-61
  Simon (b) 188-89
Spivs, The see Vitelloni, I
Splendor in the Grass
  Kael (c) 138
  Kauffmann (b) 154
  Macdonald 140-42
Split, The
  Adler 281-82, 285-86
  Kael (b) 183-85
Sporting Club, The
  Kael (a) 261-63
SPORTS .FILMS
  Schickel 272-73
Spring in Park Lane
  Winnington 106-07
Spring Madness
  Ferguson 241-42
Springfield Rifle
  Sarris (b) 71-72
Spy of Madame Pompadour, The
  Weinberg 51
Spy Who Came in from the Cold, The
  Farber 170-74
  Sarris (a) 221-25, (249)
  Simon (c) 208-10
Spy with a Cold Nose, The
  Gilliatt 247-49
Squadrone bianco, Lo see White Squadrons

Stage Door (Gregory La Cava)
   Agate (b) 149-51
   Ferguson 201-02
   Van Doren 377-78
Stage Door Canteen
   Agate (a) 248
   Agee 41
STAGE PRODUCTIONS,
   FILMED see THEATER
   AND THE CINEMA
Stagecoach (Gordon Douglas)
   Kael (d) 41-42
Stagecoach (John Ford)
   Crist (135)
   Kael (d) 41
   Warshow 149
Staircase
   Kauffmann (a) 190-92
   Reed (a) 183-84
Stairway to Heaven
   Winnington 69-70
Stalag 17
   Kael (d) 349
Stalking Moon, The
   Kael (b) 248-53
   Reed (a) 138-40
Stand Up and Cheer
   Ferguson 35-36
Standard Time
   Farber 256
Standing Room Only
   Agee 81-82
Stanley, Kim
   Simon (c) 300-01
Stanley and Livingstone
   Ferguson 266-67, 272
   Graham 246-47
Star!
   Adler xxi, 276
   Kael (b) 161-65
Star Is Born, A (William Well-
   man)
   Ferguson 176-77
Star of Midnight
   Graham 14
STAR SYSTEM see STARS
Starci na chmelu see Hop
   Pickers, The
Stark Love
   Agee (196)
   Macdonald (4), 11-13
Staroye i novoye see General
   Line, The

STARS (see also ACTORS AND
   ACTRESSES)
   Adler 32-34
   Alpert 26-39
   Crist 145, 199-200
   Durgnat 43-44, 135-45, 152-
      54
   Ferguson 52, 54-56, 74, 93,
      131, 400-01
   Kael (a) 110, 154-55
   Kauffmann (a) 75-76
   Sarris (a) 263
   Sarris (b) 23, 76, 78
Stars Look Down, The
   Ferguson 381-82
   Graham 265
   Kael (d) 349-51
Start the Revolution without Me
   Kael (a) 123
State Fair (Henry King)
   Macdonald 88
State Fair (Walter Lang)
   Agee 175-76
   Winnington 40, 42
Statues meurent aussi, Les
   Durgnat 127
Stauffacher, Frank
   Weinberg (293)
Steady
   Durgnat 101
Steel Helmet
   Farber (56)
Steichen, Edward
   Weinberg 243
Steiger, Rod
   Crist 146-47
   Kael (b) 74-75
Stella (Michael Cacoyannis)
   Kael (d) 351
Stella Dallas
   Macdonald 87-88
Steo sam cak i srecne cigane
   see I Even Met Happy Gyp-
   sies
Sterile Cuckoo, The
   Kael (a) 31-34
   Reed (a) 247-48
   Simon (b) 120-21
Sternberg, Josef von
   Durgnat 36, 95, (98)
   Macdonald 93-97, (106)
   Sarris (b) 261-62
   Weinberg (152), 161, (248),

254-55, (257), 332-34
Young 182-83
Stevens, George
Alpert 137-47
Kauffmann (a) (44)
Stewart, James
Sarris (b) 161-64
Stitch in Time, A (Robert Asher)
Gilliatt 163-64
Stolen Kisses
Farber (4)
Gilliatt 315
Kael (b) 273-76
Kauffmann (a) 137-38
Reed (a) 155-58, 221-22
Sarris (a) 427-31
Schickel 223-25
Simon (b) 184-88
Stolen Life, A
Winnington 72
Stora äventyret, Det see
Great Adventure, The (Arne
Sucksdorff)
STORIES see PLOTS
Storm, The (Marc Allégret)
Graham 191-92
Storm of Passion, The see
Tempest (Robert Siodmak)
Storm over Asia
Weinberg (152)
Storm over Bengal
Lejeune 46-47
Storm Warning
Kael (a) (297)
Storm Within, The
Kael (d) 329
Story from Othello, A
Lejeune 184-85
Story of Dr. Ehrlich's Magic
Bullet, The see Dr. Ehr-
lich's Magic Bullet
Story of Dr. Wassell, The
Agee 96-97
Story of G. I. Joe, The
Agee 171-75, (187)
Lejeune 158-59
Story of Louis Pasteur, The
Ferguson 116-17
Graham 85-86
Van Doren 319
Story of Vernon and Irene Castle,
The
Graham 225, 227

Stöten
Young 141-42
Strachka see Strike
Strada, La
Kael (d) 351
Young 64-67
Stradivarius
Graham 162
Straight Shooting (John Ford)
Sarris (b) (92)
Strange Adventure of David
Gray, The see Vampyr
Strange Affair, The (David
Greene)
Sarris (a) 377-80
Strange Affair of Uncle Harry,
The see Uncle Harry
Strange Confession see Im-
poster (Julien Duvivier)
Strange Deception, The see
Cristo Proibito, Il
Strange Incident, The see Ox-
Bow Incident, The
Strange Love of Martha Ivers,
The
Agate (b) 270-72
Winnington 58
Strange One, The
Farber (119), (121)
Strange Ones, The (Jean-Pierre
Melville)
Kael (a) 364-65
Kael (d) 262
Sontag (b) (106)
Strange Tales see Spirits of
the Dead
Stranger (Vance Lewis)
see Stranger in Town, A
Stranger, The (Luchino Visconti)
Farber 189-90
Kael (b) 35
Kauffmann (a) 46-48
Sarris (a) 331-33
Schickel 163-66
Sheed 214-15
Simon (b) 35-38)
Stranger, The (Orson Welles)
Agee 204-5
Young 411-12
Stranger in the Rain
Reed (a) 320-21
Simon (b) 222-23
Stranger in Town, A

Sarris (a) (386), (389)
Stranger Knocks, A
  Simon (c) (154)
Strangers (Roberto Rossellini)
  Sarris (a) 39-40
  Simon (b) (9)
  Sontag (b) (134), (158)
Strangers on a Train
  Farber 184, 210
  Kael (d) 352
  Sarris (a) (324)
Straniero, Le see Stranger,
  The (Luchino Visconti)
Straw Dogs
  Kael (a) 393-99
Strawberry Blonde
  Ferguson 345-46
Strawberry Statement, The
  Kael (a) 149-50
  Reed (a) 397-99
  Sarris (b) 242-44
  Simon (b) 129-30
Street of Shadows see Made-
  moiselle Docteur (Edmond
  Greville)
Streetcar Named Desire, A
  Alpert 135
  Farber 75-77
  Kael (d) 352-53
Streets of Sorrow (Georg Pabst)
  Agate (a) 149-50
Streisand, Barbra
  Reed (c) 7-12
Strictly Confidential see Broad-
  way Bill (Frank Capra)
Strictly Dynamite
  Ferguson 42
Strike
  Adler 80
  Durgnat 22
  Young 149-50
Strike Me Pink
  Graham 59-60
Stroheim, Erich von
  Agee (5)
  Durgnat 39
  Macdonald 76-77, (88-93),
    95-96, 446-47
  Pechter 297-300
  Sontag (a) (243)
  Weinberg 68-74, 142-46, 152,
    154-55, 207-09
Strong Man, The

Gilliatt 138-39
Stronger, The (play)
  Sontag (b) 143
STRUCTURALISM
  Sarris (b) 58
STUDENT FILMS
  Sarris (b) 97
Student of Prague, The see
  Student von Prag, Der (Arthur
  Robison)
Student von Prag, Der (Arthur
  Robison)
  Graham 72
STUDENTS AND THE CINEMA
  (see also EDUCATION, USE
  OF FILMS IN; YOUNG
  PEOPLE AND THE CINEMA)
  Kael (a) 145-46, 149-52
  Macdonald 169-70
STUDIOS, FILM (see also
  HOLLYWOOD)
  Alpert 13-14
  Kael (b) 93-94
  Sarris (b) 36
  Schickel 338
STUDY & TEACHING OF FILMS
  Kael (b) 93
  Macdonald 168-70
  Sarris (b) 21-22, 63, 65,
    137-43
  Young x-xiii
Study in Choreography for Cam-
  era, A
  Agee 191
Sturges, Preston
  Agee 116-17, 138, 343-45
  Farber 89-104
  Pechter (124)
Stürme der Leidenschaft see
  Tempest (Robert Siodmak)
Subject Was Roses, The
  Kael (b) 159-60
  Reed (a) 202
SUBJECTS OF FILMS (see also
  AESTHETICS; PLOTS, DIS-
  CUSSION OF)
  Adler 207
  Agate (b) 60
  Alpert 217
  Brown (c) 249-51
  Farber 61-62, 116, 121
  Ferguson 5-10, 234-35
  Graham 39

Kael (a) 59-60
Kael (b) 98
Kael (c) 45-47, 75-78, 273-
   75, 282-83
Macdonald 188, 484-85
Pechter 313
Sarris (a) 364
Sarris (b) 34-35, 59, 70, 73,
   77, 95
Young 399
SUBTITLES
   Kauffmann (b) 64-69
   Simon (c) 52-54
   Weinberg 178
Suburban Legend see Love in
   the Suburbs
Successo, Il
   Simon (c) 162
   Young 230
Succubus
   Simon (b) 150
Such Good Friends
   Kael (a) 383-84
Sucksdorff, Arne
   Young 240-52
Sudba cheloveka see Fate of a
   Man
Suddenly, Last Summer
   Alpert (17), 156, 228
   Kauffmann (b) 81-82
   Macdonald 145-46
   Weinberg (164)
Sullivans, The
   Agee 81
Sullivan's Travels
   Agate (a) 234-36
   Farber 56
   Ferguson 410-11
Sult see Hunger
Summer and Smoke
   Kael (c) 138-39
Summer Interlude
   Kael (d) 353
Summer Storm
   Agee 105
Summertime
   Kael (d) 353-54
Sun Also Rises, The
   Kauffmann (b) (73)
Sun Never Sets, The
   Lejeune 47-50
Suna no onna see Woman in the
   Dunes

Sunday Bloody Sunday
   Kael (a) 289-93
Sunday Dinner for a Soldier
   Agee 139-40
   Winnington 31
Sundays and Cybèle
   Farber 147
   Kael (c) (246)
   Kauffmann (b) 258-59
   Simon (c) 38-41
Sundown (Henry Hathaway)
   Agate (b) 195
   Ferguson 406-07
   Lejeune 65-66
Sundowners, The (Fred Zinne-
   mann)
   Alpert 161
Sunrise (F. W. Murnau)
   Sarris (b) (132)
Sun's Burial, The
   Macdonald 316-17
Sunset Boulevard
   Agee 411-15
   Farber 62, 72
   Kael (d) 354
   Simon (a) 27-28
Sunset of a Clown, The see
   Naked Night, The
Support Your Local Sheriff
   Reed (a) 167-68, 222
SURREALISM AND THE CINEMA
   Kauffmann (a) 233-34
Survival 1967
   Adler 169-70
Susan Lenox: Her Fall and Rise
   Agate (a) 107-08
Suspicion (Alfred Hitchcock)
   Agate (b) 194-95
   Ferguson 394-95
Suzanne Simonin, la religieuse
   de Diderot see Religieuse,
   La
Svengali
   Kael (d) 355
Svenska Filminstitutet see Swed-
   ish Film Institute
Svietlji gorod see Village of
   Sin
Swamp Water
   Ferguson 400
Swedish Film Institute
   Kauffmann (b) 403
SWEDISH FILMS

Young 7-8, 403
SWEDISH FILMS (1950's)
  Young 140-42
SWEDISH FILMS (1960's)
  Kauffmann (b) (403)
  Young 196, 203-04, 271,
    295-96, 298
Swedish Wedding Night
  Crist 143-45
Sweet and Lowdown
  Lejeune 125-26
Sweet Bird of Youth
  Farber 151
  Kauffmann (b) 85-87
  Macdonald 148-49
Sweet Charity
  Reed (a) 168-70, 215-17
Sweet Hunters
  Reed (a) 406
Sweet Light in a Dark Room
  Simon (c) 238-39
Sweet November
  Adler 36-37
  Kael (b) 38-40
Sweet Rosie O'Grady (Irving Cum-
    mings)
  Agee 54-55
Sweet Smell of Success, The
  Farber (117)
  Kael (d) 356
Swindell, Larry. Spencer Tracy
  Sarris (a) 434-35
Swindlers, The (Federico Fellini)
  Simon (c) 135-36
  Young 99
Swineherd and Shepherd see
  They Met in Moscow
Svinyarka i pastukh see They
  Met in Moscow
Switchboard Operator see Af-
  fair of the Heart, An
Sylvester see New Year's Eve
Sylvia
  Crist 101-03
SYMBOLISM IN FILMS
  Crist 33-36
  Durgnat 37-38, 68-69, 198,
    224-37
  Farber 71-75
Sympathy for the Devil
  Kael (a) (168)
  Kauffmann (a) 264
  Simon (b) 272-74

Symphonie Fantastique, La
  Lejeune 179-80
Symphonie Pastorale, La
  Kael (d) 356
Syn Mongolii see Son of Mon-
  golia
Synanon
  Sarris (a) 207-08
SYNTAX see AESTHETICS;
  EDITING
System, The (Michael Winner)
  see Girl-Getters, The
Szegény legények see Round-Up,
  The (Miklós Jancsó)

-T-

T-Men
  Agee (296)
T. R. Baskin
  Kael (a) 311-13
Tabu
  Durgnat 52-53
  Kael (d) 356-57
Take a Giant Step
  Kauffmann (b) (153-54)
Take It All
  Simon (c) 226-27
Take It Or Leave It
  Agee 353
Take the Money and Run
  Gilliatt 35-36
  Kael (a) 13-14
  Reed (a) 182-83
  Sarris (a) 457
Taking Off
  Gilliatt 340-44
  Kael (a) (351)
Tale of Two Cities, A (Jack
  Conway)
  Ferguson 110-12
Tales from the Vienna Woods
  Graham 174
Tales of Beatrix Potter
  Gilliatt 349-53
Tales of Paris
  Sarris (a) (50)
Tales of the Pale and Silvery
  Moon... see Ugetsu Mono-
  gratari
Talk of the Town, The (George
  Stevens)

Gilliatt 164
Tall, Dark and Handsome
  Ferguson 339-40
Tall in the Saddle
  Agee (123)
Tambellini's Gate (theater, New York)
  Faber 246
Taming of the Shrew, The (Sam Taylor)
  Agate (b) 25-28
Taming of the Shrew, The (Franco Zeffirelli)
  Crist 235-36
  Gilliatt 334-35
  Simon (b) 28-30
Tanks a Million
  Ferguson 391
Tarass Boulba see Rebel Son
Target for Tonight
  Lejeune 59
Targets
  Adler 217-19
  Kauffmann (a) 96-99
  Reed (a) 389
  Sarris (a) 382-83
Tarnished Angels (Douglas Sirk)
  Kael (d) 357
Tartu see Adventures of Tartu, The
Tarzan and His Mate
  Ferguson 34
Taste of Honey, A
  Farber 182
  Kael (c) 196-201
  Kauffmann (b) 185-87
Tati, Jacques
  Gilliatt 3-5
Tatler (magazine)
  Agate (a) 7
Tawny Pipit, The
  Agee 277-78
  Lejeune 121-22
Taylor, Elizabeth
  Durgnat 169
  Simon (c) 298
Taylor, John Russell
  Sarris (b) 21-37
Taylor, John Russell. Cinema Eye, Cinema Ear
  Macdonald 474-78
Taylor, Robert
  Lejeune 23-25

TEACHING see STUDY AND TEACHING OF FILMS
TECHNIQUES see CINEMATOGRAPHY
Teen kanya see Two Daughters
Telefteo psemma, Io see Matter of Dignity
Telemeter (television system)
  Alpert 252-58
TELEVISION AND THE CINEMA
  Adler 299-301
  Alpert 12-13, 252-58
  Crist 270-71
  Kael (a) (234), (236), 319-21
  Kael (b) 20-23
  Kael (d) 144-45, 218-26
  Kauffmann (a) 22
  Macdonald (38)
Tell Me Lies
  Adler 47-50
  Kauffmann (a) 55-58
  Sarris (a) 342-44
Tell Me That You Love Me, Junie Moon
  Reed (a) 407
Tell Them Willie Boy Is Here
  Farber 7-8
  Kael (a) 76-78
  Kauffmann (a) 209-15
  Pechter 152, 159-62
  Reed (a) 258-60
  Simon (b) 178-79
  Schickel 277-79
Tempest (Robert Siodmak)
  Agate (b) 74-75
Temple, Shirley
  Graham 276-77
Temptation Harbor
  Young (xi-xii)
Ten Days That Shook the World
  Kael (d) 357-58
  Warshow 271
  Weinberg (247), 280, (291)
Ten Days to Die see Last Ten Days, The
Ten Little Niggers see And Then There Were None
10:30 [ten thirty] P.M. Summer
  Kael (d) 167
  Simon (c) 255-56
Tender Comrade
  Agee (85), 90-91
Tengoku to jigoku see High

and Low
Tennessee Johnson
  Agee 25-26
Tenth Man, The
  Graham 123
Tenth Victim, The
  Farber 162
  Simon (c) 201-02
Teorema
  Farber (9)
  Reed (a) 173-75
  Simon (b) 146-49
Terra Trema, La
  Durgnat (64)
  Kauffmann (b) 332-34
  Macdonald 342-44
  Simon (c) 193
  Sontag (b) (174)
Terrace, The
  Simon (c) 84-85
  Weinberg 227
Terror of Dr. Hitchcock, The
  Durgnat (53)
Test Pilot
  Van Doren 401-03
Testament d'Orphée, Le see
  Testament of Orpheus, The
Testament of Orpheus, The
  Kauffmann (b) 258
Testament von Dr. Mabuse, Das
  see Last Will of Dr. Mabuse,
  The
Tetto, Il see Roof, The
Teufels General, Des see
  Devil's General, The
Texas Rangers (King Vidor)
  Graham 106-07
Thalberg, Irving
  Macdonald 129
Thank You All Very Much
  Reed (a) 237-38
  Simon (b) 323-24
Thank Your Lucky Stars
  Agee 55
  Lejeune 104-05
Thanks for Everything
  Graham 218-19
That Hamilton Woman
  Sarris (b) 265-68
That Man from Rio
  Crist 73-74
  Kauffmann (b) 236-38
  Simon (c) 124-25

That Touch of Mink
  Macdonald 112
That's the Spirit
  Agee (169)
THEATRE AND THE CINEMA
  (see also ADAPTATIONS)
  Agate (a) 28, 151-52
  Alpert 233-51
  Kael (a) 10-11, 55-56
  Kael (b) (23), 228-30
  Kael (c) 275-77
  Macdonald 4, 64-67, 366,
    445
  Sarris (a) 20
  Sarris (b) 100-01, 103, 105
  Sontag (b) 99-122, 164
  Weinberg 37-38
THEATERS, FILM
  Agate (b) 14-15
  Alpert 16
  Ferguson 229-30
  Macdonald 450-51
Theirs Is the Glory
  Agate (b) 283-84
THEMES see SUBJECTS OF
  FILMS
Theodora
  Agate (a) (17-18)
Theodora Goes Wild
  Graham 137
THEORY see AESTHETICS;
  "AUTEUR" THEORY
There Never Was a Woman Like
  Gilda see Gilda
There Was a Crooked Man...
  Kael (a) 229-30
Thérèse see Thérèse Desqueyr-
  oux
Thérèse and Isabelle
  Adler 146
  Sheed 219
  Simon (b) 141-42
Thérèse Desqueyroux
  Crist (34)
  Sarris (a) 107-09
  Simon (c) 94-95
  Young (256)
Thérèse Raquin (Jacques Feyder)
  Agate (a) (37)
These Are the Damned
  Crist 133-35
These Children Are Safe
  Graham 273

These Thousand Hills
  Kauffmann (b) 142-43
These Three
  Graham 69, 72
They Are Not Angels
  Agee (307)
They Drive By Night
  Farber (18)
  Ferguson 311
  Graham 215
They Got Me Covered
  Agate (a) 243-44
They Knew What They Wanted
  Ferguson 312-13, (403)
They Live By Night
  Kael (d) 49
They Loved Life see Kanal
They Made Me a Criminal
  Ferguson 247
They Met in Bombay
  Lejeune 67
They Met in Moscow
  Agee 101
They Must Not Die
  Kael (d) 182-83
  Weinberg 219
They Shoot Horses, Don't They?
  Kael (a) 68-72
  Kauffmann (a) 219-222
  Sarris (b) 212-14
  Schickel 280-82
  Simon (b) 81-86, 402
They Were Expendable
  Agee 185
They Won't Believe Me
  Agee 374
They Won't Forget
  Ferguson 185-87
  Graham 178
Thief of Bagdad, The (Berger
  and Powell)
  Ferguson 325-26
Thief of Paris, The
  Crist 241-42
  Schickel 132-35
Thieves' Highway
  Durgnat (59-60
Thin Man, The
  Ferguson 39, 159-61
  Kael (d) 358
Thin Man Goes Home, The
  Agee (145)
  Winnington 33

Thing, The
  Farber 59, (145)
Things of Life, The see Chos-
  es de la Vie, Les
Things to Come
  Ferguson 129-30
  Graham 54-55
  Van Doren 327-30
Third Finger, Left Hand
  Ferguson 338
Third Lover, The
  Sarris (a) 252-53
Third Man, The
  Durgnat 111
  Farber 38-41
  Graham 3-4
  Kael (d) 10-11, 358-59
  Young 27-28, 400-04
13 [thirteen] rue Madeleine see
  13 [treize] rue Madeleine
30 [thirty] Is a Dangerous Age,
  Cynthia
  Adler 68-69
  Kael (b) 63
30 [thirty] Seconds over Tokyo
  Agee 129-30
Thirty Years of Fun
  Gilliatt 174-75
Thirty-Nine Steps, The (Alfred
  Hitchcock)
  Kael (c) (294)
  Kael (d) 359
  Van Doren 326-27
33 [thirty-three] rue de Mont-
  marte see 33 [trente-trois]
  rue de Montmarte
This Angry Age see Sea Wall,
  The
This Earth Is Mine
  Sarris (b) (69)
This England
  Lejeune 57-58
This Happy Breed
  Lejeune 116-18
This Is China
  Van Doren 374-75
This Is My Affair (William Sei-
  ter)
  Graham 164
This Is the Army
  Agee 53
This Island Earth
  Durgnat 256-70

This Land Is Mine
    Agate (a) 245-46
    Agee 35-36
This Love of Ours
    Lejeune 171
    Winnington 30-31
This Man in Paris
    Graham 231
This Man Must Die
    Kael (a) 172
    Schickel 317-19
This Property Is Condemned
    Reed (b) 235-40
This Sporting Life
    Crist (40)
    Kael (c) 15-17
    Kauffmann (b) 209
    Macdonald 395-96
    Simon (c) 81-82
This Strange Passion
    Durgnat (28)
    Kael (d) 261-62
This Time for Keeps (Richard
    Thorpe)
    Agee 296
This World's in Love   see
    Liebesmelodie
Thomas Crown Affair, The
    Adler 185-86
    Kael (b) 110-12, 114-15
    Simon (b) 314-15
Thoms l'Imposteur see Thomas
    the Imposter
Thomas the Imposter
    Simon (c) 187
Thompson, E. E. A. (quoted)
    Lejeune 11-13
Thomson, David. Movie Man
    Young 328
Thoroughbreds Don't Cry
    Lejeune 28-29
Thoroughly Modern Millie
    Reed (a) 375
Those Endearing Young Charms
    Agee (169)
Those Magnificent Men in Their
    Flying Machines
    Crist 149
    Simon (c) 171
Thou Shalt Not see Thérèse
    Raquin (Jacques Feyder)
Thousand Clowns, A
    Crist 150

Kael (d) (23)
Thousands Cheer
    Agate (a) 251-52
    Agee 54
Three
    Simon (c) 254
Three Caballeros, The
    Agee (141)
    Brown (b) 97-98
Three Cornered Hat, The see
    It Happened in Spain
Three in the Attic
    Kael (b) 276-77
    Simon (b) 112-13
Three in the Cellar see Up in
    the Cellar
Three Into Two Won't Go
    Reed (a) 240-41
Three Little Pigs, The
    Lejeune 36
Three Loves (Wilhelm Dieterle)
    Weinberg 154
Three Musketeers, The (Fred
    Niblo)
    Weinberg (237)
Three on a Weekend
    Ferguson 232-33
Three Songs about Lenin
    Ferguson 56, 58
Three Wax Men see Waxworks
Three Waxworks see Waxworks
Three Women (Ernst Lubitsch)
    Weinberg 55
Three Rascals in the Hidden
    Fortress see Hidden Fort-
    ress, The
Three Smart Girls
    Graham 139-40
Three Steps in Delirium see
    Spirits of the Dead
Three Strangers
    Agee 193
Three Wise Fools (Edward Buz-
    zell)
    Winnington 61
Threepenny Opera, The (Georg
    Pabst)
    Durgnat (50-51)
    Kauffmann (b) 348
    Weinberg 42-44
THRILLERS (see also DETEC-
    TIVE FILMS)

Crist 83, 120-21
Throne of Blood
 Kauffmann (b) 376-78
 Macdonald 421
 Sontag (b) (106)
Through a Glass Darkly
 Kauffmann (b) 282-84
 Macdonald 414-15
 Young 142
Thunder in the City
 Graham 138-39
Thunder in the East (Nicholas
 Farkas)
 Ferguson (60)
 Weinberg 294-305
Thunder over Mexico see Time
 in the Sun
Thunder Rock
 Agee 122
Thunderball
 Farber 161-62
 Sarris (b) 180-82
 Simon (c) 199-201
Thunderbolt (William Wyler)
 Agee 273
Thundercloud see Colt 45
Thunderhead, Son of Flicka
 Agee 149
Tiger Bay
 Kael (c) (66)
Tiger Makes Out, The
 Crist 245
Till the Clouds Roll By
 Agee 234-35
Time (magazine)
 Macdonald 462-63
Time and Hour of Augusto Ma-
 traga, The
 Young 326-63
Time for Burning, A
 Kael (a) (207)
Time in the Sun
 Agate (b) 101-02
 Ferguson 312
 Weinberg 93-95, (140-41),
  (176), 185, 191, 197-99,
  224-25
Time of Indifference
 Crist 191-92, (209)
Time of the Heathen, The
 Macdonald 314-15
Time of Your Life, The
 Agee 307, 387-88

Time to Live and a Time to Die,
 A see Fire Within, The
Times Square Lady
 Agate (a) 150
Tirez sur le pianiste see Shoot
 the Piano Player
Tisse, Edward K.
 Young 147-56
Titan: The Story of Michelangelo
 Brown (c) 301-05
Titicut Follies
 Schickel 155-59
TITLING (see also CREDIT
 TITLES)
 Lejeune 78
To Be a Crook
 Simon (b) 249
To Be Alive!
 Crist (90), (266)
 Kauffmann (b) 167
To Be or Not to Be
 Agate (b) 204-05
To Die for Hitler see Germany
 Awake!
To Die in Madrid
 Crist (149)
 Simon (c) 189-90
To Die of Love
 Kael (a) 418-19
To Each His Own (Elio Petri)
 see We Still Kill the Old Way
To Each His Own (Mitchell Lei-
 sen)
 Agee 206-07, 225
To Have and Have Not
 Agee 121-22, 353-54
 Kael (a) (235)
 Kael (d) 359-60
 Winnington 37
To Kill a Mockingbird
 Farber (151)
 Sarris (a) 75-77
To Live (Akira Kurosawa) see
 Ikiru
To Live in Peace
 Agee 283-85, (288)
 Winnington 85-86
To Live One's Life see My
 Life to Live
To Love
 Sarris (a) 170-72
To Sir with Love
 Reed (a) 336

To the Victor (Robert Stevenson)
Van Doren   399-400
Tobacco Road
Ferguson   344-45
Toby Dammit   see   Spirits of
the Dead
Toccata for Toy Trains
Durgnat   131
Today, Tomorrow and the Day
After That   see   Kiss the
Other Sheik
Today We Live (Grierson and
Bond)
Ferguson   207-08
Together Again
Agee   130
Tokyo Olympiad
Weinberg   273-74, (289)
Tokyo Orinpikku   see   Tokyo
Olympiad
Toland, Gregg
Durgnat   79
Tom, Dick and Harry
Ferguson   362, 378-80, 389
Tom Jones
Crist   25-27, (39), (270)
Kauffmann (b)   124-26
Macdonald   392-93
Sarris (a)   98-102
Simon (c)   90-92
Tomorrow We Live (George
King)
Agate (b)   223
Toni
Adler   241
Tonight and Every Night
Lejeune   143-44
Tonight Let's All Make Love in
London
Sheed   207-08
Simon (b)   379
Tonio Kröger
Adler   14-15
Too Many Cooks
Agate (a)   83-84
Too Many Crooks (Mario Zampi)
Kael (d)   295
Top Hat
Agate (a)   168-70
Graham   30
Top of the Town
Graham   154
Topaz

Kael (a)   79-80
Reed (a)   269-70
Sarris (b)   183-85
Simon (b)   13
Topaze (Harry d'Arrast)
Weinberg   318
Topkapi
Simon (c)   131-32
Topo, El
Kael (a)   334-40
Tora! Tora! Tora!
Kael (a)   147-48
Torme, Mel.   The Other Side
of the Rainbow
Sarris (b)   269-70
Torment (John Guillermin)
Agee   (274)
Torment (Alf Sjöberg)   see
Frenzy (Alf Sjöberg)
Torments   see   This Strange
Passion
Torn Curtain, The
Pechter   191-94
Sarris (a)   268-72
Torre-Nilsson, Leopoldo
Young   12, 275, 371-72
Torrid Zone
Ferguson   304
Touch, The
Kael (a)   (348)
Touch of Evil
Durgnat   45
Farber   6-8
Kael (d)   360-61
Pechter   172-73
Weinberg   147-49
Touchables, The
Reed (a)   205-06
Toy Wife, The
Agate (b)   160-61
Toys in the Attic
Kauffmann (b)   61-62
Tracy, Spencer
Sarris (a)   434-36
Tragedy of a Switchboard Opera-
tor   see   Affair of the Heart,
An
Tragic Pursuit of Perfection,
The
Durgnat   118-19
Young   71
Trail of the Lonesome Pine,
The (Henry Hathaway)

Graham 74
Trail of the Vigilantes, The
  Agate (b) 182
  Ferguson 337
Train, The
  Farber 155-56
  Simon (c) 153
Tramp, Tramp, Tramp (Harry
  Edwards)
  Gilliatt 140-42
Trans-Europe Express, The
  Adler 145-46
Trapeze (James Hill)
  Alpert (33)
Trash
  Kael (a) 153-57
Traümende munde, Der see
  Dreaming Lips, The (Paul
  Czinner)
TRAVEL FILMS
  Ferguson 29-30
Traversée de Paris, La see
  Four Bags Full
Tre passi nel delirio see Spir-
  its of the Dead
Treasure Island (Victor Fleming)
  Ferguson 47
  Graham 42, 44
Treasure of San Gennaro, The
  Adler 59-60
Treasure of the Sierra Madre,
  The
  Agee 290-93, 398-401
  Kael (d) 361-62
  Pechter (294)
  Weinberg 220-21
Tree, The
  Gilliatt (258)
Tree Grows in Brooklyn, A
  Agee 141-43
Tree Sonata, A
  Weinberg 243
13 [treize] rue Madeleine
  Agee 242
Trelawny of the Wells see Act-
  ress (Sidney Franklin)
33 [trente-trois] rue de Mont-
  martre
  Agate (b) 232-33
Tri see Three
Tri pesni o Lenine see Three
  Songs about Lenin
Trial, The

Durgnat (103), 112
  Kauffmann (b) 118-21
  Macdonald 295-99
  Pechter 162-66, 173-74
  Simon (c) 57-59
  Weinberg 215-16
Trial of Joan of Arc, The
  Kauffmann (b) 261-62
  Sarris (a) 193-95
  Weinberg (273)
  Young 211-12
TRIALS, CENSORSHIP
  Simon (b) 132-35
Trials of Oscar Wilde, The
  Kael (c) (43)
  Kauffmann (b) 194-96
  Weinberg 157
Tricheurs, Les (Marcel Carné)
  Young (170)
Tricheurs, Les (Sacha Guitry)
  Ferguson 238
Trilling, Lionel (quoted)
  Warshow 11-22
Tristana
  Reed (a) (398)
Triumph of Sherlock Holmes, The
  Agate (a) 147-48
Triumph of the Scarlet Pimpernel,
  The see Scarlet Daredevil,
  The
Triumph of the Will
  Adler (287)
  Brown (a) 63-64
  Kael (a) (207)
  Macdonald (448)
  Young 34-43
Trocadero (theater, Elephant and
  Castle, London)
  Agate (a) 82-83
Trog
  Reed (a) 308
Trojan Women, The
  Kael (a) 300-05
Tropic of Cancer
  Kael (a) 123-27
  Reed (a) 281
  Simon (b) 55-57
Tropics
  Farber 240
Trou see Night Watch (Jacques
  Becker)
Trouble in Paradise
  Agee 155

Macdonald 83-85
Trouble with Angels, The
  Reed (a) (349)
Troublemaker, The
  Simon (c) 125-26
True Confession
  Graham 190
True End of the Great War, The
  see Real End of the Great
  War, The
True Glory, The
  Agee 175
  Brown (b) 294-99
True Grit
  Kauffmann (a) 183-85
  Pechter (95)
  Reed (a) 231-32
  Sarris (a) 454-56
  Schickel 233-36
  Simon (b) 177
True to Life
  Agee 54
Truffaut, François
  Adler 152-55
  Farber 140-42
  Kauffmann (b) 224-26
Truffaut, François (quoted)
  Alpert 197, 201
  Schickel 29
Truffaut, François. Hitchcock
  Sarris (a) 333-36
Trunk Mystery, The
  Graham 11
Truth, The see Vérité, La
Try and Get Me
  Weinberg 196
Tsubaki sanjuro see Sanjuro
Tu seras terriblement gentille
  see You Only Love Once
Tudor Rose
  Graham 73-74
Tugboat Annie
  Agate (b) 92
Tumbleweed (Ross Hunter)
  Alpert 89
Tumbleweeds (King Baggot)
  Weinberg 247
Tunisian Victory
  Agee 84
Turn of the Tide
  Graham 29-30
Turpin, Ben
  Agee (3), (5)

Tushingham, Rita
  Farber 180-83
Tutti a casa see Everybody
  Go Home!
Twelve Angry Men
  Farber (113-14), (117),
    (122)
  Kael (c) 40-41
Twelve Chairs, The
  Kael (a) 180
Twentieth Century
  Ferguson 36
  Kael (d) 362-63
24 [twenty-four] Hours in a
  Woman's Life
  Adler 248
2001 [twenty oh one]: A Space
  Odyssey see 2001 [two
  thousand and one]: A Space
  Odyssey
Twenty-one Days see Twenty-
  one Days Together
Twenty-one Days Together
  Graham 262
Twilight of the Gods (Luchino
  Visconti) see Damned, The
Twisted Nerve
  Reed (a) 153
Twisted Road see They Live
  By Night
2 [two] (Renee Taylor)
  Adler 176
Two Baroque Churches in Ger-
  many
  Durgnat 121
Two Daughters
  Crist (40)
  Kauffmann (b) 371-72
Two-Faced Woman, The
  Ferguson 400-02, (404)
Two for the Road
  Reed (a) 374-75
  Schickel 108-11
Two for Tonight
  Graham 24
Two Girls and a Sailor
  Agee 101-02
Two of Us, The (Claude Berri)
  Kael (b) 49-51
Two of Us, The (Hulbert and
  Stevenson) see Jack of All
  Trades
Two or Three Things I Know

about Her
  Adler   249-50
  Farber   233
  Kauffmann (a)   258-60
  Sontag (b)   (145)
Two Rode Together
  Farber   109-12
Two Sisters from Boston
  Winnington   111
2001 [two thousand and one]: A
  Space Odyssey
  Adler   102-04, 121-22
  Gilliatt   114-19
  Kael (b)   101, 121-24
  Kauffmann (a)   70-75
  Sarris (b)   202-03
  Simon (b)   311-13
Two Weeks in Another Town
  Farber   (148), (154)
  Kael (d)   363-64
Two Women
  Kauffmann (b)   293-96
  Young   127-29
Two Years Before the Mast
  Agee   215-16
Tynan, Kenneth
  Simon (c)   6-7
Typhoon (Louis King)
  Agate (a)   211
Tystnaden   see   Silence, The
  (Ingmar Bergman)
Tzar to Lenin   see   Czar to
  Lenin

              -U-

UPA   see   United Productions of
  America
Uccellacci e uccellini   see
  Hawks and the Sparrows, The
Ugetsu Monogatari
  Young   52-56
Ugly American, The
  Kauffmann (b)   37-38
  Sarris (a)   87-89
  Simon (c)   62-63
Ugly Dachshund, The
  Kael (d)   179
Ukraine in Flames
  Weinberg   104
Ulmer, Edgar G.
  Simon (b)   7-8

Ulysses (Joseph Strick)
  Crist   259
  Kael (d)   169-70
  Kauffmann (a)   25-28
  Simon (b)   32-33
Umberto D
  Kael (c)   (284)
  Kael (d)   364
Umbrellas of Cherbourg, The
  Crist   85-86
  Simon (c)   136-39
  Weinberg   259
  Young   259-60
Un de la Légion
  Graham   238
UN-AMERICAN ACTIVITIES
  COMMITTEE   see   "HOLLY-
  WOOD TEN"
Uncle Harry
  Agee   170
Uncle Janco
  Reed (a)   149
Unconquered, The (Cecil B. De
  Mille)
  Agee   378-79
  Winnington   101-02
Under Capricorn
  Simon (b)   (10)
Under the Clock   see   Clock,
  The (Vincente Minelli)
Under the Yum Yum Tree
  Crist   (35)
Under Two Flags (Frank Lloyd)
  Crist   (34)
  Graham   91-92
Undercover   see   Underground
  Guerrillas
UNDERGROUND FILMS (see al-
  so EXPERIMENTAL FILMS)
  Farber   247
  Kael (d)   28-29
  Macdonald   39
  Simon (c)   11
Underground Guerrillas
  Agate (b)   231-32
Underground Report
  Agee   95
Underworld   see   Lower Depths
  The (Jean Renoir)
Unfaithful, The (Vincent Sher-
  man)
  Agee   271
Unfaithful Wife, The   see

Femme Infidèle, The
Unfaithfully Yours
    Kael (d) 364
Unfinished Business
    Agate (b) 193
Unfinished Dance, The
    Winnington 119
Unfinished Symphony, The
    Ferguson (66)
Unforgiven, The
    Kauffmann (b) 147
    Macdonald 283-84
Uninvited, The
    Agee 81
UNION OF SOVIET SOCIALIST
    REPUBLICS see RUSSIAN
    FILMS
Union Pacific
    Graham 224-25
United Artists Corp.
    Alpert 13, 26, 35-37
United Productions of America
    Sarris (b) 193-94
Unreconciled
    Simon (c) 186
Unseen, The
    Agee 158
    Sarris (b) (59)
Unvanquished see Aparjito
Unwelcome Stranger, The
    Ferguson 76
Uomini del fondo see S.O.S.
    Submarine
Uomo a metà, Un see Almost
    a Man
Up in Arms
    Agate (b) 248-49
    Agee 82
Up in the Cellar
    Gilliatt 198
Up the Down Staircase
    Reed (a) 331-33
    Sarris (a) 319-20
Up the Junction
    Adler 76-78
    Kael (b) 68-70
Up Tight
    Adler 332-34
    Kauffmann (a) 122-25
Uppbrott see Breakup
Ustinov, Peter (quoted)
    Durgnat 40
Uzelac, Vera

Kauffmann (b) 404

-V-

V.I.P.s, The
    Crist 20-22
V-1
    Agee 130-31
Vacances de Monsieur Hulot,
    Les see Mr. Hulot's Holi-
    day
Vacation from Marriage
    Agee 193
Vaghe stelle dell'orsa see
    Sandra
Valley of Decision, The
    Agee 161
Vampire (Carl Dreyer) see
    Vampyr
Vampires, Les
    Durgnat 101
    Kauffmann (b) 409
    Simon (c) 185
    Weinberg 269
VAMPS (see also ACTORS AND
    ACTRESSES; WOMEN IN
    FILMS)
    Crist 78-81, 118-19
    Durgnat 140, 147-51
    Macdonald 110, 444
    Simon (c) 297-98
Vampyr
    Durgnat (103), 105
    Kael (d) 365
    Weinberg 210
Van Doesburg, Theo
    Sontag (b) 103
Van Gogh (Alain Resnais)
    Durgnat 123
Vanishing Corporal, The see
    Elusive Corporal, The
Variété see Variety [a film]
Variety (newspaper)
    Ferguson 67-68
Variety [a film]
    Durgnat (45)
    Macdonald (13)
    Weinberg 38, 50, (244), 257,
    342
Variety Girl
    Agee (282)
Variety Lights

Crist 117-18
Kael (d) 365
Kauffmann (b) 325
Vartimmen see Hour of the
Wolf, The
Vaudeville see Variety [a film]
Vaxdockan see Wax Doll, The
Veille d'Armes
Graham 58
Veliki i mali see Little and
Big
Venetian Nights
Weinberg (178)
Vengeance of the Forty-Seven
Ronin see Chushingura
(Hiroshi Inagaki)
Venice Film Festival see Inter-
national Film Festival, Venice
Venom
Adler 10-12
Vent souffle ou il veut see
Man Escaped, A
Verdon, Gwen
Reed (c) 193-98
Verdugo see Not on Your Life!
Vérité, La
Kael (c) 37-38
VERSIONS [for conversion of
novels, plays, etc. into films
see ADAPTATIONS]
Sarris (b) 61
VERSIONS, ABBREVIATED [in-
cludes discussions of length of
films]
Agee 282, 322, 338
Crist 189
Ferguson 312
Graham 38
Kael (a) 319-20
Kael (d) 99, 141
Kauffmann (a) 74, (85), 131,
164-65
Kauffmann (b) 312-13
Macdonald 130, 478-79
Pechter 9, 169
Sarris (a) 92, 274
Sarris (b) 204
Simon (c) 31
Weinberg 135, 350, 353
Young 16
Versprich mir Nichts see Mon-
ica and Martin
Vertigo

Pechter 179-80
Very Happy Alexander
Reed (a) 151
Very Thought of You, The
Agee 130
Vessel of Wrath see Beach-
comber, The (Erich Pommer)
Viaggio in Italia see Strangers
(Roberto Rossellini)
Vicious Circle
Agee (313)
Victim (Basil Dearden)
Kael (c) 201-03
Victoria the Great
Agate (a) 185-88
Victors, The
Macdonald (152)
Sarris (a) 114
Simon (c) 98-100
Victory (John Cromwell)
Ferguson 337-38
Victory Through Air Power
Agee 43-44
Vidas Secas
Young (12)
Vidor, King
Durgnat 27, 38-39, 57-58
Macdonald 78-80, (105)
Vie à l'envers, La see Life
Upside Down
Vie commence demain, La see
Life Begins Tomorrow
Vieil homme et l'enfant, Le see
Two of Us, The
View from the Bridge, A
Alpert 248
Kael (c) 172-75
Kauffmann (a) (129)
Kauffmann (b) 104-06
Sarris (a) 46-47
Vigo, Jean
Weinberg 185
Village Fair see Big Day, The
Village of Sin, The
Weinberg 61
Vincent van Gogh (Jan Hulsker)
Young 72
Vinden och floden see Wind
and the River, The
24 [vingt-quatre] heures de la
vie d'une femme see 24
[twenty-four] Hours in a Wom-
an's Life

VIOLENCE IN FILMS (see also
   CRIME FILMS)
   Adler 3-5, 92, 166-67, 217
   Alpert 230
   Crist 251-53, 267
   Kael (a) 377-78
   Kael (d) 55
   Kauffmann (a) 181-82
   Pechter 85-90
   Schickel 118, 148
   Sheed 195-201
   Simon (b) 163-68
   Sontag (b) 121, 141-42
   Warshow 151-52
   Weinberg 20
Violent Four, The
   Kael (b) 96-97
   Simon (b) (292)
Violent Summer see Estate Vio-
   lenta, La
Virgin and the Gypsy, The
   Simon (b) 62-65
Virgin Soldiers, The
   Reed (a) 274
Virgin Spring, The
   Durgnat (64)
   Kauffmann (b) 277-79
   Pechter 142-45
   Weinberg (175)
   Young (123)
Virginian, The (Victor Fleming)
   Warshow 142-43, 148
Virginian, The (Stuart Gilmore)
   Lejeune 182-83
Viridiana
   Kauffmann (b) 350-51
   Sarris (a) 53-60
   Weinberg 178, 192
   Young 161-66
Virtue
   Van Doren 378-79
Virtuous Vivi, The
   Agee 200
Visconti, Luchino
   Alpert 183
   Durgnat 64
   Sarris (a) 29-33
   Sarris (b) (51)
   Simon (b) 408-10
   Sontag (a) (245)
Visconti, Luchino (quoted)
   Durgnat 45
Vision of William Blake

Durgnat 119
Visiteurs du soir, Les see
   Devil's Envoys, The
Vitaphone
   Agate (a) 26-27
Vitelloni, I
   Kael (d) 366
   Macdonald (xiv)
   Simon (c) 26-29
   Young 61-64
Vitti, Monica
   Sarris (a) 69-73
Viva Maria!
   Farber 161
   Kael (a) 309
Viva Zapata!
   Kael (d) 366-67
Vivacious Lady
   Ferguson (10)
Vivere in pace see To Live in
   Peace
Vivre sa vie see My Life to
   Live
Vizzard, Jack. See No Evil
   Sarris (b) 256-58
Voice in the Wind
   Agee 83, 139
Voice of Anxiety
   Young 12
Voice of Britain, The
   Graham 10
Voice of the Turtle, The
   Sarris (b) 109
Voie lactée, La see Milky
   Way, The
Voight, Jon
   Reed (b) 251-59
Voina i mir see War and
   Peace (Sergei Bondaruchuk)
Voleur, Le see Thief of Paris,
   The
von Sternberg, Josef see
   Sternberg, Josef von
von Stroheim, Erich see Stro-
   heim, Erich von
Vorkapich, Slavko
   Agee 27
   Macdonald 121
Voyage Surprise, La (Prevert)
   Agee 302
Voyage to Italy see Strangers
   (Roberto Rossellini)
Vredens dag see Day of Wrath

Vynalez zkary see Deadly In-
    vention, The

        -W-

WUSA
    Kael (a) 181-82
    Reed (a) 298-301
Wachsfiguerenkabinett see Wax-
    works
Wages of Fear, The
    Durgnat (233)
    Farber (18)
    Kael (d) 165-66
    Young (78)
Wagonmaster
    Sarris (a) 41-42
Waiting Women see Secrets of
    a Woman
Wake Island
    Agee (27)
Walk in the Spring Rain, A
    Reed (a) 284
Walk in the Sun, A
    Agee 185-86
Walk on the Wild Side
    Sarris (a) 47-48
Walk with Love and Death, A
    Kael (a) 17-18
    Reed (a) (255-56)
    Simon (b) 361
Walking Stick, The
    Reed (a) 285
Walsh, Raoul
    Farber 12
Walter Sickert
    Durgnat 120
Waltz of the Toreadors, The
    Gilliatt 232-34
Walzerkönig, Der
    Weinberg 38
Walzerkrieg, Der see Walzer-
    könig, Der
Wanda
    Kael (a) 267-69
    Sarris (b) 171-72
Wanderer, The
    Reed (a) 175
    Simon (b) 355
Wanted for Murder (Lawrence
    Huntington)
    Agee 234

War Against Mrs. Hadley, The
    Agate (b) 217
War and Peace (Sergei Bondar-
    chuk)
    Adler 131-33, 136-37
    Schickel 191
    Simon (b) 38-41
War as It Was see Forgotten
    Men
WAR FILMS (see also WORLD
    WAR II)
    Agee 59, 65-67, 99-100,
        151-52
    Ferguson 60
    Kauffmann (b) 8-9
    Lejeune 157-58
    Warshow 153
    Weinberg 103-04
War Game, The (Peter Watkins)
    Schickel 102-04
    Simon (c) 249
    Young 315-17, 340-41
War Is Over, The see Guerre
    est finie, La
War Nurse
    Agate (a) 85-86
War of the Buttons, The
    Simon (c) 105
War Wagons, The
    Kael (d) 43-45
Warden, Jack
    Farber 118
Warhol, Andy
    Farber 192-94
    Reed (a) 191-95
Warrendale
    Adler 273-75
    Kauffmann (a) 102-05
    Schickel 202-04
Warshow, Robert
    Pechter 276-89
    Sarris (b) (70), (76), (79)
    Warshow 19
Warshow, Robert (quoted)
    Pechter 277-84, 301-02, 313
Warshow, Robert. The Immedi-
    ate Experience
    Pechter 276-89
    Simon (a) 286-88
Warui vatsu hodo yoko nemuru
    see Bad Sleep Well, The
Waterloo
    Kael (a) (348-49)

Waterloo Road
  Winnington 30
Watch on the Rhine, The
  Agee 53, (66)
  Sarris (b) (59)
Watermelon Man
  Gilliatt 267-68
  Simon (b) 95-96
Watkins, Peter
  Young 340-42
Wavelength
  Farber 250-52
Wax Doll, The
  Young (196)
Waxworks
  Durgnat 89
  Kael (d) 367
  Weinberg 50, (201)
Way Ahead, The
  Lejeune 123-24, 135-37
Way to the Stars, The see
  Johnny in the Clouds
Way We Live, The
  Winnington 62
Way West, The
  Kael (d) 43
Wayne, John
  Farber (147)
  Sarris (a) 454-55
Ways of Love
  Weinberg (192)
  Young 61
We Are All Assassins
  Young 80-81
We Are All Murderers see We
  Are All Assassins
We from Kronstadt
  Ferguson 133-35
  Graham 133-34, 150
  Van Doren 333-35
We Live Again
  Ferguson 53
We Live in Two Worlds
  Ferguson (207)
We Still Kill the Old Way
  Adler 60-61
  Kael (b) 55-56
  Simon (b) 291-92
We Were Strangers
  Farber 34-37
We Will Come Back
  Agee 60
Web of Passion see Leda

Wedding March, The
  Macdonald (xv-xvi), 91
  Simon (c) 184-85
  Weinberg 72-73, (177), 203,
    (262)
Wedding Night
  Ferguson (6), 69-70
Wee Willie Winkie
  Graham 276
Weekend (Jean-Luc Godard)
  Adler 251-53, 277-79
  Farber 8-9, 236-38
  Kael (b) 138-42
  Kauffmann (a) 109-12
  Sarris (a) 400-06
  Sheed 224-26
Weightman, John G.
  Durgnat 247
Weinberg, Herman
  Weinberg 10-11, 292-93,
    353-54
Welcome to Hard Times
  Schickel 115-18
Well-Digger's Daughter, The
  Agee 225-26
Welles, Orson
  Agate (b) (204)
  Durgnat (34-35)
  Kael (d) 196-202
  Pechter 310-11
  Simon (c) 56-57
  Weinberg 153-54, 158-59,
    161, 206
  Young 405-13
Welles, Orson (quoted)
  Young 323
Wellman, Bill
  Farber 12-13, 15-17, 21
Wells Fargo
  Van Doren 385-87
Werner, Oskar
  Reed (b) 108-15
West, Mae
  Durgnat (44)
West, Mae. Goodness Had Noth-
  ing to Do With It
  Gilliatt 154-56
West Side Story
  Alpert 243-44
  Kael (c) 141-48
  Kauffmann (b) 134-37
  Macdonald 286-87
Western Approaches see Raider,
  The

Western Union
   Ferguson 341-42
WESTERNS (see also NON-
   AMERICAN WESTERNS)
   Alpert 125-26, (227)
   Farber 24
   Ferguson 330-31
   Kael (a) 149
   Kael (b) 250-52
   Kael (c) (45), 242
   Kael (d) 38-46
   Kauffmann (a) 178-82
   Kauffmann (b) 141-42
   Macdonald 485
   Pechter 236, 285
   Sarris (a) 386-92
   Sarris (b) 30, 70-72, 101,
      208-11
   Warshow 137-54
   Young 395-99
Westerns--Italian Style [a film]
   Adler 239-40
What a Man! see Never Give
   a Sucker an Even Break
What a Way to Go!
   Macdonald 161
   Simon (c) 116-17
What a Woman!
   Agee 63-64
What Did You Do in the War,
   Daddy?
   Crist (210)
   Sarris (b) 188-89
What Do You Say to a Naked
   Lady?
   Reed (a) 280
What Next, Corporal Hargrove?
   Agate (b) 265
What Price Glory? (Raoul Walsh)
   Farber 5-6
What Price Hollywood?
   Agate (b) 68-70
Whatever Happened to Aunt
   Alice?
   Reed (a) 181-82
Whatever Happened to Baby Jane?
   Sarris (a) 77-82
What's New, Pussycat?
   Crist 124
   Farber 168
   Simon (c) 170-71
What's Up, Doc?
   Kael (a) 431-33

What's Up, Tiger Lily?
   Crist 202
Wheat Whistle
   Young 102
When New York Sleeps see
   Now I'll Tell
When Strangers Marry (William
   Castle)
   Agee 155
   Farber 56-57
When You're in Love
   Graham 165-66
Where Do We Go from Here?
   Agee 169
Where Eagles Dare
   Reed (a) 154-55
Where the Boys Are
   Kauffmann (b) 233
Where Were You When the Lights
   Went Out?
   Adler 204-05
Where's Charley?
   Kael (d) 367-68
Where's George?
   Graham 15-16
Where's Jack?
   Reed (a) 240
Where's Poppa?
   Kael (a) 185-86
While I Live
   Winnington 91-92
Whirlpool (Otto Preminger)
   Kael (c) 298
Whisperers, The
   Sarris (a) 303-04
   Schickel 129-31
   Young 320-21
White, Carol
   Reed (b) 266-72
White Angel, The
   Agate (b) 137-39
   Graham 121
White Cliffs of Dover, The
   Agee 94
White Colt, The see Philip
White Gold
   Weinberg (241)
White Heat (Raoul Walsh)
   Pechter 90
White Hell of Pitz Palu, The
   (Fanck and Pabst)
   Agate (a) 72-73
White Nights

Kauffmann (b) 329
White Shadows in the South Seas
    Agate (a) (44)
White Sheik, The (Federico Fellini)
    Kael (d) 368
    Simon (c) 24-26
    Young 60
White Ship, The
    Durgnat (40)
White Squadrons
    Graham 183-84
White Unicorn, The see Bad
    Sister (Bernard Knowles)
Whiting, Leonard
    Reed (b) 273-86
Who Killed Cock Robin?
    Ferguson 86-87
Whole Town's Talking, The (John
    Ford)
    Kael (d) 368
Wholly Communion
    Simon (c) 255
Who's Afraid of Virginia Woolf?
    Crist (181-82), 218-19
    Farber (5), 178-79
    Kauffmann (a) 1-4
    Sarris (a) 259-62
    Simon (b) (372)
    Simon (c) 235-38
Who's Been Sleeping in My Bed?
    Kael (c) (26)
Who's That Knocking at My
    Door?
    Kauffmann (a) 202
Why We Fight see Prelude to
    War; Battle of Britain; Battle
    of Russia [3 films]
Wicked Dreams of Paula Schultz,
    The
    Adler 1-2
Wicked Lady, The
    Durgnat (182), (197-98)
WIDE-SCREEN SYSTEMS
    Alpert 19-20
    Kael (c) 283
Wife vs. Secretary
    Weinberg 60
Wild Angels, The
    Crist 183
    Sarris (a) 272-74
    Simon (c) (263)
Wild Bunch, The

Farber 216-18
Kael (a) 133-34
Kauffmann (a) 179-83
Pechter 91-96
Reed (a) 339-41
Sarris (a) 447-50
Schickel 244-46
Simon (b) 173-76
Young 394-95
Wild Cargo
    Ferguson 34
Wild Child, The
    Reed (a) 321
    Schickel 328-30
Wild Flight see Hidden Fortress, The
Wild Harvest
    Agee 377-78
Wild in the Streets
    Adler 162-63, 173-75
    Kael (b) 89-92
    Schickel 194-97
Wild 90 [ninety]
    Adler 6-7
    Kael (b) 9-17
    Kauffmann (a) 49-50
Wild One, The
    Kael (c) 58-60
Wild Strawberries
    Alpert 62-63, 68-69
    Kael (d) 368-69
    Kauffmann (b) 270-73
    Sarris (a) 39
Wilder, Billy
    Pechter (124)
    Simon (a) (11), 23-29
Will o' the Wisp see Fire
    Within
Will Penny
    Adler 113
    Reed (a) 385-87
    Young 397-98
William Wilson see Spirits of
    the Dead
Willie Boy see Tell Them
    Willie Boy Is Here
Wilson
    Agee 110-13
    Lejeune 139-40
Wilson, Edmund
    Ferguson (4), 187
Winchester 73
    Sarris (b) 71-72

Wind
    Weinberg (250)
Wind and the River, The
    Young 252
Wind from the East
    Reed (a) 403
Windbag the Sailor
    Graham 127
Windflowers
    Adler 55-56
Windy Day
    Kael (a) (91)
Winged Victory
    Agee 135
Wings Up
    Agee (42)
Winner, The
    Crist (132-33)
Winning
    Farber 7-8
    Kauffmann (a) 174-77
    Reed (a) 230-31
Winnington, Richard
    Durgnat (62-63)
    Winnington 7-11
Winter Carnival
    Ferguson 265
Winter Kept Us Warm
    Adler 38-39
Winter Light
    Crist (40)
    Kauffmann (b) 284-86
    Macdonald 415-16
    Simon (c) 65-68
    Young 214-16, (402)
Winter Wind
    Kauffmann (a) 246-49
Winterset
    Graham 141-43
    Kael (d) 369
    Van Doren 345-47
Wintertime
    Agee 55
Witchcraft Through the Ages   see
    Häxan
With the Marines at Tarawa
    Agee 82-83, (137)
Without Apparent Motive
    Kael (a) 413-15
Without Love
    Agee 154
Without Reservations
    Agee 203-04

Wizard of Oz, The
    Ferguson 270-71
    Graham 268-69
    Sarris (b) (63)
Wolfenstein, Martha and Nathan
    Leites. Movies: A psycho-
    logical study
    Sarris (b) 73, 77
Woman Alone, The (Alfred Hitch-
    cock)
    Graham 122-23
    Van Doren 353-54
Woman Chases Man
    Graham 162
Woman in a Dressing Gown
    Kael (d) 369
Woman in the Dunes
    Kauffmann (b) 387-88
    Simon (c) 139-40
    Weinberg (250)
Woman in the Painting
    Kael (d) 231
Woman in the Window, The
    Agate (a) 268-70
Woman in White, The (Peter
    Godfrey)
    Agee (307)
Woman Is a Woman, A
    Kauffmann (b) 242-43
    Sarris (a) 167-70
    Simon (b) (8)
    Simon (c) 132-35
    Weinberg 190
Woman of Affairs, A
    Kael (a) (364-65)
Woman of Paris, A
    Weinberg (177), 195-96
Woman of the Year
    Ferguson 414-15
Woman on the Beach, The
    Agee (273)
Woman They Almost Lynched,
    The
    Sarris (a) 44-45
Woman Without a Face   see
    Mister Buddwing
Woman's Vengeance, A
    Agee 294
Women, The
    Crist (176)
    Ferguson 269
WOMEN AND THE CINEMA
    Sarris (b) 170-71

Women in Chains see Prison-
  nière, La
WOMEN IN FILMS
  Adler 268-70
  Crist 138-39, 173-74
  Durgnat 157-58, 253
  Kael (a) 341-48
  Kael (c) 36-37
  Kael (d) 96-97
  Sarris (a) 139, 390-92
  Sarris (b) 24-25
  Simon (c) 297-303
  Warshow 138
Women in Love
  Kael (a) 138-42
  Reed (a) 282-83
  Simon (b) 57-62
Women Waiting see Secrets of
  a Woman
Wonder Bar
  Ferguson 272
Wonder Man (H. Bruce Humber-
  stone)
  Agee (169)
Wonderful Adventures of Nils,
  The
  Young 196-98
Wonderful Lie, The
  Agate (b) 21-23
Wood, Natalie
  Crist (209)
Woodstock
  Reed (a) 283, 406
  Schickel 297-99
  Simon (b) 95
Woodward, Joanne
  Reed (b) 132-40
Word, The see Ordet
World Moves On, The
  Ferguson (45-46)
World of Apu, The
  Kauffmann (b) 370-71
World of Comedy, The
  Gilliatt 157
World of Henry Orient, The
  Simon (c) 115
World of Paul Delvaux, The
  see Monde de Paul Delvaux,
  Le
World of Plenty
  Agee 45-46
World, the Flesh and the Devil,
  The

Pechter (7)
WORLD WAR II in Germany
  Crist 159-61
Wrong Box, The
  Crist 214-15
Wrong Man, The
  Alpert 173
  Sarris (b) (62)
Wunderbare Lüge der Nina Pe-
  trowna, Die see Wonderful
  Life, The
Wuthering Heights (William Wy-
  ler)
  Agate (a) 196-99
  Crist (24)
  Ferguson 251-52
  Graham 219-20
  Sarris (a) (360)
  Weinberg (179)
Wyler, William
  Macdonald (xi-xii)
Wyman, Jane
  Reed (b) 30-37

-X-

X Y & Zee
  Kael (a) 405-09

-Y-

Yank at Oxford, A
  Agate (b) 151-54
Yank in London, A
  Agate (b) 257-59
Year 2000, The see Anticipa-
  tion
Years of Lightning, Day of
  Drums see John F. Ken-
  nedy: Years of Lightning...
Yeats Country
  Simon (c) (188)
Yellow Cruise, The
  Ferguson 164
  Weinberg 56-57
Yellow Rolls-Royce, The
  Simon (c) 148-49
Yellow Submarine
  Adler 289-91, 293-95
  Kael (b) 187-92
  Kauffmann (a) 117-18

Sarris (b) 191-93
Simon (b) 108-09
Yesterday Girl
  Sarris (a) 316)
  Simon (b) 375
  Young 307-08
Yesterday, Today and Tomorrow
  Crist 61
  Kauffmann (b) 296-97
  Simon (c) 114-15
Yeux Noirs, Les see Dark
  Eyes
Yeux sans visages, Les see
  Horror Chamber of Dr. Faus-
  tus, The
Yiddle with His Fiddle
  Graham 160
Yojimbo
  Farber 148-49
  Kael (c) 239-45
  Kauffmann (b) 379-81
  Macdonald 421-22, (462)
  Weinberg 190
You and Me
  Graham 195-96
You Are What You Eat
  Adler 246-47
  Kael (b) 148-49
You Can't Take It with You
  Ferguson 235-36
  Graham 203-04
You Don't Need Pajamas at
  Rosie's see First Time, The
You Only Live Once
  Kael (d) 49-50, 54
You Only Live Twice
  Gilliatt 172-74
You Only Love Once
  Gilliatt 224-25
Young, Vernon
  Young x-xiv
Young and Innocent see Girl
  Was Young, The
Young and the Damned, The see
  Olvidados, Los
Young and the Passionate see
  Vitelloni, I
Young at Heart, The
  Kael (c) (57)
Young Cassidy
  Simon (c) 154
Young Girls of Rochefort, The
  Adler 114-15, 123-24

Kael (b) 100
Reed (a) 328-30
Sarris (a) 365-67
Young in Heart, The
  Kael (d) 369-70
Young Lions, The
  Kauffmann (b) 31-33
Young Mr. Lincoln
  Ferguson 257-58
  Graham 241-42
  Kael (d) (61)
Young Mr. Pitt
  Agee 29
YOUNG PEOPLE AND THE
  CINEMA (see also STU-
  DENTS AND THE CINEMA)
  Kael (a) 145-53
  Kauffmann (a) 24, 203-04,
    243-45, 276-79
  Pechter 97-98
  Schickel 76, 101, 143, 197,
    305, 326-27, 336
  Simon (b) 90, 102-03
YOUNG PEOPLE IN FILMS
  Kauffmann (a) 178, 203-04,
    277-79
Young Pushkin
  Van Doren 383-85
Young Scarface see Brighton
  Rock
Young Stranger, The
  Farber (122)
Young Törless
  Sarris (a) (316)
  Sheed 220-21
  Simon (b) 376
  Young 300-02
Young World, A
  Simon (c) 232-34
Youngblood, Gene
  Sarris (b) (123)
Youngest Spy, The see My
  Name Is Ivan
Your Past Is Showing
  Kael (d) 294-95
You're a Big Boy Now!
  Crist 236
  Reed (a) 376
  Reed (b) 260-65
  Schickel 98-101
You're in the Army Now
  Ferguson 406
You're Telling Me (Erle Kenton)

Ferguson 36
Yours, Mine and Ours
  Adler 124-25
  Gilliatt 194
Youth of Maxim, The
  Ferguson 75-76
Youth of the Poet, The see
  Pushkin
Youth Runs Wild
  Agee 118-19, (137)
Youthful Sinners see Tricheurs,
  Les (Marcel Carné)
YUGOSLAV FILMS (mid-1960's)
  Kauffmann (b) 406

Zinneman, Fred
  Alpert 157-61
  Kael (c) (305)
Zita
  Farber 238
  Simon (b) 292-94
Zlate kapradi see Golden
  Fern, The
Zorba the Greek
  Kael (d) 160
  Simon (c) (146)

-Z-

Z
  Kael (a) 66-67
  Kauffmann (a) 215-18
  Sarris (b) 223-26
  Simon (b) 86-90, 400
  Young 349-50
Zabriskie Point
  Kael (a) 113-17, (211)
  Kauffmann (a) 238-45, (253)
  Reed (a) 278-79
  Sarris (b) 237-41
  Schickel 292-93
  Simon (b) 202-10
  Weinberg 344-46
Zanuck, Darryl
  Reed (a) 401
Zavattini, Cesare
  Kael (a) 361-62
Zazie
  Kael (d) 370
  Macdonald (330), 383-85
Zazie dans le metro see Zazie
Zee & Co. see X Y & Zee
Zemlya see Earth
Zenobia see Elephant Never
  Forgets, An
Zéro de conduite
  Agee 262-64, 287
  Kael (b) 282-86
  Kauffmann (a) (136)
  Macdonald (375)
  Winnington 69, (125)
Zero for Conduct see Zero
  de conduite
Zert see Joke, The